13708

5-

Faith Is a Song

Faith
Is a Song

THE ODYSSEY OF
AN AMERICAN ARTIST

BY

JESSICA DRAGONETTE

DAVID McKAY COMPANY, INC.
New York

ACKNOWLEDGMENT IS HEREBY MADE OF THE KIND PERMISSION OF THE
NATIONAL BROADCASTING COMPANY TO REPRINT THE POEM "DEDICA-
TION" BY BURKE BOYCE AND LINES FROM THE ODE "THIS IS RADIO" BY
JOHN LA TOUCHE.

MANUFACTURED IN THE UNITED STATES OF AMERICA

To my Husband

NICHOLAS MEREDITH TURNER

CONTENTS

Faith Is a Song

CHAPTER 1

TALL GATES

When I was almost four I sang at a church fair. "Jessica has made a sensational debut," the family said. "Now she must retire and go to school."

In the family they said I sang before I talked. Though there were no professional singers on either side, our parents loved music and often talked about the great artists, particularly Caruso. All four of us—my two brothers, my sister, and I—were musical.

One of our forebears had been a bass viol player in Beethoven's orchestra, so my brother Nicholas learned to play the violin. My older sister Nadea, whom I adored and followed like a puppy, played the piano with flair. The minute she began to practice I danced, skipping and pirouetting until I fell into a chair from exhaustion. In her grown-up way, she would remark, "If you fall asleep again I *won't* put you to bed. I'll just leave you. You should stop before you wear yourself out!" But I was never still; when I was not dancing, I was singing to anyone who would listen or to myself alone.

Our father came of a French and Italian family which gave cardinals, revolutionists, and musicians to its times. One branch, emigrating to England, changed the name to Drake and included the great navigator, Sir Francis, who destroyed the Spanish Armada sent against Elizabeth by Philip the Second and also laid claim to California for his queen. But the strain from which my father, Louis Dragonette, descended remained in Genoa "la Gloriosa," where for many generations they engaged in banking activities. My grandfather believed a background of travel was the best education for a man, so from early boyhood my father was accustomed to journeying over the Continent, Egypt, and Africa.

Mother was Italian, of the barons Baronio, from a town outside

Genoa; one of three beautiful sisters—brunette, titian, and she, Raquel, the true golden blonde of the north. Since 1400 the Baronio home has been occupied by members of the family, but with the recent death of the titian-haired sister, Irene, who never married, it is ours to claim and carry on with our aunt's adopted son—our *caro cugino*.

My parents were childhood sweethearts, but from adolescence Mother suffered from severe migraine. Grandfather Baronio sent her to Paris to consult an American brain specialist, Dr. Ernest La Place, then attracting attention in Europe through his work with the aging Pasteur. When Dr. La Place returned to Philadelphia to resume his practice, Mother, then sixteen, came here, accompanied by her older sisters, to be his lifelong patient. Father and a young cousin who was in love with the brunette sister soon followed them; before long there was a double wedding, while Irene returned to Italy.

Father, anxious that his delicate young wife have whatever alleviation Dr. La Place could give her, determined to settle in Philadelphia. He soon became an American citizen, for he quickly grew to love his new country. Although he had broken family tradition by becoming an engineer, he inherited from his ancestors a pioneering spirit that led him to the building of bridges, often in remote places. But he could never bear to be separated from his little family. So it happened I was born in Calcutta, on St. Valentine's Day, and named Jessica Valentina.

Shortly thereafter we returned to live in Lansdowne, Pennsylvania. I recall the old-fashioned garden where we played under the gentle eye of our lovely, ailing mother. The older children each had a floral bed to cultivate. I wanted one of my own, but the boys said I was too little; so when Nicholas or Fred asked, "Which garden is prettiest?" I always answered, "Nadea's flowers are prettiest."

Years later Nicholas told how, after our mother's sudden death, he found me sitting on top of the tall gate in front of our house. He was puzzled that I had managed to climb so high.

"What are you doing up there?" he asked, feeling my stillness. When I didn't answer, he persisted. "Why don't you come down and play?"

But I only sat staring. "There's no use to play," I answered finally, "Mother is dead."

Death hurts children and sets up blocks. That was long ago, but since then I have tried not to remember, and whenever anyone asks me about childhood, I can recall nothing but pain.

Though our father was inconsolable, in his positive way he turned at once to the problem of caring for his motherless children. He asked advice of his close friends, a family named English. Nadea was old enough to be sent to a local convent boarding school, the boys were soon placed with the Christian Brothers in Baltimore, and we were never together again.

The great problem was, what to do about me? I can still feel the comforting presence of Mrs. English as she sat and talked to Father in our large living room. Though I didn't understand what they were deciding, I heard her say, "Mother Mary Joseph will be glad to do what I ask."

A few days later Father helped me into my hat and coat. He had a romantic device for distracting his little girl from the idea of separation. Just outside the tall gate stood a pretty carriage with a coachman sitting up high. The two horses had long tails, their coats shone like satin, and the silver trimmings of their harness made a jingling music as we drove off. "We are going to see Mother Mary Joseph, the closest friend of Mrs. English. She is very fond of little girls like you—" But I could only think that we were going somewhere in a fairy coach and that with his black hair, green eyes, and elegant clothes, Father was really my handsome fairy prince.

The afternoon was bright and crisp, with the pleasant smell of smoke drifting from burning leaves. I examined everything carefully, for I had never ridden in a closed carriage. There was even a deep red footstool for my feet. I pushed my curly blonde hair under the edge of my bonnet, to smile gaily at Father. He smiled back, but as we went along he was silent and looked sadly ahead.

The brown satin horses brought up with a prance and a jingle at a tall iron gate with stone pillars at either side. Father said to the coachman, "Please wait," as he helped me down. We walked along a winding path to a large brick building. The door was opened for us by a Sister of Charity in a long, French blue habit, with a bright white bib, starched stiff to the waist. I had never seen a Sister before, and the cornet on her head fascinated me with its huge white wings. Mother Mary Joseph's gray eyes beamed as she said gently, "I am so glad you brought Jessica. Please come in." Father murmured something polite while I looked all around.

"Let us go to the chapel," said Mother. "All things begin with God; He will guide us." She took us up a few steps to the simple convent chapel; we passed down the aisle and Father bent his knee, waiting while I genuflected as nicely as I could. I felt tall as I stood on the kneeling bench in the pew. I put my head back to see the red roses on the white altar and the sanctuary lamp burning there in quiet beauty. Father leaned his head on his hands praying fervently while I was still as a mouse.

First Mother Mary Joseph rose from her knees, then Father. They smiled, waiting for me to genuflect again, and Mother led us to an office. Against the wall was a desk with a high stool. I climbed up fast as a little squirrel and perched. Mother laughed, "You like it there, don't you? Well, you may come here and sit on the desk whenever you like." She was rather thin and wore glasses through which she looked kindly in my direction now and then, letting me know she remembered I was there. After a few moments' talk with Father, she got up and said tenderly, "Child, come with me and we'll find a little girl to play with." She took me by the hand as I looked at Father; he nodded, "Go along, darling."

We seemed almost to billow down the long corridor with its many rooms. In one a very beautiful lady with a happy smile was sitting, a small child on her lap. From her hat a large, pale blue plume curled over her red-gold hair. Diamond bracelets sparkled on her wrists, and I could smell a perfume like roses. "Huggins dear," Mother said, "I've brought you a little playmate. My! you look enough alike to be twins!"

I loved Huggins right off. I never knew anyone named Huggins before and even the name made me feel happy. Instead of standing off from each other like stiff-legged kittens, we seized hands and ran out of the room to play. We chased each other for a minute in a game of tag. Then I hid from Huggins behind a worn piano and waited breathlessly until she found me. "Let's play the piano now," I said, and we banged on the keys with both hands. Then I ordered, "Huggins, *you* sit down and *I* will sing for you!"

After a while Mother came and took me back to Father. He was standing up, holding his hat and gloves. "Thank you very much,

Mother," he said, "for having Jessica with you. Everything will be arranged in a short time. But should you need anything before I return for her, please get in touch with Callahan."

"What was a Callahan? Where was Father going? How soon would he come for me? Tomorrow?" My doll was on a chair, but I didn't have anything for staying all night. How could I stay anywhere with only a doll that belonged to me?

"Don't worry, Mr. Dragonette," Mother answered, "she'll be fine— we'll take good care—"

Father put his hand on my shoulder, "Darling—I'll come for you as soon as—" Mother interposed, "You'll have a nice time with us, Jessica, while you wait here—" Father kissed me tenderly. "Be a very good girl—I know you will—" He went quickly out of the room.

Before I could follow him Mother took my hand. "Come, Jessica dear, let's find Huggins again." I did not see the door close behind him, but I knew Father was gone.

Later, Mother sat with me while I ate my supper: cereal, milk, a dish of prunes, a cookie. And then it was bedtime.

CHAPTER 2

DISPLACED

For several days Huggins and I played together away from the other children. Then Mrs. De Witt, the lady with the red-gold hair, came to take her home. I never saw Huggins again and I was left alone. All day long I tried to get back to the room where Father had left me, but I could not find him. That night when I went to bed I hugged my doll tighter than ever. I had never liked her as much as my other dolls, but she was all I had left.

The next morning I woke in the little room in the orphanage. Sister Angela was bending over me.

"Father will be here today, won't he?" I asked hopefully.

"He will come as soon as he can," she answered with a gentle smile. But Father didn't come—he never came. And nobody ever told

me he had been killed in an accident shortly after he left me with
Mother Mary Joseph. Nobody ever told me that in his sadness he
didn't look where he was going, and so lost his life.

Now Sister Angela took me and put me in with the other children
all living in the big building. I wore a pink dress which I liked very
much, but the other children had dark dresses all made alike. They
pulled at my pink dress crying, "That's a funny dress! Where did
you get it?" "Jessica's a funny name," another child shouted. "It's not
a saint's name. Are you a Protestant?" . . . What was Protestant?
A girl with straight black hair and freckles yelled, "Look at her
long eyelashes—if you have long eyelashes it means you'll die of consumption." A little fat jolly girl clapped her hands laughing, "Look
she's got freckles in her eyes!"
I wished I had a dark dress like theirs. I wished they would stop
looking at me and screaming "Hey!" when I only tried to answer
their questions. I didn't feel gay any more, for who loved me now,
the way everybody loved me at home?
Sister Angela had a million things to do because she was the House
Mother in charge of the children, but she was never too busy to toss
her head back and laugh happily, running to and fro endlessly to see
to our welfare.
Bells rang nearly all the time. I liked them at first because I never
heard bells ringing like that at home. Soon I found out the Sisters
knew every minute what each child was doing. Soon I learned every
time a bell rang it meant *Do this—Do that.* I felt very mixed up, like
living in a cocoon. Where were Nadea and my brothers? Did they
ever think of me? I wanted to grow up fast and be a singer, but the
Sisters said first I must learn to be obedient. They were sweet and
kind, and I ran around all the time trying to please them. The weeks
dragged on. Our days always ended with night prayers. Then, in
double file, down the long corridor we walked to our dormitory past
a large statue.
"That is Saint Anthony, child," Sister Angela explained to me. "See
the Holy Babe in his arms." The saint reminded me of Father. I
wished he would pick me up and hold me.
In the dormitory there were two rows of narrow beds with a long
aisle between. We went there before supper to remove the white

spreads and pillows and put them on shelves at the end of the room. We were not allowed to sleep on pillows, and our spreads had to be folded neatly in a certain way. If a child was naughty, as a punishment, sometimes, she would have to take care of all the spreads and pillows.

Black Bella helped the Sisters with the housework. To us she seemed an assistant guardian angel; a little round woman with a jolly round face who walked with a funny waddle. She taught us the right way to make a bed.

To Bella, a bed was a person who had to be dressed carefully. "You mus' learn to dress yo' bed jes' right, chile," she would exclaim, showing me carefully how to make every corner square and neat as a pin. If I did very well she would smile, "Come to de kitchen, chile, and lemme give you a glass ob milk to relish down yo' bread."

She had her own odd way of observing the moods of nature. Gazing out of the window, once, at a heavy snowstorm, she said, "Jes' don' know where dis awful day come from; but I hopes dey comes and takes it back!" Meeting me once just before bedtime, she said, "Come here, little Jessica, an' look out de window, dey got de moon out tonight." For a long time after getting into bed I thought about it, wondering who "dey" were.

Day in, day out, the routine of school with its endless chores went on. After every meal we filed into the lavatory to brush our teeth. When I looked at Sister Angela I brushed harder in the hope that my teeth would become as beautiful as hers.

We had morning and night prayers, Grace, and Angelus at noon and evening. Between, the Sisters would remind us, "We are all God's children, and He sees us every second." Knowing that Satan always finds work for idle hands, the Sisters taught us to mend, darn, knit, and embroider.

There was even a special way of saying the Rosary when our fingers were busy with the needle, and we could not hold our beads. Sister Angela counted out the decades, assigning to each bead a choir of angels with whom we imagined we were praying. She used to announce, "First choir of angels," and we answered, "Hail Mary, full of grace, the Lord is with thee . . ." Again she intoned, "Second choir of angels," for the second bead, and so on; but since we knew of only nine choirs, at the tenth bead she would say, "The whole celestial court," and we repeated with all our fervor, "Hail Mary, full of grace, the Lord is with thee . . ."

As the Sisters spoke of the angels all around us I remembered my mother saying when I ran after a butterfly: "Don't catch it, darling, it might be an angel." Deeper and deeper the seeds of their instructions took root in my dark mind and grew and flowered.

Whenever I could slip away unnoticed, I went to the room where the piano was and drummed on it. The sound helped me to feel better and was a change from *Do this—Do that.* Once as I rushed ahead, the Sisters were coming down the stairs on their way to the chapel, their heads bent in prayer as they walked along. Fearful of being caught, I didn't see them coming and almost knocked a Sister down. The sacred words on her lips turned to reproof, and she forbade me ever to return there. In spite of this I kept up my secret practice. How could I give up anything so infinitely dear to me, more precious than the Sister's command?

Like the piano, words were a part of my secret world—if I went up in a swing in the playground I was singing to myself, "How would you like to go up in the sky, up in the air so high!" Or I danced about my shadow on the ground, "I have a little shadow that goes in and out with me—"

The light burning all night in the infirmary across the court shone in such a way that I could see enough to read in the darkness, and I began taking a book to bed with me. While all the other children slept, and my eyes ached from reading, I climbed out of bed without a sound and leaned my head on the window sill to look at the stars. In the garden below I could see a path leading to the place where the spangled daisies grew. Was there?—there must be!—Yes—someday I would find a pathway to the stars.

CHAPTER 3

GROWING UP FAST

At the orphanage something called *adoption* was constantly in the air. The children talked about it among themselves; it meant being

taken away to live with someone you didn't know. One little girl
rushed around, shouting excitedly, "I'm going to be adopted and have
a pony of my own!" I didn't want a pony. I only wanted to sing for
people. If you were adopted, they might not let you sing. I began
trying to make myself invisible. If I wasn't noticed, no one would
think of me for adoption. Whenever I could, I ran off to hide. In my
night prayers I pleaded, "Don't let anyone adopt me," escaping into
that secret land of tears where no one could comfort me. If I didn't
belong to my own family any more, I wouldn't belong to anyone.

Once a month a lot of ladies came to the orphanage to talk and
play cards. The children helped with their hats and coats, fetched
them drinks of water, and ran to do other errands. These were the
ladies of the auxiliary; they looked us over, nodded their heads, and
said to one another, "Now she would be a lovely little girl to adopt."
The Ladies Auxiliary also provided the good things to eat for
Thanksgiving dinner which they served at our tables. Afterward we
sang, recited, and made up little plays to entertain them. I loved
singing and dancing for them, but, if any of the ladies looked at me
fixedly, I became terrified; if someone adopted me and took me
away, would my Guardian Angel be able to find me?

In one of the plays I was Snow White. My diadem was fastened
to my curls with hairpins. When I ate the fatal apple and fell upon
the couch a hairpin dug painfully into my head, but I never cried
out nor moved a muscle, for an actress must never show that anything
is wrong.

After Thanksgiving came Advent, during which we prepared for
the coming of the Christ Child. We would store up our spiritual
bouquets to lay at His feet in the manger. The choir of especially
chosen voices spent extra hours learning new hymns and carols. The
night before Christmas, Sister Mary Alice awakened us with a light
tug at our covers. We flew into dressing gowns and slippers. When
we were assembled at the door she gave us each a lighted candle
to carry and whispered the lovely secret: "You will be the Heavenly
Host, singing the glad tidings." At the stroke of midnight she led us
past the Sisters' cells, and we burst into "Adeste Fideles." Lowering
our voices to

> Oh, little town of Bethlehem,
> How still we see thee lie.

we sang to the sleepy children in the dormitories. One by one they
woke, wonder-eyed at the singing procession.

Silent night, Holy night,

we cupped hands around the candle flames as we turned the drafty
corners on our way to the chapel. Kneeling at last before the crib,
we sang like full-voiced angels,

Venite adoremus, Dominum.

As the year advanced, we became familiar with the feasts in the
Sacred Calendar and sang appropriate music to celebrate them. But
the day I received my first Holy Communion was perhaps the day of
greatest wonder and happiness for me. Everything was in white.
Garlands of snowy flowers hung from the altar rail and adorned the
altar. In white dresses and veils we folded our hands in the attitude
of prayer, as our procession entered the chapel.

After the Consecration of the Mass, at a soft signal from Sister
Angela, we began to move reverently, two by two. Ascending the
sanctuary, we clasped in our hands white candles with flickering
cones of warm, gold light. We knelt like nestling doves at the foot
of the altar, our eyes raised expectantly to the white Host held high
above the Chalice, gleaming in the light from the stained-glass window. The priest intoned, "O Lord, I am not worthy . . . only say the
word and my soul shall be healed." In breathless awe, we received
the Blessed Sacrament.

Outside the chapel, the Sisters and the other children congratulated us. In the refectory the first communicants sat together at a
beautiful white table. As we stood to say our grace, Sister Angela said
quietly, "Children, your souls are white as snow today. You are very
pleasing to God. Try to remain so your whole life." This was the second of February, the Feast of the Purification, twelve days before
my sixth birthday.

After two years I was chosen to help the Sister Sacristan. This was
a great honor. Naturally I could not touch the sacred vessels, but
I was permitted to arrange flowers on the altar. I always left one
bud leaning a little way toward the tabernacle. "Lord, when you look
down, this rose will be me," I said in my heart. And it would seem
He heard and reached out to take my hand.

I threw myself completely into whatever I was doing. Like some wild creature in the forest that has to fend for itself I made my way alone. And, though I could meet people with grace, I felt close to no one. While I appreciated the kindness of all the Sisters, I built up a fierce independence. I was determined I would make things change. I would do everything better—schoolwork, household duties, music, as fast as I could. I read and absorbed everything I laid my hands on. I was possessed with the idea of growing up quickly. Grownups were able to do as they pleased. When I was grown-up, I would be free to do what I most wanted to do all the time—SING!

The noisiest place in the orphanage was the playroom, but in one corner stood a locked piano, the only silent thing there. I stood impatiently beside it, waiting for the Sister in charge to unlock the keyboard. As I played, a few little girls hung around curiously. All the others shouted at the top of their voices; but I was deaf to the racket and went on playing.

One day a priest entered the room and stood quietly watching me. When I finished, he came to the piano. "I am Father McNally, the new chaplain. What is your name?" I got up from the piano stool, looking at him, tall and handsome. When I told him my name, he said, "Sister Angela tells me you sing very well. Would you like to sing for me now?" "I shall be glad to, Father," I said with a rush of pride. "Would you like something Irish?" I began thinking I would sing "The Meeting of the Waters" from a play we had done called *Echoes of Erin*. He threw his head back laughing. "So you think I'm Irish, do you? Well, you might be right. Yes, sing me that." I raised my head slightly and began:

> There is not in this wide world
> A valley so sweet . . .

Father McNally's thoughts seemed to move with my song.

> . . . and our hearts, like thy waters
> Be mingled in peace.

When I finished, Father looked at me thoughtfully. Then he patted my shoulder, "Child, that's nice. You must sing again for me soon." He had only recently been ordained and the orphanage was his first spiritual charge. He was happy in his priestly vocation to help mold the souls of little children, especially as his work in the chancery office confined him to the business affairs of the diocese. I could tell he was going to be my friend.

CHAPTER 4

SEMPER PARATA

Extremely precocious, at nine I was ready for high school, and Sister Angela began to worry over me. There was no way of continuing my studies at the Lansdowne orphanage, and the Philadelphia Catholic Girls' High School was too far away. Sister Angela turned to Father McNally for guidance, with a plan gathering in her mind. She was extremely practical, and her loving brown eyes glowed with longing to see all her girls properly equipped for the battle of life.

I could almost see the full-blown decision fall from her thought. "I'll ask Sister Elizabeth, one of our Sisters of St. Vincent de Paul, to take you as a boarder. She has a day nursery not far from the chancery office, and you will be able to walk to and from the high school." I could have thrown my arms about her, though I knew her concern revealed no special favoritism. She was carrying out her motherly duty in the light of her calling, but I felt I was on my way.

The day nursery was run by aging but vigorous Sister Elizabeth, whose gray eyes darted through her steel-rimmed glasses, and tall, slender Sister Frances with the delicate features and transparent skin of the true Gaelic beauty. Welcoming me to the pleasant, old-fashioned brick house on Summer Street, they gave me an austere little room on the fourth floor; its monastic simplicity was forgotten in the blessedness of a room of my own.

As I looked out the window in the morning, I could see the Sisters hurrying down the deserted street to early Mass, their arms folded within their blue sleeves, their footsteps echoing briskly in the stillness. Their great white bonnets reminded me of birds, Sister Elizabeth in staccato flight, with Sister Frances gliding beside her. Then they would come scurrying back to their fifty little charges.

My own day began when the alarm rang at five-thirty. I pulled on my clothes and followed the others to Mass. After breakfast I tidied my room, readied things for the children who were left by their mothers on their way to work, and helped the Sisters with their household tasks. Then I went off to school. After four o'clock I was free to study in the library, go to the conservatory for my piano lessons, or prepare my homework in my own room.

On the way upstairs I liked to stop in the nursery doorway to watch Sister Frances leaning tenderly over the babies in their cribs. The clatter and clamor were far below me now. Only the voices of the romping children in the back yard floated up to my window like distant music. Soon the mothers would be coming from work to take their little ones home—I was learning "the short and simple annals of the poor."

One morning as I raced downstairs, I smelled smoke. I collided with Sister Frances, flying from the nursery holding up her apron full of babies. I helped to carry out the other children, and we all stood huddled in the yard while firemen put out the little blaze. Sister Frances stood staring with her long slender fingers pressed to her cheek. I could hear her saying, "Oh, and it's often I've felt the hand of the banshee on my own cheek."

After this I loved to talk to Sister Frances about her early life in Ireland and Celtic folklore. To all my other interests I added the study of Irish folk songs, so I almost never got to bed before midnight, and the long hours began taking their toll of my vitality.

The academic requirements of the high school became more exacting, and the competition of students from the entire diocese of Philadelphia, more keen. The teachers, the very flower of various diocesan orders, taught subjects in which their communities were outstanding—the Sisters of Mercy, Latin and French; the Immaculate Heart, history and mathematics; St. Joseph, English; St. Francis, Science.

Brilliant Sister Raphael, her golden eyes the mirror of her soul, taught me Latin, which she made a living language. Of all the Sisters, she was most closely in touch with our activities and seemed to read our thoughts. She knew of my lessons at the conservatory, attended the plays in which I acted, praised my singing in the cathedral. "You are my little marine," she said, "ready for everything at a moment's notice—*semper parata*." It did not escape her vigilance that I was heavy-eyed and drowsy in her afternoon classes. She would shake her head and sigh, "Too many irons in the fire, little *semper parata*. Maybe we can do something."

About this time my high-spirited sister, Nadea, had escaped from the bounds of her convent boarding school and eloped with Joseph Loftus, the handsome son of a well-known Philadelphia family. Rejoicing in her new-found independence, she began to visit me regularly. I was heartened by the prospect of basking in her nearness, observing her style, sharing in the excitement of her many interests. She introduced me to new pleasures and always left me with something wonderful to anticipate until she came again: a Saturday matinee, a concert for my birthday, my first operatic performance, *La Bohème* with Maggie Teyte, at the Academy of Music. This was my introduction to Puccini apart from study of the score. Hearing the music with the singers and full orchestral accompaniment, seeing Mimi move through the touching scenes of her tragic life wove a spell of enchantment about me.

I ran to tell my happiness to Father McNally, the confidant of my childish joys and sorrows. His face lit up. "Next Saturday afternoon, if you are free, I should like to take you to hear the great John McCormack." Free? I could hardly wait for the day to come!

I sat impressed by the stark expanse of the stage, waiting for the artist to breathe life into the scene. Suddenly he appeared in the curve of the piano, a huge man in full evening dress. He lifted his magnificent head, dark with curly hair, and began to sing with a woodland freshness and purity which carried us away.

After the concert was over, Father McNally took me backstage to meet Mr. McCormack. I was so speechless with admiration for this great artist who could create a moment of magic in every song that I could find no words. The crowd milled around us while Father McNally chatted with the singer.

I noticed a man rubbing his hand on his trouser leg and edging toward us. "Mr. McCormack," he said in a rough voice, "I'm only a mechanic, but I would like the privilege of shaking hands with you." Mr. McCormack held out his hand with a robust laugh, "Nonsense, man, sure it's no privilege for one American to shake the hand of another."

The next day I bought two McCormack records, "Macushla" and "I Hear You Calling Me," which I carried about with me, playing them over and over on any Victrola I could find. I was on the track of his purity of tone and that moment of magic in every song.

Meanwhile Sister Raphael had been true to her promise. She had been busy exploring the possibilities of a change in my environment, a new school where the pace would be less exhausting. She did not select Mater Misericordia, a diocesan school of her own order, but applied for a scholarship to Georgian Court in Lakewood, New Jersey. In those peaceful surroundings, far from the pressures of my present circumstances, she felt I might have a less strenuous, a more suitable life.

Out of the hundreds of girls at the high school, I was at once chosen to sing in the cathedral. Everyone who heard, but most of all the students, enjoyed my voice, which also attracted the attention of the organist, Mr. Thunder. His unusual name seemed quite appropriate to the full organ climaxes of the great Bach preludes he played at special exercises.

One day Mr. Thunder asked me: "Would you like to sing for Nicola Montani, the distinguished vocal teacher and authority on Gregorian chant? I'm curious to know what he thinks of your voice."

"I'd be delighted to sing for him—and thank you very much for suggesting it." I hoped he could read into my polite words the joyous anticipation I felt at the prospect.

Nicola Montani and his wife, a former opera singer, at once became enthusiastic; and, though my lessons were infrequent, both helped me develop broader musical horizons and showered me with kindness. Through them I became interested in the restoration of liturgical music and its proper interpretation.

Our legal guardian, whom I had nicknamed "The Callahan," was shrouded in mystery. Though I never saw him or asked about him, I still remember Nadea's vehement description of financial skirmishes. She was determined I should have some new clothes to go away in. Bearding "The Callahan" in his den, she emerged in triumph with money to take me shopping at Wanamaker's.

I ran from saleswoman to mirror. Never had I dreamed of possessing such an outfit for my very own, and I was ecstatic. A pale blue silk dress, a matching hat of crushed velvet, a coat of sapphire blue, also velvet, buttoning on the side and edged with light brown fur; patent leather shoes, long stockings of silk, dark blue gloves—I put everything on so I could walk out of the store all dressed up. Never had I been so elated with a sense of my own chic!

It struck Nadea as an excellent time to go on a round of visits, so her friends could admire me. The moment also seemed right for paying a call of my own.

Proudly smoothing the shining folds of my blue coat, I rang the bell of the chancery with a flourish, listening as it tinkled back at me. My new clothes were a most appropriate costume to pay a visit of congratulations to the recently appointed Right Reverend Monsignor Thomas F. McNally. Would he be surprised that I, too, had an announcement to make?

There on the steps I rehearsed my lines: "Monsignor, tomorrow I am leaving for Georgian Court, in Lakewood, New Jersey."

CHAPTER 5

GEORGIAN COURT

Georgian Court! Georgian Court! The words made a lovely chime of joy in my heart, though seething in my frightened little head were a million doubts and fears.

Did I look too young? Could I compete with girls brought up in families from the cities of the world? Would they laugh at my clothes? I was wearing my wonderful blue outfit; but in my suitcase were only an old Peter Thompson and a little wool suit with pleated skirt, Eton jacket, and round-collared white blouse.

September was advanced to the time of thin silver nets of early morning frost; of moonstone smoke from burning leaves; of birds on the long flight south. As we passed the lake and rounded a curve, before us loomed Georgian Court surrounded by a high fence of iron spikes. Nadea and I rode through the massive gate and between bright borders of fall flowers to the white and shining mansion house.

A Sister swung back the heavy grilled door. "You are one of the new girls," she said, with the mysteriously sweet smile of the religious. "I am Sister Bertrand. You are very welcome; I am sure you will be happy here."

The term was opening, and many things demanded her attention; but after introducing me to Mother Mary John, the Superior, Sister Bertrand took a few precious moments to lead us from the foyer to a tiny chapel.

I said my prayers with a happy rush of devotion. I had never imagined a place so heavenly as the chapel, light and exquisite in tone; the afternoon sun filtering through the delicately colored stained-glass windows threw shafts of light over the Lourdes grotto with the kneeling Bernadette and the statue of the Little Flower of Jesus. I sighed, "quiet as a nun, breathless with adoration."

"Now I will turn you over to one of our older girls," said Sister Bertrand gently. I noticed her queenly bearing, the swift grace with which she moved, the now flashing, now roguish glance of her green-gold eyes. "Marie has been with us ever since she was a little girl; she will help you settle comfortably. We want you to feel at home."

"Thank you, Sister." Could this really be happening to me?

Back in the foyer again, waiting for Marie, I turned around slowly, drinking in everything: the warm brightness of ruby damask hangings; the purple twilight streaming in at the tall windows, bringing out reds in the Canterbury Pilgrim murals; the high carved marble fireplace with the coat of arms of the Gould family; the iridescent crystals of the great chandelier.

A slim blonde girl with a reserved expression came down the curving staircase. "Please, Sister?" she said. And, turning to me with a shy smile, "I'll be glad to show you to your room."

There was contentment in Nadea's eyes when she kissed me good-by. "Be sure to write soon," she reminded me. I picked up my suitcase and followed Marie Tobin up the marble steps, holding the gold balustrade to steady myself.

Alone in my small room under the gables I knelt later to say my night prayers. My heart was overflowing with gratitude. "Thank you, dear Lord," I whispered over and over. Outside my dormer window a big bright star hung low in the dark blue sky.

The loveliness and peace of my new surroundings took me in hand, soothing and encouraging me. Gradually I discovered my own way in the variegated pattern of the campus; the lagoon dazzling in the morning sun, the Apollo fountain with the gigantic god driving his sea horses against the background of the dark spruces, the tall pines of Cathedral Lawn, the hidden Japanese garden, the casino where five thousand people would come to hear us perform in the Musicale. I felt attuned to the great bell ringing for early Mass. After what seemed a long, frightening journey, I had come home at last, to a place where I belonged.

In the first weeks of finding a foothold in routine I was puzzled that Sister Bertrand addressed me as Jessica "Plantagenet." Did she really think that was my name? Did she think I was of royal blood? I never questioned her, for it was romantic, and I was studying the Plantagenet kings in history class.

From the time Sister Bertrand welcomed me at the open door at Georgian Court, she stirred my devoted admiration. Intuitively I sensed the warmth of her interest, yet I found it difficult to confide in anyone. Biding her time, she watched me patiently. By her strong, serene ways, by the gracious authority with which she presided over our activities, by movement and speech, we could see she lived close to the lifeline of prayer. How could we show that devotion to God which was Sister Bertrand's vocation?

Whether she taught history, mathematics, philosophy, she seized our interest, showering the golden moments of her classes with knowledge and wisdom. The inner light of her brilliant spirit made her an inspired teacher. To us she seemed a Wingèd Victory. Her classes were never long enough, and we left them walking on air.

In my eagerness to continue the study I had begun at the conservatory I lost no time commencing my piano lessons with learned Sister Beatrice, a doctor of music at a time when very few women had the degree. Sitting close beside me, her long musician's hands folded in her lap, she said, "Play me something, so we can see what you have been doing." I played a Chopin polonaise. Without commenting on my performance, she reached up and took a book from the shelf, opened it and placed it on the music rack. Creasing the pages with her positive fingers, she said: "I want you to learn this Bach invention for your next lesson, besides some Czerny finger exercises. In addition, you may select anything else you wish."

She was a little surprised by my choice of the Chopin D-flat minor étude. "Why do you choose that particular étude?" she asked, fixing me with her brown-eyed, penetrative gaze.

"At the conservatory one of the boys played it—I liked its harp-like quality—"

"Very well; prepare a few pages of what the boy played." Then she grew serious, "You understand, don't you, that I require my students to practice two hours daily? You will find your practice schedule on the wall inside your cubicle." It was Friday afternoon, and Sister Beatrice stood up, "It's time now for Holy Hour, so we'll cut this lesson short; get your veil and meet me in the chapel."

The Sisters and pupils were already kneeling in their pews. While Sister Beatrice played the organ, I stood beside her and sang the special hymns to the Blessed Sacrament. I joined in the fervor of their devotion, pouring out my soul in the sacred words.

After "O Salutaris" and "Tantum Ergo," the priest, dressed in his white and gold cope, rose. He adjusted the humeral veil to cover his hands, and lifted the jeweled monstrance in benediction, while we bowed our heads in deepest reverence. The mystical joy lingered as the sacred Species was locked away in the tabernacle. Then we stood, and in unison our voices welled out in a mighty flood of praise,

> . . . Fill the heavens with sweet accord
> Holy, Holy, Holy Lord.

Our services did not always reach the heights of the Holy Hour. Sometimes we gathered for May devotions in homage to the Queen of Heaven. Sister Mercedes, drawn to the oratory by my singing, would be carried away and burst into song. I loved her for it, but her old-fashioned style of singing threw me into paroxysms of stifled giggles. Despite all my control, the shaking of my shoulders betrayed me to her.

"You were laughing at me today in chapel," she said with mock severity, meeting me in the corridor. "Aren't you ashamed to laugh at the singing of a poor old Sister?"

"Oh, no, Sister—I would never laugh at you—something very funny came into my head—"

"Oh, yes you would!" she insisted, cornering me with playful accusation. "But I forgive you. Here—"

Like a prestidigitator, she opened her wide sleeves drawing from one a bowl of cold chicken, and then—to my utter amazement—from the other a bowl of layer cake. "You can't live on Divine Love alone, you know."

The omniscient Sisters had doubtless observed how little I ate in the refectory and how often I absented myself from meals. They could not know that this was a habit I had formed in the orphanage when talk of adoption was in the air.

The girls used to worry about it, too. They always asked me to sing at the parties they gave when boxes of goodies came from home. Their plans miscarried, for I would sing so much I would forget to eat. They would flop on the floor, munching and listening. "Sing us 'Peggy Take Me,' Jessica," they would plead. This amusing ballad ended with a showy high note. It probably led to Sally McKeon's inviting me to a family celebration for her sister, Peggy, just returned from Dublin.

The girls, and their brother Joseph, lived with their uncle, Monsignor McKeon, who often visited the convent. A North Ireland newspaperman, he had been converted to Catholicism. I was delighted at the prospect of seeing his little church which Sally mentioned so much, a replica of the flawlessly carved church of Gray's *Elegy*.

It was a very gay party. We were greatly amused when the irrepressible Sally addressed the dignified churchman with "Hey, Unc', you must have had a hard time rearing us when we were little. Remember how you used to order our clothes by mail from Sears, Roebuck?"

The companionship of girls like Sally McKeon was good for me. My instinct for fun, under other circumstances, probably would have made me a tomboy. But the goal that I had set for myself demanded every moment of time, every ounce of energy that I could give. The girls thought I was allergic to mischief.

"If you want Jessica to come to your room, you'll have to send her a gilt-edged invitation," they teased.

How could they know I was possessed of a single ideal—to give to the world the song in my heart? How could they know I was jealous of every minute that took me from this dedication?

I worked so hard I had no time for the little intimacies of school life—a complete lack of worldly experience contributed to my shyness and unbelievable innocence. When I was given a roommate, and the girls discovered I undressed in the closet, they pulled me out with shouts of "Ho, we'll help you get your clothes off." The girls were much taller and stronger than I. The only way I could cope with them was to crouch down on the floor and butt my head at the middle of whoever tried to touch me. They could not budge me.

"How are you going to be able to live in the theater and play roles like Traviata, if you're so modest," they shrieked. "You'll never do it."

"I will, I will!" I cried. "I know how those women feel, I don't have to be like them. I shall sing before great audiences all over the world."

These great expectations were hard for them to swallow. "I shall go to Paris, too!" I added desperately. "And have lovers!" This was something I had read about artists. I hadn't the faintest idea of what it meant, but my schoolmates must understand that nothing was going to stand in the way of my dreams.

I moved through the days in a trance. The only person whose absent-mindedness matched my own was a new German maid who came in to care for my room one morning. Busy with her thoughts, she did not see that I was sleeping and began making me up in the bed. Sitting bolt upright at the touch of her hands, I yelled, "What are you doing?" Frightened out of her wits, she ran screaming out of the room and never came back.

The girls were still determined to break up my preoccupation. One evening a group of them swooped down, snatched me bodily from my chair, stretched me full length on top of the desk, and rolled me for a spin to the end of the corridor. As they clattered along at hair-raising speed, the other girls came running out of their rooms to join the uproar.

At the height of the commotion someone caught sight of Dorothy

Mulgrave. Dorothy, now a professor of education at New York University, illumined the one school year she spent with us like a brilliant shooting star. An ambitious student, she had many extracurricular studies and took frequent home leave. She could manage this on account of her father's illness, but at the same time we were envious of her.

"What are you doing here, stranger? We thought you were in New York! What do you do there, anyway? Why do you go so often, you lucky stiff, when we can't get permission to go at all."

"I have a season ticket to Grant's Tomb," reported Dorothy dryly.

The general laughter was an impetus. The girls whizzed me all the harder down the corridor, shouting, "Oh, they laid her bier in the chapel! In the chapel they laid her bier! Whose bier? Why Jessica's, of course!" Expecting to be whirled off into space, I closed my eyes and gripped the edges of the table.

Suddenly a new vibration struck them simultaneously. In a flash every single one vanished, leaving me to scramble off my "bier." As best I could I dragged it back to my room. Just then the faint sound of cincture beads materialized into the form of Mother Mary John, on the way to her cell.

We liked to fool ourselves into thinking she was oblivious to our pranks, but she was a born psychologist, with the most acute powers of discernment. Mother Mary John kept close watch, sometimes encouraging our mischief by staying out of range. Still she never let us overindulge this freedom. We were kept constantly busy, and when hard put to find another occupation for us, Mother would say with quiet authority, "Girls, get your instruments," and we would be consigned to playing the mandolin for an hour. She dearly wanted all to be good pupils, and her mind never left us for a single waking moment. She knew everything there was to know about us. She had eyes in the back of her head.

Periodically the news would fly through the dormitory rooms: "Bishop Walsh is here!" We would go at once to the foyer to greet the Bishop of Trenton. He would stand benignly in the doorway as we knelt to receive his blessing. Then, while we watched in a respectful semicircle, he would ascend to the suite reserved for his visits.

Now called the Bishop's Suite, in the time of the Goulds it was known as the Green Rooms, because of their rich green hangings and commanding view of Cathedral Lawn. An aura of romance and mystery still hovered about them. A tale is told to newcomers at the convent about how Edith Kingdon Gould left a note written to her husband in the corner of her desk blotter. The same day she fell dead at his feet on the golf course at Georgian Court; the note was never opened, and finally vanished.

During his stay we would entertain the bishop with a concert or a musical play. His Grace spoke most beautiful Italian. Indeed, his great interest in Italian missions had impelled him to bring a community of Sisters to Trenton to establish the Villa Victoria. Mindful of these interests, when I was asked to sing for him, I would especially choose an Italian aria, something like "Un Bel Di Vedremo" from *Madama Butterfly*.

He always seemed quite pleased with these official visits, and made a point of thanking me personally for my songs. One day he said, "I want you to be sure to have a talk with me every time I come."

As I knelt to kiss his ring and bid him good-by, I murmured demurely, "But Your Grace is always so busy when you are here." I never went to have the talk with him. I was afraid to. What if he were considering me for Villa Victoria?

Together with the Sisters we had numerous distinguished lay teachers. Their latitude of experience, outlook, and temperament expanded our imagination and thinking, striking a healthy balance between the discipline of the contained convent world, and a concept of the outside, practical world.

A colorful Viennese, Professor Moric Stoehr, taught us science. He appealed to me because he also was a musician, both a pianist and a singer. His inventions all applied to music. Eagerly we observed his experiments with a musical typewriter and a magical device for transposing from one key to another. In class we liked to divert him from our lessons to his experiences with musical celebrities: Caruso, Godowsky, Kreisler. He amused us when he alluded to his talented wife, the concert pianist Herma Menthe, as "a crazy woman with an artistic finish."

The heart and soul of kindness in the classroom, he tried earnestly never to give anyone a poor mark or even a word of rebuke. It so happened that Professor Stoehr taught in a nearby boys' school. One day after our class he noticed one of the girls bending nervously over his hat and coat and wondered about this sudden, unusual interest.

"Mademoiselle," he said politely, "what are you doing with my hat and coat?"

"Oh, Professor—" she stammered, on the verge of tears. "I implore you—please don't tell on me—please!"

"Tell on you? What have I to tell, Mademoiselle?" He put on his coat, ready to leave for the other school. Before he could pick up his hat she had it in her own hands.

"I've—you see, Professor, I've been sending notes to Johnny—I—we —hide them in the lining of your hat—and—" She began to cry hysterically—"Please don't report me—I know there's a note from him in the lining for me today. I was trying to get it out without your seeing—"

Professor Stoehr was almost in tears himself. He felt about in the lining anxiously and pulled out the note. Then agitatedly he extended his hand. "Take it! I give it to you on one condition—" He shook his finger at her like an exasperated father—"I forbid you to tell a soul what has happened, Mademoiselle. Neither shall I!"

The French-Italian blend in my blood gave me an instinctive leaning toward languages. I could speak French and Italian, some German and Spanish. For the sake of my music I lost no chance to use them. With happiness I saw the homesick Spanish girls' eyes brighten whenever I spoke to them in their native tongue or sang their native songs.

Our French Mademoiselle was a pretty blonde and possessed a sophistication which to my inexperience was quite daring. I was shocked to find her smoking a cigarette in the sunken garden!

Fräulein Klauss's national pride was not to be outdone by Mademoiselle's triumph with her student production of *Cyrano de Bergerac;* so Fräulein arranged to have us play an act of Schiller's *Wilhelm Meister*. With Teutonic zest she helped us design our costumes and build the scenery. The night of the performance she invited a covey of German nieces and nephews to enjoy the results of her labors.

Abruptly the scenery collapsed. Fräulein strode on the stage and urged us to start over again. Undaunted, we doubled our efforts to do justice to her pride in us. The play resumed. Fräulein's relatives poised themselves to act with spirit as a claque.

When they heard the wavelike cadences of Schiller's lines as declaimed by American girls they were convulsed with amusement. And when the scene reached the apple-shooting climax they threw off all restraint and roared with derisive laughter.

"Speak your lines louder!" we whispered wildly among the cast. "Drown them out!"

An actor shouted:

> . . . This feat of Tell, the archer, will be told,
> While yonder mountains stand upon their base,
> By heaven! the apple's cleft right through the core. . . .

But it was of no use. Their unbridled mirth broke up the performance, leaving nothing for us to do but lower the curtain.

Trite, Hiatus, Pithy, Pungent, these were the words I saw Professor Haney writing large upon the blackboard as I entered my first class in English composition. What did he expect us to do with the words? Was this some method of his own for teaching us to write? A paralyzing silence fell upon us for we could see we were going to have a hard time with him. But to me his approach was a challenge.

He lost no time with textbook study, plunging us at once into the actual writing of prose and verse. His first assignment was a quatrain on a subject of our own choosing. A quat—what? The task was too preposterous for words! Some of the class simply gave up in disgust and handed in nothing. Inspired by my love of Keats, I tried to emulate the poet in four lines whose title "Happy Insensibility" I pilfered bodily; at least I was honest enough to leave my paper unsigned.

When Professor Haney read the verses to the class for criticism, Keats to the contrary, they were received with scornful snickers. I tried to be nonchalant, but my blushes betrayed me. On the margin of my paper, however, Professor Haney had written a charming reassurance, "Have no fear; Providence helps the moth out of the chrysalis." Over my shoulder Ann Noonan complained, "Well, I like that! Look what he says on mine. 'Not written with a graphic pen'—and I used my best Waterman!"

Only Regina Codey appeared to understand. The incident gave

me a new appreciation of her Sapphic gifts, a new respect for this frail poetess with the scintillant peridot eyes of one driven by the Furies to ecstasy. A luminous quality also permeated her prose, which I read ardently before settling down to write my own themes.

I had none of the worldly experiences of my classmates and I drew heavily on my imagination. One paper I turned in, *A Ride in the Subway*, received the highest mark in the class. At that time I had never ridden in a subway nor even seen one from the outside.

Professor Haney never allowed us to become conscious of any lack. Instead, he struggled to open up new vistas for our burgeoning minds, inspiring us with his constant emphasis on the deep integration of the arts, the living pulsating language which is music. He fired me to make this idiom so much my own that I might faithfully communicate to the world the beauty of the great composers.

We were all very fond of Sister Consolata Carroll, then Viola Carroll. She had come to Georgian Court fresh out of Pratt Institute, with the last word in home economics. Pretty and fun-loving, she established herself quickly in our affections.

Viola was apt at dashing off parodies on all kinds of subjects—a talent we depended on when there was a revue. Once, when a musical was in rehearsal, she made a happy use of the coincidence that an economy wave had struck the dining hall. Day by day the butterballs were becoming smaller. Viola dressed her protagonist in yellow, had her carry a huge tray with a single tiny butterball in the center. Over this she held a large magnifying glass while she sang "Poor Butterball" using the melody of "Poor Butterfly." The Sisters always attended our performances. On this occasion, the poor Sister in charge of the dining room did not relish the humor of "Poor Butterball." Before the first lines of the parody were finished, she hastened away from the gymnasium in great embarrassment.

One evening we received from Viola Carroll invitations tied with blue and pink ribbons, reading, "Come to my room; I have something to tell you."

"Oh, she's going to announce her engagement!" we chattered. "And no wonder—she's so gay and attractive."

To our amazement she announced, "My dears, I'm going to leave you for a while; very soon I shall enter the novitiate at Mount Saint Mary to become a Sister of Mercy."

We all cried. Dear Viola would be lost to us forever! But after a few years she came back to us, where she is today, teaching English at Georgian Court—Sister Consolata Carroll.

We could not long remain sad or discontented at Georgian Court, for the Sisters planned an over-all program of range and versatility. Besides academic work, we rushed to speech seminars, lectures on art, Wagnerian music, current events, instrumental rehearsals—every girl at the school was required to play an instrument—gymnasium practice, which included dancing. Sister Miriam had charge of our choral training, but once a month, to my delight, Nicola Montani came to supervise our proper singing of Gregorian chant, which, he explained, he had perfected at the Benedictine Monastery on the Isle of Wight.

Though I was by no means carefree, I was no longer a displaced person but oriented, beginning to be rooted. In this good and comfortable life, I gained assurance and confidence in myself. But were my ambitions leading me in the right direction?

During the soul-searching annual retreats, usually conducted by some prominent member of the Society of Jesus, I worried a good deal about my chosen vocation. A singing career did not fall into the two categories designated by the Sisters as most pleasing to God. The first aim of every Catholic woman should be sainthood. But I knew I did not intend to be a nun or marry and dedicate myself to a family. These very thoughts seemed sacrilegious and caused my heart to beat violently against my ribs.

"Now when the crocus and daffodil shed their winter wrappings, and the trees burst into jade newness," the retreat master was exhorting us, "do you not feel the fresh impulse to love God anew—and resolve to make a better life?"

As I knelt before the tabernacle in the exquisite chapel no ritual of words gathered to my lips. Rather I tried to reach out directly for the hand of God. "—Ask and you shall receive—" I prayed fervently that my chosen way of life would be compatible with the ideals I had been taught. In the light of all that had happened I knew the way would not be easy. I hoped, I believed the beatitude would be fulfilled in

my life of song. So it was in my struggles, prayer supplied the daily
steady flow of power that sustained me.

CHAPTER 6

ON THE THRESHOLD

All winter long and into spring we practiced for the culminating
event of the year, May Musicale. Sister Beatrice drew up the program
to include the music students in piano arrangements of works played
on seven pianos simultaneously; orchestral selections, harp ensem-
bles, chorales, vocal solos, and always a closing tableau dedicated
to some universal theme like *I Am An American* or *Our Lady of
Fatima*. It was a tremendous undertaking for Sister Beatrice, whose
nerves must have been rubbed raw, caught as she was in her studio,
enmeshed in the web of practice cubicles.

One day I was intently polishing the breezelike cadenza in the
middle of Liszt's "Liebestraum," my solo at one of the seven pianos,
when I heard a quick timid knock at the door of my practice room. I
opened, to find Regina Codey standing there, that characteristic
ravished look on her countenance. My own out-of-this-world expression must have frightened her, for she stood there an instant open-
mouthed. Then she ventured, "Mother Mary John wants to see you
in the mansion house at once." Simple enough words, though ominous
in Regina's sober speech.

Meekly I fell in with her and we retraced the long path to the
mansion. The wind in the walk whipped up color in our cheeks. I
didn't always understand Regina but I was fascinated by her brooding looks. She had the entrancingly blue-black hair of the Irish, worn
curly and short, the high ivory forehead conforming gently to her
heart-shaped face.

"The girls say you are going to be a nun," she remarked slowly as
we hurried along. "Then your music—"

"Oh no!" I exclaimed, "They're mistaken—for me music comes first,
last, and all the time!"

She smiled with marked satisfaction. I thanked her for coming to fetch me and went straight to Mother Mary John in the morning room.

"Come in, dear child," she said, seeing me hesitant on the threshold. Drawing me to her visitors with an inclusive gesture, she said persuasively, "Mrs. Buckhout—Katherine—I want to introduce Jessica Dragonette. Rest a minute, girls; then, Jessica, show Katherine about. If she likes Georgian Court well enough Katherine will stay—so you have a responsibility." For the austere Mother Mary John this was a surprisingly light touch.

We smiled and forthwith our hands reached out in a warmth of greeting. We talked as though we had known each other for a long time. Mrs. Buckhout studied me appraisingly, with curious intentness. She was handsome and smartly dressed.

A scene long-forgotten flashed before me. In place of Mrs. Buckhout and Katherine, momentarily I saw Mrs. De Witt and Huggins that first day at the orphanage. Mrs. Buckhout had the same aroma of perfume; Katherine, the ash-blonde curls and laughing cornflower blue eyes of Huggins. For a dizzy moment the rush of memory burst the floodgates of the past. I must have turned pale, for Katherine said, "May we go now? It's awfully warm in here."

I led her first to the sunken gardens. "How lovely," she said, stopping wide-eyed on the steps to stare at the blue-green lagoon. When she turned, however, to see the statue of the Sacred Heart in a niche below, she became thoughtful. "Jessique," she said, "you don't mind if I call you that instead of Jessica? It seems to suit you better. Are you a Catholic? You don't look like one!"

The puzzling experiences of the day were mounting one on another! "How should a Catholic look?" I laughed. Yet deep inside I sensed troubled waters. Even so, her remark did not disturb me. I thought, *I have been Catholic for centuries.* Evidently Katherine is new wine.

I went on uncovering gardens, to beguile her; and this became, I think, the touchstone of her decision to stay. Each day forward gave something new to our ripening friendship. She had been out of school for some time before coming to Georgian Court. It was difficult for her to adjust to convent discipline; besides, she was homesick. Nevertheless, with gallantry and courage she threw her energies into all her studies, especially sculpture and painting.

For my Valentine-birthday she made a colorfully decorated paper ship bearing a pretty cargo of gifts, among them a booklet designed to prophesy my future life, and a sealed envelope containing two tickets, from her parents, for a Metropolitan Opera performance of *La Tosca*, with Jeritza and Gigli.

The heady impact of being in the great world, sitting in a box close to the stage in the Diamond Horseshoe, was like champagne. Gazing at the impeccably dressed men and women all around me, with their air of sophisticated poise, I longed to take my proper place among them. As the golden curtains parted, revealing the magnificent stage, I was transported to the church of Sant' Andrea della Valle. Breathlessly I waited for the entrance of the impetuous prima donna, her arms full of red roses for the Madonna. The "Te Deum" finale of the first act with the Cardinal and Swiss Guards in processional advance while all the bells of Rome chime harmoniously, was so exalting that at the intermission I could not move. Mrs. Buckhout, gracious and intuitive, broke the spell with the suggestion that a cool drink would be nice before the second-act curtain.

When it came time for the "Vissi d'arte, vissi d'amore," the glamorous Jeritza—her golden hair falling about her face, covering her shoulders—flung herself prone on the stage and in that revolutionary position sang, "For art and love, for these alone have I lived." Its like had never been seen before!

When Tosca placed the candles at the head of the murdered Scarpia and when, later, she leaped from the parapet, her hair flying like a golden cloud in the radiant night, I could have cried out as the tenor did: "E non ho amato mai tanto la vita." ("I never loved life more than at this moment.")

The incomparable showmanship of Jeritza, supreme even among celebrated artists, made a profound imprint on the aspiring amateur. I could hardly wait to include her in my repertoire of imitations. Alas, when Mother Mary John observed that the mimicry required me to lie stretched full length on the floor, she asked me to "eliminate this unladylike performance."

Mr. Buckhout must have been very much amused at the "unladylike" effect of Tosca upon "the little one," as he affectionately called me. "Why didn't you bring her home with you," he asked the following week end, as the large family gathered for dinner about the big round table.

Katherine answered, "That would be as hard as extracting a turtle from its shell. She's completely snowed under with lessons."

"Oh, that's not fair," said Mr. Buckhout. "She ought to have a little bit of fun. All work and no play—"

The next mail brought me a matinee ticket for *Pelléas et Mélisande* with Bori and Johnson. I selected from my frugal wardrobe a black velvet dress with delicately pleated collar and cuffs of *café au lait* georgette Nadea had sent me for singing occasions at the convent. I felt elegantly grown-up as I stood at the head of the orchestra aisle, ticket in hand, waiting for the usher to show me my seat. To my surprised confusion, a man pushed his stubs in my face, saying "Please, Miss, my seats." Before I could stammer a word, the regular usher appeared in the nick of time. "Follow me, Miss, your seat is right here." The stranger's profuse apologies drifted after me; but I had already forgotten him, for I found myself sitting right beside John Charles Thomas! I had seen him on the concert stage, but when he looked up from his program and smiled genially at me, my heart skipped a beat. Delighted at the flutter he had caused, he brought me back to equilibrium with, "Is this the first time you are hearing *Pelléas et Mélisande?*"

"I know 'Mes longs cheveux descendent—'" Just then the house went dark, an arc of golden light moved upward along the curtains, and I was alone in the world, listening to the opening chords of the forest scene.

This introduction to Debussy was a new musical experience. It was like wandering in fairyland, hearing the eternal symphony of the sea through a shell held to the ear. I went back to Georgian Court with another ambition. One day I wanted to sing Mélisande.

We awoke to find May fifteenth, the day of May Musicale, waiting for us in the sunshine and flowers Sister Beatrice had diligently prayed for the whole year. After early Mass and breakfast we hurried for last-minute practice. We were on the way to our performance.

Around us everywhere was the hubbub of arriving guests, clergymen, and Sisters from all points of the compass; people taking their leisure or promenading, dwarfed by the giant spruces. I was looking forward to Nadea's coming. She had promised to bring her music-loving newly-wed friends, the John Alden Smiths.

Along an undulating path in the formal gardens I tried to hasten to the casino building, but every few feet I had to stop, for the scent of lilacs in full bloom intoxicated me—

> Le temps des lilas et le temps des roses . . .
> Ne reviendra plus à ce printemps-ci;

The very flowers seemed to be singing with me. Sister Beatrice would be standing impatiently on the gymnasium stage to give us instructions for the Musicale about to begin. But she could wait—

> Heaven's breath smells wooingly here—

In just a few days the lilacs would be spilling their pink and lavender tacks over the dark green velvet of the lawns, and then be gone until another spring!

Above the flowering shrubs I could see bronze Mercury striding the skies over Raymond Hall. I wanted to sit in a lilac tree and fathom the portent in my mind, the something tugging at my heart. In the world within the world in which I had so long isolated myself, my sensitivity had become exaggerated. Besides, to confide in others always seemed an intrusion upon their lives.

I worried a good deal about making right decisions, but from time to time in unpremeditated moments, often after prayer, the answers sprang up from within, like a flash of insight, before the reasons were at all clear to me. So I had come to listen for these inner voices, to whatever it was that Coleridge called the "creatrix" at work—"frequently establishing a center, a sort of nucleus in the reservoir of the soul."

As I lingered in a springtime daydream, imagination bodied forth "the forms of things unknown." But Sister Beatrice was waiting! Believing that I had been snared by the romantic fragrances, I thrust the presentiment from me that at this Musicale I should be standing on the solid threshold of my professional career.

I stood on the stage bowing, waiting for the introductory measures of my first aria. I took in the colorful picture of Bishop Walsh in his

magnificent red robes of state, as he leaned forward in his special
chair, flanked by clergymen and close by a group of Sisters from
Villa Victoria. Behind them, row upon row of parents and friends; in
the overhanging balcony, all our beloved Sisters of Mercy.

The expectant hush that fell upon the audience charged me with
inspiration. I heard the silence melt into Musetta's gay waltz song,
carrying all hearts with it:

> Quando m'en vo'
> Soletta per la via—

Sister Beatrice, concealed in the wings, resolutely beating out the
time for every number, would feel rewarded for her labors by the
enthusiastic applause.

The long performance was over. Proud relatives and friends rushed
backstage to congratulate teacher and pupils. Nadea and the Smiths
found me, and we walked down to enjoy the rainbow colors of the
Apollo fountain in full play.

Mr. Smith was particularly cordial in his congratulations. "I enjoyed your singing very much. Have you ever thought of following
singing as a career?"

"Oh, yes, I think of it all the time. But first I should like to have an
audition with an outstanding authority who could judge whether my
ambitions are justified."

Something in his mind responded to my need. "Dr. Tertius Noble
of the Juilliard Foundation is a fraternity brother of mine. I see him
sometimes at the club. I'll make a point of speaking to him." I
thanked him with tears of joy in my eyes and tried to possess my
soul in patience, knowing that every day would seem a year.

I wanted to make every moment count in my time of waiting. As
stage director of our dramatic club, I persuaded Katherine Buckhout
that she was well suited to the part of the Madonna in our proposed
version of Massenet's *Jongleur de Notre Dame*. Though she was not
a music student, she was interested in dramatics and dancing and
gladly gave up week ends at home to attend our rehearsals. I loved
playing the wistful little juggler, tumbling, juggling his balls, and finally dancing himself to death before the altar of the Blessed Virgin.
Katherine was touching in the moment when the statue comes to life

in blessing—a living reproof to the censuring monks. I felt in the little juggler my own poor talents that would achieve greatness only through their dedication.

Our teachers were very proud of this ambitious performance of the old legend and looked forward enthusiastically to our next dramatic presentation. By way of contrast, we felt we should do a modern play and promptly sent our ten-dollar fee to Samuel French and Company for *Summer Boarders*. All went well until the curtain was going up. Mother Mary John, coming backstage to spur us on, was startled to see some of her young ladies dressed in men's clothing. Her expression changed to a horrified gasp, and she told us with finality: "You will have to dismiss the audience; I forbid you to go on with the play unless you change your attire."

We were in despair. We had to do something. I was elected to fill in the gap while the girls hastily improvised a miscellaneous program. I sang a few numbers, but still they were not ready. Suddenly Katherine Buckhout, her arms full of pink and blue chiffon, came toward me excitedly.

"Here's your costume. You will have to do the dance you've been practicing."

Before I had time to think, it was poured over my head and I heard Veronica Scott playing the opening measures of the Chopin "Butterfly Waltz." I stood stark still, afraid when I looked down and realized my lovely gown was nothing but diaphanous draperies. Somebody pushed me onto the stage. Shivering with apprehension, I turned and pirouetted, hurrying through the languorous dance. Oddly enough, I was not reprimanded as I expected to be on this occasion. I could only imagine that the rapid swirling of the veils protected me, and I fell half swooning into the arms of my comrades in crime.

Clothes were indeed a recurring problem, for Mother Mary John was strict on the subject of modesty. She severely reprimanded one of the girls for devoting sewing class to the latest fashion and making a *sleeveless* black lace dress! The smart clothes brought back from week-end visits were a constant wonder to me. None more than another *sleeveless* dress of emerald green tulle. We ah'd and oh'd over it, wondering whether the girl would be forbidden to wear it.

Before "an important date" the owner of the green dress, a beautiful blonde, shut herself up in her room for three days, playing sick. A sign on the door warned away all visitors, so we left our sympathetic offerings of fruit and flowers on her threshold. At the end of three days our invalid emerged with her hair a bright red. In answer to our absolutely stunned expressions, she explained calmly, "Well! It goes with my green dress."

There was a time, too, when curious to see ourselves in the habiliments of a nun, we "borrowed" Mother Mary John's laundry, which had been left outside her cell. We put on our academic gowns backwards, tied on the bib and wimple, and draping improvised veils over our heads, we took snapshots of each other. Nobody seemed surprised when the mother of one girl wrote back asking about my picture, "What is the name of *that* Sister?"

These innocent pranks prevented us from taking ourselves too seriously; but they never diverted me from music, the main current of my heart's desire. I was conscious that I did not know people well and that I would have to understand "all kinds and conditions of men" when I went to live among them in the world outside the convent walls. To supply this lack, I avidly turned to reading.

Katherine and I sat in the pergola under a canopy of flowering wisteria. We made a pact as she read aloud from the slim volume of Italian verse I had given her: "You sing for me, Jessique, and then I'll read for you out of the *Crock of Gold,* the Brownings, or anything you want." Katherine was much more sagacious than I in her reading and was greatly amused over the impervious naïveté with which I read Benét, F. Scott Fitzgerald, and Hemingway.

But Mother Mary John, in on everything, shook her head sadly, seeing me pore over the *De Profundis* of Oscar Wilde. "That is no book for you, my child. If you want to read *De Profundis,* I would rather you turn to the *Psalms of David.*"

Nadea and her busy husband were now living in Atlantic City. She was so anxious to have me spend the summer vacation near her that she secured a post for me as governess at Dr. Madeleine Hallowell's school for retarded children in Margate Park. It was a great honor to be associated with Dr. Hallowell in this baffling pioneering work. Although the hours were long and arduous, my heart went out to these little ones; and I was gratified seeing what could be accomplished with music. But I was still awaiting the good word that did not come. Had Alden Smith forgotten his promise?

Meanwhile I practiced diligently. When I was singing at Nadea's home one day, a new neighbor called to ask if I had a teacher. A white-haired, dominating personality, conversant with managers and professional people, she was bent on impressing me with her competence to take the entire situation in hand. My instinct not to become involved with anyone was aroused, and I avoided her. Finally she gave up in the face of rebuffs, which seemed very odd to her in one so ambitious to get ahead.

Later my intuition was confirmed; for though I never discovered her real identity, it was rumored that, mixed up in shady dealings in New York, she had come to hide out under an assumed name. More and more I became on guard against entanglements.

Up to this time John McCormack and Galli-Curci were my teachers. I listened endlessly to their recordings, trying to unravel the secret of their flawless singing. A poster now announced a concert by Galli-Curci on the Steel Pier. I was one of the first to buy a ticket to hear her—the only time I ever heard her in concert.

She reminded me of a Spanish infanta in some fine old painting, removed and precious, in a crimson dress that made a splash of color against the black ebony of the piano. But when she began to sing, she was like "the angel of spring, the mellow-throated nightingale."

The sound of that enchanting voice lingered with me for days— and, since I had had no word from Mr. Smith, an impulse moved me to write her and ask if she would suggest a teacher "who in your opinion is the best." By return post Madame Galli-Curci replied graciously: "In my opinion, the outstanding teacher in New York is unquestionably Estelle Liebling."

A strange coincidence brought me another letter in the same mail. It was a note from Alden Smith saying that Dr. Noble had arranged an audition with the teacher who passed on applicants from all over the United States for the Juilliard Foundation. Her name was Estelle Liebling.

One Sunday early in October, my arms full of scores, I appeared at her West Fifty-fifth Street studio in New York City. Miss Liebling opened the door for me, and I entered her artistically appointed rooms, with their musical souvenirs and inscribed photographs from great artists. Dr. Noble and Mr. Smith were already waiting.

Miss Liebling smiled at the many scores and seating herself at the piano said encouragingly, "So, what have we here?" As she accompanied me in Mimi's first aria, I felt new courage and joy in singing. In our musical rapport I forgot that I was there to be evaluated.

When I finished, Miss Liebling said, "Will you sing something else?" I opened the *Tosca* score to "Vissi d'arte." Her large brown eyes flashed with amusement, and patiently she heard me through. "Now what?" I timidly brought out "The Last Rose of Summer," recalling that she herself had sung it in the opera *Martha* with Caruso.

"You have a very beautiful voice, which you would do well to cultivate. But why do you sing those dramatic arias? You are little and blonde. You should sing the things that suit you better and will preserve that velvet-pansy quality you have." Then, turning to Dr. Noble and Mr. Smith, she added, "Don't you think I'm right, gentlemen? It's a delicious quality! She would develop greatly here."

Miss Liebling seemed to understand the dreams of the young. It was apparent she would accept me as a pupil, for she began to chat about her own early study in Berlin, where she sat all day long in Frau Nicklass-Kempner's studio just listening—"an excellent way to find out what some singers have and others lack." In Paris she had studied with Marchesi.

Into the atmosphere of this rich musical heritage I was to come in a few weeks and begin my first serious vocal study. Mother Mary John, perceiving that nothing could shake my purpose, arranged for me to commute from Georgian Court.

One day, after I had been in the studio about two weeks Miss Liebling said, "Max Reinhardt is casting for *The Miracle*. He is holding auditions in the Century Theater. I think you ought to go and try for the voice of the angel."

There were already more than sixty applicants waiting in the green room when I arrived. Max Reinhardt sat quietly in a corner listening, while his musical director conducted the auditions, explaining that true pitch was essential as the angel voice would float down unaccompanied from a high balcony.

I was one of the last to sing. As I finished, Mr. Reinhardt ran his fingers through his hair and pointed: "That one—she will be the angel."

CHAPTER 7

THE MIRACLE

It is a long road from the Middle Ages when men and women thronged the great cathedrals to witness the birth of dramatic art to *The Miracle* of Max Reinhardt, acted out in chancel, choir, and shrine. The thousands who forced their way into the old Century every evening to witness this religious spectacle saw a Gothic church set in the heart of a twentieth-century theater.

Reinhardt gathered a constellation of impressive associates about him. Among them was the youthful architectural genius, Norman Bel Geddes, who completely transformed the gaudy place into a vaulted expanse of pillars, great trinity arch, apse, transept, nave, high altar, pulpit, and cloisters. Illumination poured in from towering, rose-stained glass windows and dimly glowing sanctuary lamps. Long before the play began, the audience finding their places in pews, felt themselves part of a great congregation. This vibrant scene Reinhardt filled with people of an olden time: priests, nuns, sacristans, peasants, nobles, men-at-arms, the halt and the lame—each living out his own role in the pantomime of the miracle-working statue of the Madonna and the wayward young nun, tempted by the pleasures of the world.

The artistic success of this complex venture depended on many men; the book was allocated to Carl Volmoeller, the music to Humperdinck of *Hänsel und Gretel* and *Koenigskinder* fame. Reinhardt himself worked with the principal actors and actresses; Michel Fokine arranged the incidental dances, while Richard Boleslavsky of the Moscow Art Theater handled the unwieldy mass scenes. Reinhardt, directing the multifarious happenings from a loft scaffolding, was like a captain on the bridge of a mighty ship, clearing the way for smooth passage among the seething currents below.

A quiet, polite, expert man, he was a continuous example of good theater manners. He was never rude, never wasted time or energy by blowing up. I have been grateful all my life to Reinhardt for what I learned by observing him, especially in the rhythm of a scene, the tempo of the walk, carriage of the body, and most important in pantomime, the thought prompting the action.

Rehearsals were held in a vast warehouse, around the corner from the Century Theater, on Sixty-third Street, between Broadway and Central Park West. One day, Ethel Hart, a member of the sixty-five-voiced choir remarked, "Dull, isn't it, sitting around like this for hours and hours?" The gigantic cauldron I was swimming in was anything but dull to me. With every breath I sucked in wonder the like of which I had never dreamed of in my career-filled convent reveries. Studying the chubby, black-eyed Welsh girl, I sought to divert her boredom. "Sit down and I'll sing you an act of *La Bohême*."

Ethel's fascinated eyes followed me, wondering what in the world I was about. Hurriedly I arranged a table, two chairs, and to an audience of one, in an isolated corner of the huge studio, I sang Mimi's heart out from the first "Scusi"—indicating the other parts as they came along.

Such industry in one so young was a spur to this lovely singer. Ethel began bringing scores to the long rehearsals, and together we would sing Italian, French, or Spanish, whenever we were not required onstage.

Until rehearsals commenced, I continued living in the indulged hospitality of the Buckhout home. Now I needed to be near the theater, so I moved into an apartment, a kind of student pension, where seven pupils of Miss Liebling's lived under the chaperonage of Mrs. Funk, the mother of one of them. The large, many-roomed apartment, on a high floor of a building overlooking Central Park, was inside—with the exception of the community living room; and mine, a monastic dark little chamber was on an inner court. Yet within its narrow compass, high schemes were fashioned. Expenses quickly ate up my pittance-salary; the other pupils frequently carried tales to Miss Liebling of how I always managed to disappear at mealtime. I do remember that I ate as little as possible in the best tradition of sacrificing for one's art.

Mother Mary John, seeing I was determined, at any cost, to win my goal, granted me a leave of absence from Georgian Court, with the understanding that the forfeited time from school would be made up after my sojourn as Reinhardt's Angel. Therefore, I continued my studies together with my nights in the theater and lessons with Miss Liebling. It was difficult entering the theater-church to realize I was not still in the convent, but in the great world of make-believe in New York. Seeing the effect of the pantomime upon the audience, I sensed with a start that where religion once gave birth to dramatic art, dramatic art might here in turn give birth to religion.

High above the cloisters, a long ladder reached clear to a fly-loft under the roof of the theater. On a narrow ledge with room for only one person, I stood to become the Voice. As I stepped out on the little platform, with its frail, narrow railing, waiting for the music cue, I saw before me the kind, understanding eyes of Max Reinhardt; I could not fail him. After a fragment of pause, I began in true pitch and intonation, without accompaniment. It was as if I had always been singing that quaint, other-worldly song. Joyfully, fear a sponged-out mark on sand at the ocean's edge, I enacted that moving role, an angel from heaven, singing to all listening hearts.

Wrapt for an instant after I finished, I listened to the eerie silence far below me. By its heavenly illusion, message, mystery, my song had stirred a great audience. How sweet to my ears that pearl of silence, sweeter than any audible applause. As the orchestra made a bridge from my dying note, I carefully descended the ladder with an ejaculation of thanks in my heart. Opening night was over, and I had not failed!

Later the New York *Staats-Zeitung* made note of a musical coincidence, reporting:

Of the great number of beautiful voices I cannot forget the indescribably tender, sweet, and at the same time, distinctive voice of a young unseen member of the choir . . . I had to think of the great singer Angelina Catalini, who as a child in a convent attracted so much attention by the seraphic beauty of her voice that the little singer finally was permitted to leave the convent and adopt a professional career.

This little piece was heartening to Nadea, ill and far away in Arizona. My brother Fred soon followed her there, remaining to marry and go into the banking business. Nicholas, likewise marrying and following the family business tradition, remained in the East, but our interests were diverse and kept us all apart. Meanwhile Nadea's letters spoke of the wide-open spaces, but they were full of concern and constant worry over my being alone in New York. My open space of sky was a handkerchief piece of blue over Central Park, but I wrote every day to reassure her.

"I am in very good health and advancing in wisdom," I revealed importantly. "I am happy, but not as happy as I shall be in the days to come, when my dreams come true. . . . I am very busy with performances and between times I am studying and having such diversions as I can to keep my spirits where they should be. . . . I am learning, learning from everyone. I am not worried, not afraid, and I have a splendid mental state. Things are going to work out marvelously. . . . Helen of Troy wouldn't have to ask twice if I love life! It is wonderful just to live! My singing is improving steadily, and I am developing a sense of humor that I never dreamed possible. . . . I enjoy the company of men very much when they are not stupid, which they rarely are, even though women think so. Women are much more petty than men. Of course I understand that it is because they must be, and we can only pity them for it. I am in marvelous spirits and feel that I am maturing."

One of the mobsters in *The Miracle* production made a striking impression on me—not alone his tall handsome figure, his dark, Byronic head, but his fine, colorful speech. I almost tripped over him one evening as he sat buried in a book on the steps of one of the high balconies.

"I beg your pardon," I said, ashamed of my clumsiness.

"Don't give it another thought," he said, looking up smiling. "I'm rugged enough, I can take it. What's your hurry? Sit down for a while."

I sat down beside him and saw he was reading Aldous Huxley's *Antic Hay*. The title started a strange stirring in my brain, and he seemed to see the satyr-image forming in my eyes.

"You look at me as if I had cloven hoofs. Don't be frightened. They're only papier-mâché."

It was flirtation on a lofty plane. We would ride on a Fifth Avenue bus to the Forty-second Street Library where I would sit quietly reading while he did research for his master's degree at Columbia University. Then, on the upper deck return journey, he would extemporize on Elizabethan poetry, placing a nimbus around Marlowe, or he would talk of his current reading—*The Education of Henry Adams* and the daily Greek newspaper—while I listened in awed attention, drinking in every word.

We saw each other only in the theater and on the brief walk home, for I never accepted his invitations for refreshment afterward. This was mystifying to him. "I can see," he would say, "that, when you are scandalizing the nations, I shall be a pillar of the church."

In the theater he kept changing his name—sometimes he was Morton Herbert, again Robin Morton, but his real identity was David Morton. Apparently, he was part of the brilliant group including Clifton Fadiman, John Gassner, and Lionel Trilling, interested in literature, who frequented the classes of Mark Van Doren, poet-lecturer at Columbia University. Sometimes it is difficult to be then-minded, but a page of a diary I kept reveals much:

Saw Morton at 6. We walked and then took a bus ride. It rained and rained, but we didn't pay any attention. Had tea at the Revonah, a Dutch place. He talked until 10. He spoke of the Scotch bond of sympathy between him and a Witticar Chambers whom he considered the most wonderful poet in America. A short slim man, wears a little mustache and carries a cane. Spent last year in Paris. For 6 mos. he lived on 13 dollars. Just lived in his room and read: Montaigne, ancient history etc. Morton was most interesting; he spoke of his brother's place in Seattle, his grandfather, his wealthy father who died when they were young. His days in Shanghai. What he thought about me—

I mentioned Morton in a letter to Nadea, taking care to leave no room for misunderstanding. "He is most unusual, and of course there are few unusual people in the world. However, my first and dearest thoughts are with my music."

Usually I stole about like a timid child studying with admiring eyes the blonde porcelain beauty of Lady Diana Manners, who alternately played the Madonna and the young Nun. Contrasting hers with the other portrayal by the warm, Mediterranean-looking Princess Matchabelli, I observed a different background philosophy in their reading of the part; yet both women, each in her way, were truly miraculous.

No one, however, could have played the impetuous Novice with more verve than the lithe, Junoesque American, Rosamond Pinchot, Reinhardt discovered. There was always a swift, desperate heart-wringing quality about her that made one think there was only a hairbreadth line between reality and artifice. Was she acting out her own life? I was inconsolable some years later when I read of her suicide and thought of the canker that may have been gnawing at her center while we all unknowingly looked on.

For 287 performances I never failed to climb the steep ladder to the distant skies while the audience heard me, but had no idea what I looked like, for I was never seen. One night the great Russian basso Chaliapin, calling on Lady Diana Manners and her mother, the Duchess of Rutland, in a pause during the performance, inquired after the unseen Voice.

"She is lovely, but can I see her?" he asked Lady Manners. The Englishwomen sent for me and presented me to the blue-eyed giant.

"Allow me to thank you, child, for your exquisite singing," he said, bending to kiss my hand. Then smiling from his great height, "But you're only a cherub—half an angel. Maybe some day, if you work hard, you'll be full-fledged." Just then the call-bell summoned me, floating on air.

Rudolph Schildkraut, father of the then young, romantic actor Joseph, was also in the company. The elder Schildkraut became a target for my youthful sympathy; I tried to draw him out whenever possible, and he would tell me tales of his roles in the theater. He was old enough and, by long, distinguished service to the stage, entitled to retire, and but for the war, he would never have come to America. Now, in his autumn years, his whole life centered moodily around his son. Joseph made a point of driving his father to rehearsal, roaring up to the theater entrance in an imposing foreign car. I was always touched, seeing this handsome young star, oblivious of the stares of women and idlers, tenderly waving a kiss on the tips of his fingers to his aged, unhappy looking father.

We were ever on the lookout for the few extra singing jobs that offered an opportunity for displaying our talents. On one occasion, Gloria Swanson returned home from Paris having completed *Madame Sans Gêne*, and made a new marriage to a young nobleman, the Marquis de la Falaise. The Paramount Company, generously grateful and publicity minded, too, arranged a colossal dinner in her honor.

Besides the Fokine dancers, four singers from *The Miracle* company, including Ethel Hart and me, were asked to present a Chinese novelty number as part of the entertainment. If we gave our services, we were told it might lead to a future stage-show engagement at the Rivoli Theatre.

Gloria Swanson was such a fabulous star that I doubt if anyone at the dinner paid attention to our little number. In her spectacular lavender and silver dress, her short cropped hair, she struck me as a precious, lively little music-box bird, set down for a moment for the admiring gaze of the vast assembly. She stayed only briefly, and the light of the dinner dimmed abruptly with her leaving.

Hugo Riesenfeld, however, managing director of the Rivoli, was as good as his word, and soon we were invited to join the stage show, this time *with* pay. The first time I arrived backstage, I noticed with trepidation a group of men playing cards at a table in the wings. Among them, one in particular—the position of his stocky hunched-over body, the thick cigar clamped at an aggressive angle between his teeth—gave me the idea he was some sort of gangster. Would we be safe in the vicinity of such an individual? It was such a relief when I saw him in the orchestra pit at the first rehearsal, playing for us—Ben Bernie, gentlest of men!

Ethel Hart, a lovable harum-scarum child, was always amused when she found me in the wings, constantly perfecting the flutter of the fan for our Chinese novelty. That was only half of the story. I was also drawn there by the marvelous dancing of a boy, dressed as a scarecrow, while under an autumn moon in a field of pumpkins, he stylized new gyrations in macabre steps. I never missed a performance, nor did his father who always stood in the opposite wing. This was possibly the first professional engagement of that remarkable artist, Ray Bolger.

The months of *The Miracle* engagement were filled with surprises and many problems for a girl on leave from the convent. And I would not have been able to weather them, had it not been for a tiny legacy augmenting my salary, the residue wrung from the remote hand of Callahan! I coddled my meager wardrobe and maintained an intimate acquaintance with cheap restaurants. I could hardly believe my ears one day, when Mrs. John J. Jackson, who had taken back the student apartment, told me her niece was in New York for a visit.

The girl had heard of that exciting nickel-eating machine called the Automat.

"Jessica, would you take Chérie? She will be thrilled to see how it works."

"Of course, I shall be glad to," I said with a sickly smile, wondering about the ignominious quirk of fate that permitted such puzzles; and presenting a gay exterior to the North Carolinian, I accompanied her on a spree to the Automat.

The girls' dressing-room talk had opened my eyes to many things, and when *The Miracle* closed in mid-fall to go on to Chicago, I wondered whether the Broadway managers, who had only heard my voice, would want to engage me after they saw me. I loved beauty in all things; being nothing but a child and small, I felt unable to command the attention of important people in the world in which I must forge ahead.

"How does she look on the stage?" I could hear them inquire. "Will the people out front—especially the men—like her?" And only finally, "How much talent has she got?"

"No," I agonized. "Singing in the dark will not help me much toward my future."

To keep up my spirits, I spilled out my thoughts in letters to Nadea: "I feel as if I have lived five years in this less than one. My observations are astonishing; every day I am learning that life is devastating, and we must master it. . . . I expect to be the most charming, mysterious, clever, artistic, sane, attractive, ravishing creature possible when I am thirty."

The whole drama of this evolution was being played out from day to day. The impact of the worldly was sometimes harrowing; like a searing firebrand that marked my soul. I could not forget the sight of one of my friends in another show, an exceptional beauty, wealthy and talented, who called me late one evening. I went immediately to her apartment and found her, beautifully gowned and bejeweled, in an atmosphere overcharged with excitement. Before I could even question her, an ashy pallor spread over her olive skin, and a wild look filled her black eyes.

"The man I expected to marry has just been here and left," she cried out. "He has no interest whatsoever in my condition. He advised me," she said, sobbing, "'Do what other girls do, but count me out. Besides, I'm already married.'"

In her despair, she threatened to take poison and end her life rather than face her mother and stepfather, who had been so good to her.

"Dear God," I prayed, "why has she sent for me? How can I possibly help her?"

My inner quaking I covered with calm words while I groped along the uncertain keyboard of her mind searching for some responsive chord she could hold to in her drowning effort. Cautiously I proceeded, differentiating between what might be her conscience and my own.

"Would you have the courage to face these possible courses?" I asked her gently, "even a way dangerous as your premeditated suicide? In the end, you know, the decision must be yours alone."

Trying to shake her from her lethal purpose, I asked if she had ever had any religious ties in her life. She had only a vague far-away remembrance. Heavy in sadness she sat like a beggar drinking in the alms of my words: "God always leaves the door open." She looked at me skeptically. Rich with every good gift of life, she was pitifully poor in her extremity.

In the early morning I left her, noncommittal to the last as to her intended course, but convinced at least she would not take her life. "Thank you for the passport," she said wearily. "I'll let you know how I make out."

I never saw her again; and many times I wondered—two years later she wrote me after a European trip that she had married and was very happy. But I never forgot—it put me doubly on guard in my attitude toward men.

Shortly after this experience that had so depressed my mood a musician swain called me on the telephone and with surprisingly little preamble made a proposal of marriage. I cringe at the memory of how cruel I was.

"How can you propose over the telephone?" I demanded angrily. "It's grotesque. No! No! And no! Even if you came on a white horse, it would still be no!"

My sense of the romantic was outraged; I hung up the receiver in his ear. Hurt and confused, I went scurrying back to my music, clinging desperately to shut out the jungle of the world, holding more firmly than ever to my high purpose.

The existence of something called radio had become known to me in a vague way, on an overnight visit to Georgian Court, when I learned that one of the music students had gone to Newark to broadcast. Our chaplain, Father Baldwin, had a little set he brought into the study hall, so we all might listen.

"That isn't Veronica Scott," we laughed, completely unbelieving when the music was over. "It must be somebody playing a record."

Now that there was no sign of a new part for me, I left my pension existence and fitted myself back into my studies at Georgian Court. All the time I had been in New York, in addition to my performances and studies with Miss Liebling, I worked to keep up as far as possible with my classes. I had no wish to throw education aside, for I believed it would help my career. Mother Mary John was cautiously sympathetic whenever we discussed the practical aspects of my ambitions. She knew I was in the throes of a powerful drive and she was willing to free me within reason, to go in search of my objectives.

It never entered my head to apply for a chorus job with the thought that I might work into a role. To start only at the top was my high aim. There were many road companies of *The Student Prince* besides the one playing in New York. A dozen understudies could be drawn from them at any time; consequently, no one needed me for the role of Kathy in Manhattan. Nevertheless, that was what I wanted. If I could play one leading role, it would establish me in the theater. It would be a record to point to, an answer to the manager's eternal question: "What have you done?" I haunted the producers and stage managers until finally they gave me permission to watch every performance, and from that time I never missed one.

Then, suddenly, my chance came to sing Kathy. I was transfixed with excitement. To some extent I was among friends, for many boys in the company had been in *The Miracle;* Emil Coté, who later worked so much with me in radio, played captain of the student corps. The stage manager found me tractable, but demure. He was not sure I would be able to project the called-for abandon in the dramatic second act.

"The first and great quality of a true artist is to capture and hold the sympathy of the audience," he told me, as I practiced alone with him in a high, isolated studio above the theater. I felt competent of being able to do just that, when the time came, and my whole being sang at the thought of it!

Howard Marsh, sure, graceful, famous, who had created the role of *The Student Prince,* was a little bored at the constant stream of Kathys playing opposite him. While I was sympathetic to his mood, I was soon lost in my own portrayal of the little Heidelberg waitress in love with the prince. In the first-act passage, accordingly, I kissed Mr. Marsh so realistically, I left half of my "mouth" on his make-up! At the next offstage opportunity he took me aside.

"See here," he said indulgently, "I look like a boy who's been eating cherries. We can seem just as fervent without actually being so intense—"

"I'm so sorry. I'll try hard," I mumbled self-consciously. How could he know he was the first man I had ever kissed in my life!

Half the company stood in the wings when I was on stage. In their interested kindness, each one added something to my performance; one, a bit more rouge to fill out my thin little face, another, an encouraging word—I felt them all with me.

I fairly glowed in high key through the dramatic second act, crying real tears and playing the parting scene with surprising abandon. Only Howard Marsh jolted me back to earth—I could feel him stiffen and withdraw from my fervid kisses as the audience wildly applauded.

In a box sat Miss Liebling, with Mr. and Mrs. Paul D. Cravath, and Galli-Curci, who stayed only a few minutes—the others came backstage long enough to comment that Kathy had a rare stage talent. I was elated, having accomplished my goal of singing a leading role on the Broadway stage; but I kept an eye on myself lest I attach too much importance to this one thing, for it was only the beginning —I still had a long way to go.

Monsignor McNally in all this time had kept in touch with me; now he sent me word he was coming to New York to see me and if time permitted he would take me to the theater. When he arrived, he announced happily, "It wasn't easy, but I have two tickets for a wonderful show, *The Student Prince.*" I didn't have the heart to tell him I had seen its every performance night and day for weeks. I sat through the show acting as if I were seeing it for the first time in my life, and to this day, Monsignor McNally has never found me out.

As a respite from my hermetic solitude I would often hang about Miss Liebling's studio in off hours, to see what the magnet was pulling from some musical direction. Late one evening I timidly tried the outer door and though I found it unlatched, not a soul was in the anteroom. Perhaps Miss Liebling was entertaining in the studio—she wouldn't welcome the sight of me at such an hour. Strains of *Romeo and Juliet* came wafting from behind the closed door of the inner sanctum—voices I knew, but couldn't place, piqued my curiosity and made me sure this was not mere sociability.

Suddenly the door opened, and through the parted space I could see Edward Johnson of the Metropolitan Opera Company standing upon a chair, an accompanist at the piano, while a dark young girl at his feet looked up in adoration. The great singer was patiently coaching her in the fourth-act balcony scene. As Miss Liebling came through the door I tried to scamper, but she caught me.

"Oh," I sighed, "Edward Johnson—I have heard him in *Pelléas*, *Bohème*. Isn't he wonderful—and—but who is the girl?"

"Joan Ruth," said Miss Liebling, smiling at my exaltation. "They will tour together—isn't that a lucky break? Now go home and study hard, and maybe something like that will happen to you."

"Joan Ruth." I kept repeating her name to myself, as I went down Fifty-fifth Street. At last I made the association. She was the lovely girl, the lovely voice, I heard in the Fenway movie house in Boston during one of the Georgian Court Christmas vacations, when Mother Mary John permitted me to go home with one of my classmates.

She was so fortunate, I thought, carried away with excitement. Think of what she will learn from association with such a consummate artist!

My letters to Nadea contained bits from the musical arena that I hoped would amuse and cheer her restless days in Arizona. "Raquel Meller is here," I revealed to her, feeling very *au courant;* "she is a Spanish woman who has been singing in Paris for a number of years. She is, I think, more a *diseuse* than a singer. In the Paris music halls she is heard for the equivalent of fifty-five cents, but for many dollars here." I added mischievously, "Will I have to do some serious gold digging in order to get to hear her? My swain of the telephone proposal would have taken me, but I couldn't take him. . . . I am reading the life of Sarah Bernhardt. She was very ugly, but marvelously magnetic. . . . I have been able to get some very nice clothes at greatly marked-down cost." I was very anxious not to have Nadea worry about my being provided for. Though I thought it best not to tell her the whole story, here is how it happened.

Hope Hampton, the cinema star, a pupil of Miss Liebling's, knew well that many of us had a hard time making ends meet. Hope had exquisite clothes, and a great many of them. Often her generous heart sent her to winnow out her wardrobe, and she would give Miss Liebling practically new dresses to distribute among students who might have occasion to sing.

"Look at these beautiful things Hope Hampton left today for the students," Miss Liebling would say, leaving the piano and opening the studio closet. "I think this one would make a lovely singing dress for you, Jessica."

"They're gorgeous," I sighed, "but you know, Miss Liebling, I couldn't accept one without paying for it."

Accordingly Miss Liebling, acquainted with my fierce pride, charged me five dollars apiece for Hope's magnificent creations. The five dollars I would save by cutting down in the Automat, and then I would preen myself with a clear conscience, knowing the dresses were paid for.

During this time Frances Paperte, a Chicago Opera Company singer, and to me, therefore, a creature of a golden realm, came flying into the studio one day. She looked around for a second and exclaimed airily, "Anybody want a sandwich? It cost a whole seventy-five cents; I bought it at Reubens', then somebody invited me for lunch. Someone ought to eat it—it's simply full of chicken and things—" Frances' eye fell on me—"wouldn't you like to eat it—just to keep it from going to waste?"

I was so hungry I wanted to grab and greedily devour it; but I sat quietly hoping no one would outbid me! "Well," I said gravely, "if you really can't—I'll be glad to help you out—I think I can manage to eat it."

Meanwhile Nadea fed her solicitude on the New York headlines. At the death of Rudolph Valentino, the movie idol whom I never saw on the screen, she sent me an anxious letter, special delivery. "Don't get into those dreadful, insane crowds!" she besought me. "You'll be injured." The breath of hysteria in the city was close to me—Ethel Hart's brother, Michael, had been engaged to sing for Valentino's funeral at nearby Campbell's Funeral Parlor—where Pola Negri was weeping over his bier. But I never wandered out of my door, and by return mail I wrote to Nadea: "I am by now a blasé New Yorker and would not dream of getting caught in crowds."

While I was singing in *The Miracle,* I had gone down to the Neighborhood Playhouse to audition for a Chinese operetta called *Yuan Yin.* The Lewisohn sisters, quite taken with my voice, offered me the lead, but since they would go into rehearsal immediately and I was occupied in the theater, I had to forego the role. However, Miss Irene promised to send for me again in the late spring when they would do their usual summer revue. The Playhouse, subsidized by the Lewisohns, was a repertory theater whose permanent company put on five plays a year. As a witty relief from the serious productions of the season, the summers were devoted to a "Follies"—the *Grand Street Follies* after the name of the street in which the little playhouse stood. Irene Lewisohn did not forget; she sent for me to audition, this time for the musical director of the show, Howard Barlow, and I was cast for the summer revue. There would be (wonderful to relate) only three weeks of rehearsal. I hurried off a bulletin to Nadea. "I am now rehearsing at the Neighborhood Playhouse which is interesting and congenial," I importantly informed her.

Mrs. Jackson, having moved to Euclid Hall at Eighty-sixth and Broadway, invited me to go with her. It made a long ride down to the theater on Grand Street, changing from the El to a crosstown bus each day, but all new and wonderful to me, a life of color and sound I had never imagined. Anything the Grand Street neighbors happened not to want they threw out their windows; riding the bus, I might easily have to duck or receive a corncob on the nose! Never having seen such tumultuous life, I reveled in it. When I went home after the performances, I often left the El near Washington Square and rode the rest of the way uptown on the top of a Fifth Avenue bus. I fell in love this way with the exciting vertical city and the shining mirror of the Hudson, which in the dark night reflected the golden lights of the Palisades, which were like filigree tattooed upon the sky.

I became acquainted with Playhouse standards during the rehearsals for the *Grand Street Follies,* though they were something of a holiday for the members of the permanent company—Dorothy Sands, Vera Allen, Paula Trueman, Junius Matthews, George Heller, Albert Carroll, Edla Frankau (daughter of Aline Bernstein); beneath an air of frivolity and lightness lurked a somewhat subtler philosophic emphasis. It was a feather in my cap to be engaged, and I tried to absorb what I could in the atmosphere of skilled theater and association with versatile players of established place.

The 1926 edition of the *Grand Street Follies* was topical, building around Admiral, then Lieutenant Commander, Richard E. Byrd and Floyd Bennett, who had made the first flight in history over the North Pole and back. On his return, Byrd made another long journey down to Grand Street to see the revue he had inspired. The entire cast gathered about him in great excitement to exchange congratulations. I recall the tall, slender, quietly magnetic figure, the farseeing gray-blue eyes, filled with visions of unconquered polar space.

Cast as "Everybody's Sweetheart," perhaps a prophetic label in the light of later radio events, I was given several specialties in the show with music by Arthur Schwartz, the lawyer turned composer, and Randall Thompson. Aline Bernstein designed a luscious pink velvet costume with pink ostrich collar, matching hat and shoes for the "Little Igloo for Two" hit song by Arthur Schwartz, which I was able to write effervescently to Nadea "stopped the show Saturday night." For the Northern Lights Art Club scene, there was a hilariously amusing take-off on *Uncle Tom's Cabin* in which I was an angel singing and guiding distracted Eliza over the ice. But from the standpoint of my own choice, the greatest opportunity came from being assigned to do an impersonation in the "Arctic Night Club" number.

Helen Hayes was then appearing in Barrie's *What Every Woman Knows* at an uptown theater. Though I had a wealth of admiration for her artistry, I had scant money for theater tickets; in what seemed the nick of time Nadea sent me a gold piece with which I sped off to see Miss Hayes play Maggie. I couldn't wait to work out an impression of her for the *Follies.*

Since I had no Maggie Wylie dress, I wore the lovely pink velvet "igloo" outfit and in the impersonation I used Maggie's famous answer to Aleck's question about charm:

Oh it's—it's a sort of bloom on a woman. If you have it you don't need to have anything else; and if you don't have it, it doesn't much matter what else you have. Some women, the few, have charm for all; and most have charm for one. But some have charm for none. . . .

To my surprise, no one commented on my inappropriate costume. Even Lumsden Hare, who coached Miss Hayes and played with her, thought I did the bit very well and arranged a meeting. Her wistful shyness almost matched my own, until we began to talk of Barrie and the play. Then we took fire in the whimsy, the canniness, the poetic tenderness, the subtle characterization of the Scotsman's women. With renewed insight, I went back to the Playhouse to impersonate her.

Once the *Follies* were over, my spirits ebbed. I made frugal plans to buy the pink hat and shoes of my "Little Igloo" number as a memento of progress, a talisman for the future. I could not afford the coat, much as I longed to possess it. After each engagement came a letdown—and then a beginning all over again.

Miss Liebling, seeing me droop a little at a lesson, suggested I go to see her lifelong friend Daniel Frohman, whose brother Charles had discovered Maude Adams. Knowing my sensitivity to inspirational people, she felt in her uncanny way that it might be a battery recharge for me to have a talk with a man so steeped in the tradition of the theater.

Tall, thin, faintly satanic in appearance, Daniel Frohman looked like some eccentric recluse I had met in my reading. He lived on the top floor of the Lyceum Theater. Tremulously I rang the bell of the elevator and waited; presently the wire cage slid into place, and at the control stood Frohman himself. Annoyed, he opened the door—"Who are you and what do you want?" he abruptly demanded.

"I'm coming to call on you, Mr. Frohman," I said timidly. "Estelle Liebling asked me to do so."

"Why in heaven's name did she send you to me?" he snapped, eying me sharply. "She knows I never give anyone letters of introduction—"

"I don't want any letters—or anything at all," I said imploringly.

"Well—get in then—" In silence he took the controls again, and we rode up to his floor past the greenery of pastoral scenes painted on the whitewashed walls of the elevator shaft.

I looked around the beautiful, dust-cluttered room: there were many lovely ornaments, interesting-looking books, elaborate furniture, bric-a-brac, statuary, and paintings, all pell-mell.

Mr. Frohman barked out a few penetrating questions while I complacently told him what I hoped my career would be. "I have been the voice of the Angel in *The Miracle*, but eventually I want to sing in opera and on the concert stage."

"You are a pretty little girl," he said at last, impatiently, "but I advise you to forget all this. Go home—in time marry some nice boy —have a big family—and be happy. The struggle isn't worth the candle."

"But that is exactly what I am *not* going to do, Mr. Frohman," I replied calmly.

He studied me thoughtfully with his piercing glance. "Your name's too long!" he began ruminatingly. "It would look awful in lights. Besides, no one would accept such a name—they would play on it— you'd better think about changing it."

He had begun pacing up and down like a caged lion, and seeing him grow eloquent, I laughed. "First you try to discourage me, Mr. Frohman, and now you're already seeing my name in lights! I don't think I want to change my name—"

Seeing that I was not easily swayed, he took up another subject. "You certainly have a mind of your own," he rapped out. "Ask Miss Liebling to send you to see me again. I've enjoyed talking to you," and then still convinced that he was right, "the next time we'll work on the name."

Samuel Rothafel—the famed Roxy—was gathering one of his "Gangs" to go on the road to stimulate national interest in the big theater he was building in New York, and Miss Liebling had me sing for him at her studio. Roxy, a graying thick-set man, intimated, in his peculiarly brusque though engaging way, that he liked my singing. When Miss Liebling saw that his interest was aroused, she asked me to leave the studio and wait outside until she sent for me.

These "waitings outside" were always ominous, but I had steeled myself to them.

After Miss Liebling called me back, Roxy said in a gentle manner: "Jessica, I like you very much, and I am definitely going to use you—but my theater won't be open for quite some time. It's not fair to keep my artists waiting without pay"—he took a bill from his bulging wallet, and when he placed it on the piano I could see it was a hundred dollars—"I would like you to have this in advance."

Outraged at what I interpreted as his patronizing air, I glared at Miss Liebling for what she might have told him. Then furiously eying Roxy again, I said hysterically: "I thank you very much, Mr. Roxy—but it won't do! I shall never sing with your Gang!" and I whirled out of the studio like a wild tornado.

Outside in the street I shook from head to foot. All of a sudden I realized I had no standard of worth for a man like Roxy. It did not matter to him whether I was good or not; whether he would use me in his theater or not. In a trance of despair I ran all the way from the studio on Fifty-fifth Street through the Park to Eighty-sixth and Broadway.

Once inside my room, I threw myself on the bed in a paroxysm of sobbing. In the fixed anxiety that did not permit a moment to be sacrificed in wrong decisions, had I misinterpreted Roxy's simple kindness? Had I ended my career before it was fairly begun? I didn't know what to do! It was a sink-or-swim act to go to Miss Liebling in the first place. Now I had antagonized her, too. I felt trapped and for my bad behavior, guilty—I could not go back and face her. What would become of me now? Was this the ending of an auspicious start? I answered my own questions. My beginner's luck had run out!

CHAPTER 8

PHANTOM OF THE AIR

Only the timid and aspiring can understand the agony I endured for weeks. While I had displayed high spirit to both Roxy and Miss

Liebling, my behavior was extremely rude. Now I was consumed with remorse over my cowardice. I could not go back and face my teacher and friend to apologize for flouting Roxy's interest. I was afraid to have Miss Liebling tell me that by my actions I had ruined any future chances at what I most wanted, a singing career.

Bewildered and miserable, everything seemed to fly from me at once—courage, money, inspiration. I lived through the ensuing days with difficulty and privation, fervently praying for a way to meet my problems. Then, one day, I was ready to go back to Miss Liebling.

Waiting pupils crowded the anteroom, and I could hear a lesson progressing. I sat close to the studio door; I might have to wait all day to catch Miss Liebling's attention; but, when the moment arrived, I would be on the spot—

The telephone rang inside—the lesson stopped—and Miss Liebling opened her door—

"Well, Dragonette," she said in brisk surprise, "where did you come from? I thought you had thrown yourself in the East River."

We always liked it when she called us by our last names. It was a signal that she believed in our talent. Narrowing her eyes thoughtfully, she put on what I called "that dealer-in-fine-arts look" I had seen on her face many times: she was measuring a talent—making an estimate—where it would fit—the element of chance involved.

Then forgetting the past completely, with one of her inspirational impulses she hazarded, "They're holding auditions at WEAF down at 195 Broadway. If you think you'd like to go and try your luck, tell Mrs. Bushman, the program director, I sent you."

"Thank you, I would like to go, Miss Liebling," I whispered repentantly and, relieved that she had not washed her hands of me, I rushed out and ran all the way to the subway. This might prove to be the psychological moment I was waiting for, the turn of the tide. It was sink-or-swim again, and I was determined to hold my own.

Mrs. Bushman, a slim, blonde, blue-eyed Scottish woman, and very chic, was waiting for me. "Come into the studio," she said, after talking to me for a few minutes. "I'll call Harold Sanford, director of the Musical Comedy Hour. We need a prima donna for the program, which is sponsored by Colonel Green and sent out over his Massachusetts station Saturday nights, then repeated Sunday nights for New York listeners."

Harold Sanford led the way into the studio where an accompanist was already seated at the grand piano.

"Stand about here," he said, placing me about a foot away from the microphone. "Now just sing naturally." Then looking over my music, he pulled out the "Indian Love Call." "This will be fine, we're featuring light opera music. If we ask you to do a second number, what will you do?"

"How's 'Estrellita,' a Mexican folk song?"

"Fine—fine," he said quickly and disappeared after Mrs. Bushman into the control room back of me.

It was Sanford who broke the silence following the audition. "Yes," he was saying impatiently, as if he were glad to have the matter settled, "we'll put you on October 26th. Report for rehearsal at three the 25th."

"You understand, don't you," Mrs. Bushman interposed, "this constitutes an engagement. You wouldn't think of leaving, would you, without giving us two weeks' notice?"

Think of leaving? Nothing in the world could have taken me away, but I looked at her composedly and murmured, "Oh, no indeed."

This summed up my contract, which for some time remained entirely verbal.

"Now come with me," said Harold Sanford, leading me down the corridor, past the studios to the small, neat music library. He lifted some sheet music from a high shelf. "Here," he went on, nervously handing me the music. "I want you to learn this 'Babes in the Wood' duet; you'll sing it with the baritone, Theodore Webb, as well as the other songs you auditioned. If everything goes well, we'll use you regularly."

As Sanford guided me to the elevators after this brief interview, I studied his clean-cut head, the iron-gray hair, the platinum colored suit, the large tortoise-shell glasses framing his restless gray eyes, his entire harmonious person impressing me as exactly what a musical director should look like. He bade me a hasty good-by, and that was that.

No red tape existed in those days when the National Broadcasting Company occupied three studios in the Telephone Building. There was no triple line of defense—sponsor, account executive, "time"

salesman—all bent on repulsing the radio aspirant. A program director could engage one on the spot.

Excitedly I hurried back and reported to Miss Liebling that I had
been accepted. Then, as the afterglow of the thrill subsided, I was
caught up again in my practical problems. I wanted to work now
harder than ever, but I had no money for lessons or clothes, only a
pitiful subsistence for food and shelter. The savage energy of the
city, the tensions I had been living through, the pressure of decisions,
my vaulting ambition, anxiety over Nadea's illness, the struggle for
equilibrium in the maelstrom produced a kind of combat fatigue. I
longed to take refuge in the blessed peace and security of the convent, but I fought back even more fiercely this impulse to run away
from the life I had chosen. In nervous exhaustion, I completely forgot the date for my first broadcast.

Several days later I was crossing Seventh Avenue in a blinding
rain storm. When I reached the middle of the street, a blast of
drenching wind swept up behind me, turning my umbrella inside
out. I stopped and grabbed for the rim, holding my music case against
me. When I started walking again, I found a sheet of newspaper
plastered around the back of my galoshes. I tried to kick it off, but
a new blast of wind glued it to my feet. Fearful lest the traffic light
might change and find me unguarded, I hobbled across the avenue,
irritated every step of the way by the annoying newspaper. Finally
on the sidewalk, I stooped down forcibly to disentangle myself. As
I did, I saw a picture of a girl smiling at me.

"Why, that looks like me," I said half aloud. I examined the caption that read "Jessica Dragonette will be singing her first broadcast
over station WEAF in four days." I could not believe my own eyes.
I must have been a funny spectacle on the corner of Seventh Avenue
and Fifty-fifth Street, puzzling over that rain-soaked piece of news-
print.

A young man walking by said, "Hi, sister. Did you lose something?"

"No," I replied automatically. "I've just found something."

"Whatcha find?"

"Myself," I answered, transfigured. It struck me suddenly that an
invisible hand, perhaps my guardian angel's, had reached out to remind me that I had a rendezvous with destiny.

"Well, I'll be darned," he commented with disbelief, "she doesn't even hear me." As the young man continued his way up Seventh Avenue, my mind was already turned to the broadcast.

With a joyous prayer I sped up Fifty-fifth Street to Miss Liebling —I couldn't wait to tell her about my picture in the paper, to remind her that next week I would be appearing on the air. There were people waiting as usual—men, women, boys, and girls. The group was never the same, though over a period of time I had become familiar with quite a few of them. Without a word of greeting I sat down opposite two girls whom I had seen several times before, intent on the tenor inside singing an aria from Massenet's *Manon*.

"What a *beautiful* pianissimo," I sighed to myself.

"How's *your* pianissimo?" one of the girls teased.

"Just wonderful," I bantered, "in fact, it's my forte."

"Why whaddyaknow," the other girl roared, "she talks as well as sings."

When I passed through the reception room to the studio for my first broadcast, I noticed a man whom someone called Graham Mc-Namee. He was talking animatedly to an executive, and I caught the words "Babe Ruth's spindly ankles." I had never seen Babe Ruth hit a ball out of the park nor had I heard McNamee describe a ball game over the air, but his warm laugh was heartening and gave me assurance as I walked to the microphone.

Suddenly I realized I should be singing to a forbidding instrument, cold and lifeless, instead of to a warmly expectant audience. The dry, uninspiring atmosphere of the studio was depressing. I wanted to run away—

Directly before me, Harold Sanford with poised baton, his eyes riveted to the control room, awaited the cue to begin. As he led the orchestra in my introduction, I abandoned myself to the song. Then I experienced something I had never known before: I felt myself being pulled in all directions, simultaneously this way and that. What could it be? Ignorant then, I know now this was a beginning in "spatial thinking."

Now it was over, and there was not a shred of human response. Beyond the microphone, had anyone really been listening? Would I ever know how my voice came over the air? I wondered. I felt completely let down. The next day I repeated the same broadcast as a sustaining program for the New York listening area, and by Monday when I reported to the studio, I was greeted with an armload of letters.

"This is your fan mail," they explained to me, laughing at my stunned expression.

"You mean—people did hear me?" I said.

"Hear you?" they inflected. "Of course they heard—they loved you —read for yourself!" I put down the letters and began examining them. Was I worrying about people's hearing me? It was surprising what they heard in my voice. These letters told me what I looked like, my character, my breeding, my tastes, and my daily life. Ears have eyes, too; these letters proved that they saw me; that the voice is the most powerful medium we have, depicting the personality far better than the visible appearance.

Radio had given the world a second pair of eyes—eyes of the spirit. I warmed to the thought pervading my mind—suddenly out of this intricate device had risen a spiritual force, flooding the world with romance and beauty. It was impossible, I went on, to calculate the extent of this new influence, as it gradually reached out to the hinterland. Music pouring so freely into our homes might give us another singing century like the thirteenth. The vision began to grow, gaining momentum; this most intimate and spontaneous communication would, with the flick of a knob, make me a visitor in every home.

"I am young," I told myself, "and radio is young—we will develop together."

As my voice had materialized me for my listeners, their letters in turn gave me a picture of them—a cycloramic picture of sincere and wholesome people, taking me into intimate and poignant scenes of their everyday life: a father asking for Brahms's "Lullaby," the first music he wanted his six-weeks-old daughter to hear; the Norwegian parents in Indiana who would not raise their eyes from their evening paper, their librarian daughter wrote me, lest the rest of the family surmise how much they were enjoying the radio; the farmer from Pennsylvania, who spoke of the feats of his dray horses and the relaxation of listening to music when the day's work was done; the two young brothers working on models for streamline trains; the housewife from Akron, Iowa, arranging her linen closets and hanging her curtains while listening. There was really no way to classify the letters—they were from bank presidents and errand boys, business girls and sportsmen, shut-ins and students, the old and the young.

"What does it mean?" I asked myself. These glimpses of many homes evoked awe at the animation breathed into stone and wood and the familiar things of daily living. If I decided to stay in radio, I should be part of it all. "How wonderful!" I thought. "The lives of people around us are packed with nobility and fine dreams they keep locked up and dare not confide, waiting for the right moment —a song perhaps—to release them. It is the human urge, 'Build thee more stately mansions, O my soul.'"

I began to see the microphone in a new light: I began to regard it as the most alive audience I had ever known. In a rush of fervor I wanted to dedicate myself to wooing it, to learn all I could about this new medium, and while I was learning, I could also be earning.

To many around me radio was only a passing fad. Remembering my neglect of the stage, they chided me for staying away from my "proper place," for the questionable rut of this medium of sound and fury, whose future was uncertain.

"You should not hide yourself back of a microphone," they said scoffingly. "What good can you possibly do there?"

"I don't know yet," I said, absorbed. "But something quite different, I'm sure. I'm in on a dream—a challenging enterprise, sailing an uncharted sea."

I was absurdly content. In their concern, they overlooked the extent to which radio offered a fresh outlet for my innate talents, a natural voice, a love of music, a sincere desire to use these gifts to the best advantage, and, most crucial, the opportunity for an American girl to train on this side of the Atlantic. Oh no! *My friends were mistaken;* I wasn't detouring but moving out along a new road with the pioneers.

The lack of established tradition appealed to me. I would create and help mold the new medium of expression, instead of following the accustomed practice of the theater. I could see a long way winding—not yet clear, but worth exploring; for pioneers go first to meet and solve the mysteries.

I was not aware until years afterward that when I did my first broadcasts, radio was already in its second stage of development; but the newly formed National Broadcasting Company was only a month old. The networks of A. T. & T.'s station WEAF and RCA's station WJZ had already been operating concerns. The old broadcasting group, consisting of A. T. & T., General Electric, Westinghouse, and RCA was now dissolving; and in the RCA conference rooms, amidst much rich blue smoke, a new corporation came into being. RCA (with the consent of its parent company General Electric and its affiliate Westinghouse) bought A. T. & T.'s radio properties, WEAF and its network for the sum of $1,000,000, and on November 1, 1926 the National Broadcasting Company was born. The visionary utterances of David Sarnoff, then general manager of RCA, laid down the policy of the new subsidiary—"a great force for the cultural improvement of the American people." Owen D. Young, chairman of the board, turned to more practical action. He summoned Merlin H. Aylesworth.

"We intend to build a radio broadcasting network, Deac," said Mr. Young, calling Mr. Aylesworth by his nickname. "We would like you to take charge."

"Why me?" asked Aylesworth. "I don't know a thing about broadcasting."

"Because," rejoined Young, "as managing director of the National Electric Light Association, you have visited every community of ten thousand or more in the United States. You know people, and as a network, we want to give them what they want. Otherwise, the novelty of broadcasting will soon wear off."

Aylesworth never forgot Young's parting words, "Always remember this, Deac, the dollar follows the service."

It was in the cyclonic atmosphere of this exciting venture to capture the imagination of the American public and to promote network broadcasting that I began my first radio appearances. Aylesworth cleverly capitalized on the name of the newly formed organization whose initials were identical with those of the National Biscuit Company:

"I may be able to sell them some programs; they'll be able to say they are broadcasting over NBC and will get double value."

The newly aligned network, having a total of nineteen affiliated stations throughout the country, caught up many loose ends and made for more effective control of executive and technical problems.

A formal première celebration went on the air fifteen days later, with five added stations; more than 10,000,000 listened in to the all-star entertainment, while in the ballroom of the old Hotel Waldorf-Astoria at Thirty-fourth Street and Fifth Avenue, an audience of social, political, and industrial significance assembled.

I had a program that evening and though not invited to the dinner I had permission to look on. As I hurried into the balcony, Graham McNamee was at the microphone, poised for the signal inaugurating the network ceremonies. Mary Garden, picked up from Chicago, had already sung, but McNamee referred glowingly to "the divine Mary Garden," and to Titta Ruffo, who likewise had been there and left, as "the greatest baritone of his time." The famous Will Rogers, facing a microphone in the dressing room of an Independence, Kansas, theater impressed the audience with his realistic impersonation of Calvin Coolidge, but even more remarkable was the feat of bringing his voice from such a distant place. McNamee introduced Joe Weber and Lew Fields as "these comedians of other days, who are still going strong."

Never before had I been able to reach out and touch in a single New York performance such a variety of illustrious personalities as Dr. Walter Damrosch, conducting the Symphony Orchestra; Harold Bauer, concert pianist; Edwin Franko Goldman; George Olsen and his orchestra. By remote control Vincent Lopez and his band came into the ballroom from the Casa Lopez; B. A. Rolfe and his orchestra, from the Palais d'Or; Cesare Sodero, staff conductor of grand opera, WEAF, and many others. The renown of the artists, the caliber of the industrialists, and the brilliance of the audience confirmed my decision to stay with radio. I felt I was on the threshold of something epoch-making.

Besides the impact of this memorable première on the entire assemblage, it was an astounding awakening for millions of Americans, causing them to realize that for the price of a radio set they could have the finest entertainment in their own homes. The new invention was the first step toward the world's becoming ear-minded.

Now I was immune to all but *radio's calling*. Everything else was crowded out to give way to my own artistic development and radio unfoldment. My voice was a natural for this medium. My solid musical heritage, knowledge of languages, interest in original entertainment made it a "hand-in-glove" situation. I was in the studios from morn 'til midnight, trying to solve the riddle of microphone personality—searching out the secret of good radio entertainment to fill eighteen hours a day, learning that two minutes "on the air" is an eternity.

The stop watch was ever in the hand of the director, and every second had to count. Studio directions like Indian sign language are to this day delivered in gesture: "on the nose"—"speed up"—"slow down"—"OK"—"cut." The electrical symbol itself was so beautiful that years later I commissioned a twenty-five-foot-wide mural batik depicting radio's history, utilizing it for the first time in a work of art.

I was rhapsodic in my youthful description of the Sponsor, who to me was the modern equivalent of Maecenas, ancient Roman patron of the arts. Commerce and industry saw "the instrument" as a shining new tool of advertising, and in a trice there was an "air-rush."

Semper parata, I personally ushered in a series unique in its way —"brought to you by the courtesy of Coca-Cola," I played the first original singing-acting serial written for the kilocycles.

Whereas most programs on the air at this time handled operettas, and do to this day, by having two people play the same role (an actor to read the lines, a singer to continue with the lyrical portion), Coca-Cola wanted one performer who could manage both, smoothly and appealingly. Their hour was to be a continued serial concerning the adventures of two fellows and a girl named Vivian (the Coca-Cola girl). At a high point of suspense each week the audience would be left to wait with baited interest until the next installment.

Having been chosen as Vivian was an advance in many ways. It gave me great opportunity for work and growth in the new medium. Vivian's adventure lasted a whole half hour each week wherein I sang seven solos and duets. I spent hours finding appropriate songs to fit the story and the feeling of the lines.

My salary was augmented so that now I could resume my singing lessons. Besides these advantages I was asked to sign a five-year contract with NBC—my first written contract, and I had only been broadcasting a month.

I knew by now that the region beyond the microphone was not at all illusory. Listeners took Vivian and her singing-talking series very much to heart, and let me know by letter just what I could or should not do in a given situation. One installment called for a night-club scene. The director gave instructions that I was to be written out, being too young to fit suitably into such a place. To me this implied a lack of artistic versatility; I persuaded him to put me back in, undertaking to write the scene myself. The idea was that a big Broadway manager would offer Vivian a part—with hinted-at strings.

Immediately the mail bag bulged with admonitions: "Remember, dear child, all is not gold that glitters. Cling to your present course which is the right one—" What nobler proof of the cliff-hanging potential of our stories? As "Vivian" I even heard about my *alter ego*, Jessica Dragonette. "Dear Vivian," ran a letter from a listener, "There is a song which Jessica Dragonette sings—a very fine artist, by the way—I wish you would sing it in one of your stories—"

Thus began a correspondence with the American public that has lasted many years. A house painter never forgot that, when he couldn't get tickets for a broadcast, I personally admitted him to the studio. Ever since then, I have been his "sweetheart." After years of writing to me, a young girl, confused by world problems and conflicting religions in her own family, followed my advice and found a way of life in studying music. Working in a local orchestra opened up her destiny, too, for playing the violin next to her sat a young medical intern, and later they became engaged. These were a few of the thousands who gave and received in the exchange of inspiring friendship.

The radio fascination kept me spellbound! I could see things change under my very eyes—the whole picture was a seething mass of increasing cell growth—technical, financial, educational, historical, world-shaking.

Absorbed and captivated in learning the nature of this provocative world of communication, I began to wear formal dress for my performances. After what the letters told me, I was sure the audience could see what I was wearing; besides, the right clothes helped me project with more artistic effect. I had been warned: beware of all enterprises that require new clothes—and not, rather, a new wearer of clothes! Nevertheless, I wore the loveliest gowns I could find to match my songs.

One of the earliest "good music" programs was the Atwater Kent

Hour. It featured stars of the opera and concert hall, and through
its annual radio auditions for young singers, it created tremendous
interest throughout the country. Many of these aspirants, unfamiliar
with the mysteries of radio, actually believed they had to buy an
Atwater Kent set to tune in these hours; naturally the sponsor did
nothing to disabuse them.

The Sunday evening broadcast of the world's finest music was
presented through effective collaboration of NBC and the Arthur
Judson Concert Bureau. Since I had exchanged the stage for radio,
it was interesting that both the opera and Broadway now came to
me via the microphone. This began very early through the Atwater
Kent series. Significant, too, was the opportunity given to American
singers only half-emergent on the musical scene at this time. While
we were still at 195 Broadway, Grace Moore, Mary Lewis, Anna
Case, Albert Spalding, Rosa Ponselle, came to broadcast in the Atwater Kent series. Uniformly they were terrified by the mike, for
their training and artistic balance had been keyed to projecting
across the footlights.

Time was to point up interesting differences in the careers of two
of these American singers acquainted with radio through the microphone of the Atwater Kent Hour. Grace Moore—beautiful, yet not
as beautiful as Mary Lewis—went dauntlessly on, as she had vowed
she would, while Mary—the perfect type for opera—lacked the in-
dispensable drive; she was a touching enigma, evidently bent on destroying herself, in spite of excelling gifts.

Aside from the satisfaction of having a personal part in this series
by way of later guest appearances, it was encouraging to me that,
in the public consciousness, the competitive talent of American-born
artists could be heard and received with acclaim on its own artistic
merits. This marked the first nibbling away of the old superstition
that a singer could only succeed in America with European training
and a foreign-sounding name.

The social peak of the studio year was Miss Liebling's Christmas
party. Having been brought up in New York, she had a wealth of
friends; but primarily she felt solicitous about her many pupils from
all parts of the country who could not go home for the holidays.
She would take over a whole restaurant, decorate it festively, fill

one corner with an enormous tree ornamented with shining baubles and stunning gifts for everyone, then cram the place with friends, pupils, celebrities from every walk of life: opera singers, impresarios, actors and actresses, painters, writers, poets, and dancers.

I was delighted when she let me know she would be pleased to have me add to the informal entertainment some of my impersonations of the guests. Ever since I was a small child, I had loved mimicry. Perhaps I escaped from shyness by imitating others.

Miss Liebling was often formidable in the studio, but as hostess at her Christmas party she led the gaiety and laughter, while I portrayed her in the act of giving a lesson with its constant interruptions. Playing the part of both teacher and pupil, I stood by a piano with four telephones. Over soft music I began to enact Maria Jeritza, whose idiosyncrasies included calling Miss Liebling, "*Geliebtes,*" and, like the King of Siam with the "et cetera," overworking the phrase "all of a sudden."

Loosening my hair so that it fell carelessly about my forehead and cheeks, I walked and posed à la Jeritza entering the studio, with her dramatic "*Geliebtes*"; then, after vocalizing "Mah-Ma-Ma—" I broke off, interrupting with another "*Geliebtes.*"

"All of a sudden, *Geliebtes,* vot you tink hoppen? I am singing auf Baltimore mit die Metropolitan spring tour—undt I have für dis dressing room—die tird floor. Undt I say to Honor [one of her three maids] 'Warum?' Undt Honor she say, 'Aber madam, you are the big star und you need lots of room.' Undt den, *Geliebtes,* der are tree bells—die first is to got ready—die second is to hurry hup, undt die tird—it is too late!

"So Honor, she take die rouge, undt Liselle she take die powder undt mine oder maid she take die pineapple juice undt we get in die lift. Hup undt down—down undt hup ve ride. All of a sudden I say: 'Dis is no joke—I must sing Tosca!' All of a sudden I hear tree bells vot mean it is too late! I come on to the stage undt I sing to the tenor 'Mario—Mario,' but Mario shakes his head undt sings 'Nein, nein! Didn't you hear die tree bells, it is too late!' Undt I say 'Never mind—all of a sudden I vill sing "Vissi d'arte."' *Geliebtes,* vot you tink?"

Then I flung myself on the floor, like Jeritza singing the aria as I heard her on that never-to-be-forgotten first time when I was still in school. When I made my exit, with the diva herself a part of the vociferous applause, I was already adjusting large pearl earrings, tying a scarf about my throat.

Now, my impersonation was Galli-Curci who, oddly enough, liked to call Miss Liebling "Stelchen Carissima." She had just had her hair bobbed, so I wore a short skirt and, running my hands through my curls and mocking her high lyrical voice, I said:

"Well, Stelchen Carissima, how do you like the kid with her hair bobbed? It makes me feel just like a girl again—like a girl again!" Then I patted my larynx. "The voice is coming fine; the support is splendid; play this for me, Stelchen"—I whipped out "Clavelitos"— "and listen to me biff these notes right on the coco!" Knowing Galli-Curci was a golf fan, I then interrupted the song to say, "I played golf with the old boy Rockefeller in Florida, and what do you think, Carissima? He gave me a dime!"

So I went on with other celebrities, but it was as Miss Liebling herself that I most amused the audience. Her tact and eagerness to please the managers was famous, but in my imitation of her I would carry this to extreme. No matter what happened, she was equal to the occasion. A third telephone would ring and I, as Miss Liebling, would pick it up and say in dulcet tones:

"Hello? Yes, this is Miss Liebling. Oh, good morning, J. J. Shubert, I'm sending down twelve tall girls; they are *beautiful* and sing just *wonderfully*." Then taken aback: "You don't want *tall* girls this season?" She continued undaunted, "Well, I have thirty-two *small* ones. No? Well, I have any kind you want—even a group of seventeen called the Liebling singers—they are *every type* imaginable. Let me send them down right now—ah—how kind! Good-by—J. J.!"

Henry Bellaman, sitting with his wife Katherine, led the applause. Succeeding Dr. Noble, he was now director of the Juilliard School of Music; a gifted pianist, poet, and later author of the successful novel *Kings Row*, he came to congratulate me.

"Jessica, it is rare to find singers with charming speaking voices. I'm going to repeat what I told you that day at tea before you began to broadcast, 'Some day people will pay you a great deal of money just to hear you speak.'" I thanked him. "But where did you learn those accents?" he was asking. "With your fine speaking voice, I would not have believed it possible."

I couldn't help laughing over the buried memories unearthed by Bellaman's question. The countless auditions I had attended without success loomed—one especially, when I tried something different just to see what would happen. After listening to quite a few applicants sing and hearing them dismissed with a polite "Thank you," I hung back, afraid to face the barrage of indifference. Then as a kind of "whistling in the dark," I decided to "put on" a French accent. At that moment, one of the managers seeing me hesitate, called directly to me to perform.

"I do not care to sing, sank you, because I am *Franch*," I told him in my broadest accent. In a second both men were at my side and asked me to wait until they were through with the other hearings. Then, like an ill-matched jigsaw piece, they endeavored to fit me to the part they were casting—which did not call for an accent.

"What a pity," they clucked. "You think you are saying the words correctly, but you're not. You put your tongue up against your teeth— Americans don't talk that way." They spoke to me indulgently as if I were a pampered child and raised their voices as if I had difficulty hearing as well as speaking.

"Too bad," one said shaking his head, "we would love to use you— but the accent, no matter how we figure, is not for this part, it doesn't make sense."

Here was one audition that wasn't disappointing. Though I was unsuccessful, I felt I had played a part to the hilt!

At Miss Liebling's Christmas party—soon after I began singing on the air—Daniel Frohman was also present. He stood in saturnine silence in the shadows watching me during the impressions. When they were over, he stalked around to me.

"It is perfectly ridiculous for you to be in radio," he remarked sternly. "You should be in the theater. You have something definite to give."

I couldn't resist laughing slyly, "But Mr. Frohman, don't you think my name is too long to be in lights?"

Radio began giving signs of drawing people from the speak-easy back into the home, and keeping them there absorbed by what cynics called a new toy. Most Americans, however, especially those away from the large centers, soon learned that the microphone was their passport to the world—in time they would know what the world was doing every hour of the day.

As radio grew so did its stars. The newspapers began to carry my name in headlines. Said the Philadelphia *Inquirer:*

AMERICA HAS A NEW LOVE—SHE'S THE RADIO GIRL

Like some lovely phantom with her exquisite voice, her mystery and charm, the maid of the air is ascending that throne from which idolized favorites of the public have held sway. . . . As proof, consider the story of little Jessica Dragonette, a girl in her teens. . . . They call her the "Jenny Lind" of the Air; the girl with the dimple in her voice. They hang her picture over the radio so they can pretend she is actually there when she sings. . . . How the unseen singer, product of the machine, could blossom into favor as human and personal as that of any star who won popularity with beauty and charm of appearance is the interesting phenomenon unfolded in this story.

In the differentiation between the two networks, WEAF carried commercially-sponsored programs, and WJZ was "sustaining," a public utility concentrating on the public culture. Strictly speaking, being a WEAF contract artist on a sponsored program, I belonged to the mercantile network. However, in my own mind I was determined that as an individual artist my performances would reflect the cultural ideal. It was a form of madness to think I could remain apart from the spirit of commercialism; yet that was my preoccupation.

The Philco Company, for reasons of availability and coverage, decided to buy an hour's broadcast time on the Blue Network, whose key station was WJZ. They were interested in a Theater Memories series—featuring famous operettas.

They let it be known, "We want Vivian, whoever she is." In spite of their merger as NBC, WEAF and WJZ still rather stiffly maintained their accustomed separateness. Philco's demand for me posed a problem. It put the WEAF Artists Bureau, with which I had a contract, and Bertha Brainard, program director of WJZ, on the horns of a dilemma. Miss Brainard tried to solve it with her uncommonly clear thinking. "At least," she said to Philco, "let my WJZ artists compete in audition."

It was reported later that her WJZ contestants evoked no interest on the part of the Philco representatives. But when I began to sing, Sayre Ramsdell, vice-president of the company, began to smile, and when I had finished he was boisterously enthusiastic. "That was Vivian," he remarked, "yes sir, that was Vivian, and she's our girl."

CHAPTER 9

THE AIR RUSH

Now moving uptown from the cramped quarters in the Telephone Building, we went on the air from NBC's new home, 711 Fifth Avenue. In the third month after my radio debut, I was inaugurating the new Philco Series, broadcasting light operettas for the first time. Here was a new concept in entertainment, for by the amplification of the voice radio carried to the largest imaginable audience the most intimate form of expression.

A dazzling prospect to me was the initial plan of having as guests, members of the original cast of each light opera. Having separated myself from the stage, I would still be in contact with Broadway through its artists, crossing over the footlights into the ether world.

The Merry Widow brought us Donald Brian, who had created the prince's role in the original company. However often I was subsequently to hear this operetta, I never knew anyone to play Danilo to such perfection.

At rehearsal, Brian was dashing, full of sparkle and bravura, and when he sang "There Once Were Two Princes' Children," I was moved to tears. But as I stood at the microphone as Sonia, *The Merry Widow*, in my red velvet dress, trimmed with ermine tails, he became quite another person. He grew pale, nervous, and terrified of this unaccustomed method of projection. Experienced in the demands of the theater, he had not had the occasion, as I had had, to woo the instrument. I seized his hand and held it to prevent him from gesticulating and turning his head in every direction. When he observed me speaking my lines and singing, he could see I was playing to the microphone and not to him. Then the innate artist rose to a fine performance. When the broadcast was over, he had a new respect for the "little girl."

"Whew!" he sighed, nonplused. "You certainly know your onions around that microphone." In addition to the compliment, Donald Brian had given me a brand new expression.

It was a personal joy to be rejoined with Harold Sanford in the new Theater Memories, during which he was eventually to teach me how Victor Herbert wanted every measure of his music sung. A violinist in the Metropolitan Opera Orchestra under Arturo Toscanini, Sanford, from the age of twenty-two was associated with Victor Herbert, a cellist in the same orchestra under Anton Seidel.

A strict disciplinarian, Sanford tolerated no untoward musical liberties nor any irreverence for his idol's scores. In every way the association proved to be marvelous training for a young singer. Henry M. Neely, the "Old Stager" who held the thread of the story, a first-nighter at most of the operettas we presented, could draw on many personal experiences for his part in the programs. Our permanent company also included Doris Doe, Mary Hopple, Muriel Wilson, Colin O'More, Walter Preston, Charles Robinson, and Dan Gridley.

Dan, who had come from California, greatly wished to make a fine impression. His radio bow was in *The Vagabond King*, where he had but one line to speak. The role called on him to herald the royal presence in stentorian tones: "His Majesty, the King!" Rushing toward the mike with upraised arm and excited voice, Dan cried out, "His Kadjesty, the Ming!" Poor fellow, he never lived down the slip, and all of us had a hard time going on with the show that evening.

When I was engaged for the series, I did not know a single one of the operettas and had to learn over seventy-five of them from beginning to end. Each week, I found it an exciting challenge to sing and act the contrasting roles with their dramatic range of music and varied feeling of locale—among them: *The Quaker Girl, Sari, Naughty Marietta, Only Girl, Count of Luxembourg, Princess Pat.*

Now we were broadcasting weekly over a chain of thirty-nine stations, and thousands of letters were pouring in after each presentation to this first series of the Red Network, a coined name derived from the *red ink* engineers used in making up their charts. This gave us a tremendous audience, and we were not yet in Radio City. Before we could catch our breath, the ribbon of the NBC outlets spanned the Continent, like two halves of a circle, one encompassing the

South—the other, the North. After two and a half years with Philco, we had forty-nine stations.

The nation was contained in a small floating studio! With the speed of light, streaming out of the vibrant steel towers, were voices—music, drama, news, commercials. The carrier-waves were becoming the voices, and the voices began to speak the truths and wisdoms of the ancient faiths to people everywhere, even in the remote corners of the world. The studio, in turn, penetrating steel and stone, was dissolving into a vast cathedral of the air.

The air rush amounted to an overnight boom. Along with Philco, I was also doing a Hoover Sentinels Series; guest appearances for Maxwell House; children's stories, experimenting with countless sound effects; reading the first poetry on the air; taking part in the first variety shows, beloved by listeners; the first Shakespeare—ideal for radio because of the many short scenes; acting in the first modern plays.

I saw the radio dream glowing and expanding. Only a student, I was reluctant to meet the press, for I did not feel I was a finished star. Legends began to spring up—I was becoming "Radio's Mystery Lady." When cornered, I spoke about my visions: one world—radio, an instrument of peace; possibly through radio, a standard English for the first time; a music-conscious America—radio, the instrument of education; surely there would emerge a school of the air—but these things were never quoted until Stokowski said them much later. They were superseded in the press by "the girl with the plaid eyes"—"the girl you would like to take to your next prom." "She's pretty, but refuses to go into the movies." No matter, my compensation was in the materialization of many of these dreams.

Appearing in a new operetta every week, I could lose no time, so I formed the habit of beginning study on the score the minute it was in my hands. Leaning against the wall in the studio corridor, one day, I was so engrossed in *Sweethearts,* I never noticed a man who passed me and went into his office. Several hours later he walked by again on his way to luncheon—and I never looked up. He came back, and I was still there, oblivious of his passing. Finally, in amazement and curiosity, he sent his secretary out to investigate me.

"Go and find out who that girl is and what she's doing," he said. "I never saw such concentration in my life."

The secretary led me back into his office. Confronted with George McClelland, vice-president and general manager of NBC, I did not know what to expect.

Biting down on his cigar and with his blue eyes severely holding my gaze, he demanded sharply, "What have you been doing out there in the hall, all day?"

"There's no studio available, sir, and I wouldn't have time to go all the way home before rehearsal. I must study where I can," I said quietly.

"Are you sure that's all?" he asked suspiciously.

"Oh, yes," I answered, surprised.

"Well, if that's the case," he responded with a sudden smile, "I'll listen in on Friday and hear how you do."

"Thank you," I replied demurely, but an inward glow told me in a secret way I had found an understanding friend.

George McClelland did listen, and from then on I was free to go to him from time to time for help in interpretations of company enigmas.

Whenever we presented a Victor Herbert operetta, Ella Herbert Bartlett, the composer's daughter, attended the performance. Now we were planning to give *The Only Girl* with Wilda Bennett, who had created the role on Broadway. She was a raven-haired statuesque beauty whom Ella told us her father had especially selected for the part because of a brilliant high B natural. We could hardly wait for the broadcast, but alas, the microphone was overwhelming to Wilda. With a gay, spirited, little song called "Personality" I played the ingénue to her lead; sometimes standing directly behind, I tried to keep her in line with the microphone, but she was unable to prevent the hint of nerves from coming over.

After the hour, Ella Herbert congratulated me: "You certainly saved the day, and I'm looking forward to hearing you sing the lead in Father's *Sweethearts* next week."

By the time we gave *Mlle. Modiste* and Fritzi Scheff joined us, Harold Sanford was openly apprehensive. He had felt all along that guest artists interfered with the well-rehearsed, carefully coordinated performances of the permanent company. Besides, remembered circumstances around the original stage production of *Modiste* affected him. Fritzi Scheff entertained a like anxiety—this was her first radio and she wanted to appear to advantage. Tension mounted between conductor and singer; when they rehearsed the scene "If I were on the stage," it was plainly visible that Sanford had a flashback of what had happened twenty-five years before. The action of the number gave Fritzi Scheff, playing the part of Fifi, the little French hat girl with operatic ambitions, several differing characterizations: first, a country girl, singing a simple air; then a marquise, vocalizing a showy polonaise; and finally the modiste says:

> . . . but best of all the parts I'd play,
> If I could only have my way,
> Would be a strong romantic role,
> Emotional and full of soul.
> And I believe for such a thing
> A dreamy, sensuous waltz I'd sing.

To fit the wish, Herbert composed the famous "Kiss Me Again." And true to the line "A dreamy, sensuous waltz" in the key of G, beginning on a low B natural, he wrote, "Sweet summer breeze, whispering trees . . ."

A high soprano from the Metropolitan Opera, Fritzi's Musetta in *La Bohème* was a favorite. Furious, outraged, and sure that Herbert was plotting her ruin in her operetta debut, she left the theater in a temperamental outburst and was not seen for several days. When she did come back, Herbert cajoled her with the idea that the emotional quality of the song called for a low cello-like melody. The ovation she received for "Kiss Me Again" on opening night made up for all her misgivings, and the fact that the song has followed her throughout her life proves Herbert was right.

Nevertheless, not even the magical results of her identification with the hit had erased the incident from her mind. Sanford, always the serious musician, and not a notably diplomatic man, in a forthright admonition, warned us: "There's no going back to correct a broadcast. It has to be perfect."

But it was Fritzi Scheff's remark that made a lasting impression on me. Tilting her chin to Sanford, she said quietly, "Of course I'll do my best." Then with a rapier thrust she added, "Artists are like children, you only have to know how to handle them."

After this, the simmering antagonism between Fritzi Scheff and

Sanford worked creatively to good effect. The high-gear, volatile prima donna and the meticulous conductor succeeded in bringing off beautifully the presentation.

The Philco Series was a new *Westward Ho!* The telephone lines carrying it over the thirty-nine-station network constituted a great ganglia of nerve cells of communication. The scope of radio could still be only dimly envisioned, but fan-mail response proved it was taking hold, affecting the lives of people everywhere. On this New Year's of 1927 the first cross-country broadcast was a football game in the Pasadena Rose Bowl. New lines, not yet connected, but ready and waiting, were a dramatic implication.

Advertising agencies were having to find means of meeting demands of their clients for radio advertising. Buying time was only the first step; the agencies had also to write radio copy, act as musical consultants and impresarios. A few took the easy way out of this challenge to their knowledge with trivial programing. Others went about it more conscientiously, even taking lessons like children to acquaint themselves with music. Soon they solved the problem by recruiting people from radio—Annette Bushman was one of the first to leave NBC for the agency business.

Not long after the Theater Memories had been in full swing, the account executive from Erwin Wasey, Radcliffe Romeyn, took me aside one day and revealed he was considering abandoning the guest-star plan. Rehearsals were often complicated, delayed, or interrupted by the people from the stage, and he was turning over in his mind a plan to knit more closely the little repertory company.

"As an artist in great demand," Mr. Romeyn asked me, "how do you feel about the idea?"

On the spur of the moment, I replied, "You don't know how good I am for Philco. Up to now you've not had a chance to find out. But five programs are after me at once. I can do a much better job by concentrating on one. Why don't you sign me up exclusively and be different? Of course, you'll have to pay more money, which won't affect me, but it will please the Artists Bureau."

What I meant to say was that I would only receive a percentage at the end of the year on the excess over my salary guarantee.

Mr. Romeyn shot a shrewd look at me—I had been doubtless coached by some sharp Mephistopheles on the NBC staff. He took the suggestion; and thereafter, instead of guest stars from the original companies for Theater Memories, I played all the name roles. But he could not fathom how a "green girl" dreamed up what the advertisers hadn't thought of—the first exclusive contract in radio. Soon it became the fashion, but boomeranged many times, always to my disadvantage!

The General Motors family party in 1927 was the equivalent of 1951's Big Show emceed by Tallulah Bankhead. Willie Collier, "end man" for General Motors on that occasion, was a famous comedian, a versatile actor, who began as a call boy at the old Augustin Daly Theater. Nora Bayes was the star of the first broadcast produced at Carnegie Hall Chambers. The advertisers captured public interest by calling attention to the presence of "Willie Collier Himself" (not "in person"); "Miss Nora Bayes Herself." It was an all-around feast of entertainment, with Joe Green's Marimba Band, Nat Schildkret's Orchestra, B. A. Rolfe's Orchestra, Pat Conway's Band, and a number of other specialties. Lewis James, the tenor of the Revellers, was featured, and Deems Taylor, who had written the score for *Beggar on Horseback*, helped with the programing. Original music was written especially for this broadcast, and Alois Havrilla was the announcer.

I will always remember the sparkling vitality of Nora Bayes. She made a wonderful picture with clearly chiseled features, handsome blue-white coiffure, her fringed white dress adorned with the Légion d'Honneur and other decorations. When she sang the songs for which she was famous—"Just Like A Gypsy," and "Has Anybody Here Seen Kelly?"—the effect was electrifying. I felt she gave me a mark to live up to.

When we were introduced, she said, "Oh, I know you—you're the girl with the smile in her voice." Later, she remarked on it again. "When you sing, I can actually see the dimple."

I was featured in some of the original music written for the hour: "June, Moon and You," also a song called "Naughty Baby." Immediately after the broadcast I had a note from a priest who told me that seeing in the newspaper I was to be on a big new program, he gathered a group of people to listen. He felt sure I would sing only "good music."

"What was my consternation, dear Miss Dragonette," he wrote, "to hear you singing 'Naughty Baby'! But never mind; we enjoyed it as much as if it had been the 'Ave Maria.'"

George McClelland, present with the General Motors officials from all over the United States, came afterward to congratulate me. I sensed a growing coolness between him and Annette Bushman who through the Campbell-Ewald Agency was connected with the program. He interpreted her asking me to appear on the program as an agency overture, trying to wean me from NBC. Keeping myself aloof, I disregarded agency-company politics, business intrigue and antagonisms.

All in all I felt I had made the right decision by staying in radio. However, the sponsor wasn't always too sure. I remember vividly the remark of one General Motors executive: "Maybe radio will be usable in time."

Rehearsing Lehar's *Count of Luxembourg* for Theater Memories one afternoon, I was handed an unsigned note, a call to Studio A at four o'clock no matter what I was doing. It read "Discuss this matter with no one." When I asked Harold Sanford if I could leave, he seemed primed.

Nine men were in Studio A when I arrived, but nobody said anything to me about what was in progress, and I was puzzled when they locked the door. At a given signal, four of the men went into the control room. Another sat down at the piano, the remaining four took a position near the microphone. One was Mayor Jimmy Walker, another, Owen D. Young; I did not recognize the other two, but later learned they were Dr. F. W. Alexanderson and McFarlane Moore.

It was Jimmy Walker's little speech—one of those incomparable impromptu gems of his—which told me why we were there: this was a first television experiment. When Mayor Walker finished, I heard a cheery whistle, and my picture was transmitted on a small crank-turned apparatus, fitted with a roller. It traveled twenty-five miles, to the home of Dr. A. N. Goldsmith who, with Alexanderson and Moore, was responsible for the equipment at this stage, hence vitally concerned with the results. After the sending of the picture, I was instructed to sing Friml's "L'Amour, Toujours L'Amour." It was rather startling to have all this sprung on me, but I tingled with the air of conspiracy—fate had again counted me in on an exciting new venture.

As it turned out, the photograph sent through space collected static marks. *The New York Times* commented that the apparatus was extremely simple and the pictures, recognizable though crude, were of vast interest to people all over the world.

This personal association with the pioneer TV experiments of February 5, 1928, emphasizes how closely television has developed side by side with radio. TV, the broadcasting of sight, repeating the same pattern as the beginnings of radio, the broadcasting of sound, has been unrestricted; writing my own scripts, testing make-up and wardrobe, selecting my own music, routining scenes, I got to learn something about everybody's job. Today, however, TV tends more and more to circumscribed forms, though the addition of color will doubtless delay the stalemate.

Now I began to worry about losing my French; and, since it was impossible for me to go to Paris, where I could breathe the language in by osmosis, I decided to create Paris here. I soon found a room with a delightful French family, the Brugells.

Madame Claire Brugell was a French teacher and translator; at the moment, she was working on Louis Bromfield's novels and Thornton Burgess' animal stories. Thus I first became acquainted with both authors in French, being particularly carried away by Bromfield's *The Green Bay Tree* and *Early Autumn*.

All in the spirit of *La Vie de Bohême,* the Brugell family nicknamed me Mimi Pinson. I had a Mimi room on the fourth floor, a casement and window seat, a narrow bed, an upright piano, a trunk covered with a piece of black taffeta appliqued with red poppies, cut from one of my costumes. With zest I wrote Nadea, still ill in Arizona, all about my special blue sky and *"il primo sole e mio."*

We spoke only French; and I learned much from Madame Brugell's realism, her typical Gallic sagacity. She knew my dreams were boundless and was careful never to discourage me, though sometimes after gazing around my bare room, she would commend me to destiny with an eloquent shrug of her shoulders, *"Qui vivra, verra!"*

There now began a period of huge radio shows to stimulate the selling of sets to listeners. To liven up the display of the latest equipment and machines, artists who were making radio listening interesting were asked to appear in person. One of the first was held in Pittsburgh, where commercial broadcasting began over the great local station KDKA, and I was selected to appear.

I chose my clothes for the event with excitement: to travel in, a beige lapin coat with a small muff, a sports dress of tan wool with red leather belt and white dice buttons dotted in red, a brown grosgrain skull cap; and for my appearance, a white satin concert dress.

Graham McNamee and Milton Cross came on the train with me to Pittsburgh. As we pulled into the station, I noticed a number of men running up and down the platform peering at the cars, but it never occurred to me that they might be looking for me, and I went straight to the hotel.

There was an immediate telephone call from the radio editor of the Pittsburgh *Gazette*.

"I met you in Chicago—remember?" a loud, hurried voice began. "I'm very anxious to see you again. How did we miss you at the train? Can you come to the office at once; we want to go to press with a story?"

"Yes, I will come," I said accommodatingly. But I was wondering how he could have met me in Chicago, since up to this time I had never been there!

In the office, the radio editor rushed to greet me effusively. "So good to see you again," he said, wringing my hand. Dumbfounded, I echoed, "Yes, yes, so good!" knowing full well I had never laid eyes on the man before.

During my stay in Pittsburgh he never left my side, which further piqued my curiosity. He even saw me off at the train with flowers, which I later learned was a new high for a newspaperman. Now that we were driving to the railroad station, I could no longer resist.

"Tell me," I said, "who *was* it you did meet in Chicago? You know it really isn't very flattering to confuse me with someone else." He spun around like a gyrating top.

"Gee," he exclaimed, "you're a good sport—you really helped me out! I'm supposed to know you very well, and for weeks I've been answering all kinds of questions about you in my column: the color of your eyes, your hair, everything your fans want to know. I never cared much for Catholics, but let me tell you—I don't care if you're the Pope's cousin, I'm all for you!" I had saved the day for the radio editor of the Pittsburgh *Gazette*, but he still wasn't satisfied.

"Who would you say is the handsomest man in the studios?" he asked.

"Oh," I said discreetly, "I couldn't possibly answer that as I haven't seen them all."

He studied me, bit his lip, snapped his fingers, "You win again—that's exactly what a smart girl like you would say."

Shortly after this I made a personal appearance at a radio show in Louisville, Kentucky. This time NBC sent with me William Burke Miller, who had left his paper to join the staff of NBC in New York while he made up his mind between continuing a career in journalism or singing. As a boy, it had been Miller's ambition to go to West Point, but difficulties with mathematics somewhat changed his perspective; instead, he got a job as cub reporter on the Louisville *Courier-Journal* and put his beautiful baritone to work between times, singing over the paper's key station WHAS.

During the tremendous drama of Floyd Collins' entombment in a Kentucky cave, Miller, very slim and built like a jockey, crawled snake-like to the imprisoned man, pinned between two boulders, bringing him food and human sympathy until finally Collins died. Miller's heroic bravery and daily report gave his newspaper an exclusive scoop on the story and won him the Pulitzer Prize for the year's best reporting.

From time to time at NBC he had been assigned to interview me for publicity releases. His intense seriousness aroused my sense of mischief.

"What are you going to do when you retire?" was his first question.
"Retire," I said.

Miller sighed with exasperation and decided to try again. Looking me straight in the eye, he inquired, "What color are your eyes?"
"Scotch plaid," I answered.

"There's no such thing," he snapped back. "At least I've never heard of it."

It is entirely to Miller's credit that from this unsatisfactory beginning we could become friends. He was amazingly modest about having won the Pulitzer Prize and always shied away when anybody grew sentimental about it.

Another time he invited me to luncheon saying, "I hope you're not accepting because I'm in the press department." This rather rubbed me the wrong way, and it was a very long time before I saw him again. Now he was sent to Louisville with me primarily to report in detail on the radio show and also keep an eye on my press relations.

The Louisville Show was far and away the finest I had ever attended, and for the entertainment part 30,000 people were seated in a vast auditorium. At the close of the first evening, Dr. David Morton gave a midnight supper for me at his home in Mockingbird Valley. I was enchanted by the stately Southern colonial mansion some distance from the city, by the magnolia-scented night in that soft climate, by the marvelous Southern hospitality, and by a supper quietly and expertly served by liveried servants. Among the sixty guests were Credo Harris, director of WHAM, Judge Robert Bingham, later our ambassador to the Court of St. James's, and his wife. The judge recognized radio as a coming force, but did not particularly believe in its future, and my relation to it puzzled him. As we sat in the library, leading by four steps to the veranda, we talked.

"Why are you in radio?" he asked. "You are gifted with a charming stage personality. I wondered as I heard you sing tonight why you are not in the theater."

"I have a dream, Judge, a vision of thousands and thousands of people sitting together in their own homes or alone in the nooks and crannies of the world, with their memories and dreams ready to be touched off by the beauty of a song. I am not in the studio when I sing—but in the hearts of all who are listening."

Judge Bingham grew thoughtful, but made no specific comment. The next day at a meeting about buying another radio station he is reported to have said, "Let's buy the station—it will open up a new life to the mountain people." Then he smiled, nodding his head, "Now I understand what the little girl was trying to tell me last night. 'Radio is a magical thing.'"

The following spring, we lived out an unbelievable fairy tale. A smiling Missourian in an airship called the *Spirit of Saint Louis* flew the wide Atlantic nonstop to Paris, and while the whole world watched and waited, he brought down his plane at Le Bourget in Paris and handed the customs officers his passport and letters of introduction. The long-waiting French, amused at this boyish modesty, asked the tired airman to sit down. Lindbergh quietly refused; adding to their further amusement, he smiled, "Thank you; I've been sitting."

On his return to America, all the NBC artists stood by for a day-long salute to the conquering flier. Between our programs of aviation music, Sanford joined us as we listened in to the welcoming city outside.

"Bravo Lindy!" They shouted above the din—"Welcome Home!"

Hearing Charles A. Lindbergh's own voice later, I wondered if he did not feel an exile from the skies? For no one else ever had the stars as he had them. How could he enter our earth-bound joy when he had "chased the wind along and flung his eager craft through footless halls of air"?

In a sense, I thought, he and I shared a pioneership of the ether.

Just about this time the engineers of the Brunswick Recording Company asked NBC if I could record for them: "She comes over the air so beautifully—with real microphone personality! We would like to have her voice on records."

For the audition I recorded a little Gershwin song called "Do It Again" and the Mexican folk song "Estrellita," and learned that the president of the company, Thomas D'Arcy Brophy, asked when he heard it, "Who is that girl? She burns up the records with temperament!"

At the time I didn't even own a Victrola and carried the records around looking for a place to play them. Afterward I brought them to Miss Liebling. She had already heard from Mr. Brophy, about the "burning temperament." Laughing, she pooh-poohed him with, "Why, she's only a little convent girl!"

Miss Liebling gave me a mock scolding, "You naughty girl, how could you sing those songs so shockingly?"

To which I replied in all seriousness, "How should they be sung, Miss Liebling, like a Sunday-school teacher?"

It was the same "Do It Again" that I sang with a French accent one night on an air guest appearance. The next day I was summoned before the board of NBC and sternly forbidden ever to use that "risqué" song again.

"What are you trying to do," Mr. Aylesworth asked, "corrupt the youth of the nation?"

I was still seeing the vision of the miracle of entertainment broadcasting and spent every moment I could developing the unknown quantities of this fascinating medium: suitable radio formats and use of the microphone. Evidently I was succeeding, for people were certain I possessed some secret weapon—my voice "came over so well." They wondered what was back of my microphone personality. "How does she do it?" They gave me credit for technique instead of a God-given voice. They begged the secret, and believing I withheld it, came and sat under my nose while I was broadcasting, to catch it.

Newspapermen wrote, asking for my "trade secrets." This surprised me, for what I had learned about radio applied in essence to any art form. "Sincerity," I wrote back, "is the first requisite—color of voice is all-important! The microphone loves beautiful and gentle tones—*no forcing*—maximum of quality, minimum of quantity —effects are a matter of tempo rather than dynamics—only genuine feeling comes across. The voice must be used with perfect control and direction. The psychology of broadcasting is an intimate mental picture of singing without projection, in contrast to singing across the footlights."

Frequently I suggested to the program directors that we were not making the best use of the microphone as yet.

"Instead of talking and singing at one level, we should experiment with the distances and several microphones. It is monotonous to live at one level."

"Let's try it," they would respond.

Now with radio's slender fingers drawing melody out of the night and flinging it across a continent, we demonstrated in an adaptation of *The Nightingale and the Rose,* how the unseen singer, product of the machine, could emerge as a warmly human personality.

The gossamer story, iridescent as a butterfly's wing, required no special handling to make it believable. As we heightened ideas for ear appeal, we found that the spoken lines of the allegory really told us what to do, and I seemed to the listeners most human when I was playing the part of the bird.

"If you want a red rose," said the Tree to the Nightingale, "you must build it out of *music* by moonlight, and stain it with your own heart's blood. You must sing to me with your breast against a thorn. All night long you must sing to me, and the thorn must pierce your heart, and your lifeblood must flow into my veins, and become mine."

I found an ideal opportunity working with Raymond Knight, director, and Wilhelm Schaefer, composer, on this original musical production. Ben Grauer played the Student; Aileen Berry, a Broadway actress, the Girl; and I, the Nightingale in the Oscar Wilde story. The first plan was to have a lyric writer set words to the melodies. Could any lyric writer, I wondered, match the spoken lines of Oscar Wilde? Further, would it not be disturbing to hear words coming from a bird? I asked, therefore, that I be allowed to go from my speaking lines into the bird song, suggesting by gaiety or sadness the mood color of what was being portrayed.

Reluctant to appear and mar the delicate fantasy, we decided to broadcast by remote control from another part of the building to the audience assembled in the large studio, 8H, at 711 Fifth Avenue. To intimate a change of character and to heighten the dramatic effect, lights were played on the soft gray hangings that curtained the loud-speaker—a colorama, suffusing the presentation with subtle imagination, heightening the illusion for the audience.

We had a flood of response; yet no message touched me more than one from my long-time friend, Monsignor McNally:

"Superb," he wired me. "I always longed to hear a nightingale— now I can die content."

For me it was not only the most romantic role I had ever played, but one ideally suited to radio. As the Nightingale, I sang through the ether from an unseen bower with the stars as footlights. In the poetry, music, and fantasy of the story I was permitted to live for an instant the mystery of the birth of a rose.

Now in December, 1929, we were preparing to finish our series of Theater Memories, and for the holidays we would present *Babes in Toyland*. After two and one half years of building up a popular program the audience eagerly awaited from week to week, I was

abruptly shifted to another hour. Though I did not know the-behind-
the-scenes reasons, Philco was leaving NBC for the Columbia Network and would like to have me go with them. But unfortunately,
much as I loved the program, I was not free to do so, for I had a
five-year contract with NBC. George McClelland consoled me, explaining they had other plans that would be announced the following
week.

I was facing a major turning point in my radio career, but the
momentous broadcast of the next day, distracting me from its import,
seized my entire attention. *"Hello, Germany"* was as significant as
Lindbergh's legendary flight to Paris, as revolutionary as atomic fis-
sion, a long-awaited climax of concerted effort, changing our physical
world and expanding our spiritual horizons. As part of this stupen-
dous event, I recall the incredulous excitement accompanying our
realization that we could be heard simultaneously on both sides of
the world. We thrilled at talking across the oceans. Soon we should
be able to hear the heartbeat of Everyman. There would be no more
separateness, loneliness, misunderstanding.

What dark adversary, fiery and threatening, roaming the universe,
stepped between to impede our progress? What evil threw us into
a catastrophic era, rendering impotent this greatest mass medium of
communication? What diabolical force still prolongs the human tragedy of man's failure to understand man, overwhelming us with the
sense of loss and separation that accompanies this failure?

CHAPTER 10

MUSIC FOR THE MILLIONS

In the short interval between December 27, 1929, and January 3,
1930, I not only had to prepare a new program—work with new associates—but I also had to prepare a new contract! The Artists Bureau,
calling me to a conference, read off a press release which first
acquainted me with my new sponsor, Cities Service, and in dis-
cussing the terms they told me there would be no change whatsoever

from my previous financial arrangements. It was not easy for me to leave a well-wrought program like Philco, so firmly placed in the listeners' affections, and now the dreary outlook given me by the Artists Bureau was most disappointing.

The public always marvels at the huge salaries paid artists, but rarely do they realize how many debts may be incurred through the artists' continuous training; their responsibilities and liabilities; how stringent the conditions under which they are forced to work. From the beginning my burden had been a heavy one. In 1929, on the edge of the depression, the newspapers talked of millionaire radio stars and included me in the group. Actually I was so far from qualifying that it is laughable. Under the terms of my contract with NBC I received an advance of seventy-five dollars a broadcast; and only after it was earned, did I receive at the end of the year a percentage of what the sponsor was actually paying for my services. Many people had claims on me. Besides I had contracted to pay percentages out of future earnings.

After futile discussions with the Artists Bureau, I felt compelled to take a hand in my own affairs. I went directly to George Mc-Clelland—he could always be depended on for a straightforward answer. After I explained my dissatisfaction with the terms of the new contract for Cities Service, Mr. McClelland looked straight at me: "Write your own contract." For a minute I was taken aback. I knew he would be fair, but I didn't expect him to go so far. I gulped very hard, then plunged desperately: "I think I should get double my present salary." Before he could answer me, I plunged again: "What's it to you—you don't have to pay it." My answer made him laugh so heartily that he got up from his chair and left the room. I sat there ill with the thought that again I had done the wrong thing.

He came back with a contract in his hands: "You see, it shall be just as you wish. Go and relax now; we haven't much time. Your Cities Service program begins on the third of January. Fortunately you'll be where your audience expects to find you Friday nights."

That was true as far as the night was concerned, but not so with the station. The Cities Service program emanated from the Red network, which was WEAF. This led to some confusion as people kept tuning in to WJZ, and thousands of letters arrived asking: "What has happened to Jessica?" A lively correspondence ensued between the vice-president of NBC and Mackenzie King, the late premier of Canada, whose every note concluded: "What has happened to Jessica? Where can I find Jessica?"

The Cities Service concert program had been in progress for some time before I joined it. The audience was continually wondering why I was not presented in dramatic scenes where I could speak as well as sing. When I brought this matter up with the agency men, they said: "We don't want you to speak at all on this program. Why should we remind the audience of your former sponsor?"

Whatever my disappointments over their attitude, it was a privilege to sing with Rosario Bourdon and the forty-piece orchestra of "hand-picked men." This was decidedly a step up. Again I felt the musical horizon changing and widening. With Rosario Bourdon I was working with the director whose beautiful accompaniments I had been enjoying for a long time in the Victor Red Seal records of the greatest musicians—Galli-Curci, John McCormack, Tito Schipa, Rosa Ponselle, Fritz Kreisler, and many others.

The hour's concert, from eight to nine on Friday evenings, included the Cavaliers, and later the Revellers Quartet. Kenneth McGregor was our program director and Frank Williams, the engineer. I remained with Cities Service for seven years, doing over 600 broadcasts. We never repeated a number under six months' time—a self-imposed rule. Of the seventeen selections given I was usually involved in eight—solos, duets, features with the quartet—singing operatic arias, classics from the song literature of the world, operetta music, ballads, and the best of the popular songs, concluding with the hit of the week—precursor to the present Hit Parade. In all this period, we rehearsed the whole program in three hours, which meant one run-through with the orchestra; it also meant we all had to be expert to accomplish this feat, for it was a feat!

Timing was the sword of Damocles hanging over our heads. We could not be ten seconds overtime without infringing on another sponsor's territory. Time is fugitive, but however fast it ran, Rosario Bourdon could keep up with it. He could pour the infinite into the finite.

Speaking of time reminds me of a ride with Stokowski once in California. My watch did not agree with his automobile clock. Glancing at my wrist, I asked, "Is that the correct time, Maestro?" He looked at me indulgently: "My dear girl, is there any such thing as correct time?" There was, indeed, to Rosario Bourdon. In this, as in many other ways, he was a genius. He steered us gently, but firmly, between the first and last numbers, the Scylla and Charybdis of an hour's voyage of melody, without ever taking more than fifteen seconds overtime in the seven years I worked with him.

No one who has not sung and performed on the radio over an extended period can realize the strain, difficulties, and special problems of broadcasting. It is like tightrope walking in the need for perfect adjustment, balance, and concentration. Bent on expressing everything through that one medium, the voice, we could not let our attention wander one minute from the microphone, for up to this time the microphone was largely directional; this meant we had no latitude, we had to stand exactly in front of the mike. A glance out of the corner of our eye to the director had to suffice, to say nothing of the difficulty of hearing the orchestra which was placed differently from the customary concert arrangement.

The range and variety of the music included in the year-long programs called for its own special handling. A two-octave aria, for example, had to emerge from the listener's loud-speaker with the same caressing smoothness "in the highs and lows" as a little one-octave song, in right proportion, too, and every note clear against the orchestral background accompaniment. Even with the best efforts of the expert Frank Williams, we could not be sure how the broadcast would come from the control room. There was constant adjusting to the instrument like juggling ten balls at once while balanced on the tightrope.

Singing as I was to the vast audience that is the world, I now began to receive fan mail from New Zealand, India, South America, Great Britain, the West Indies, and other far-off places. As I reached out to the Italians, Germans, French, and Spanish, I was of necessity rooted in traditional music; but as Americans we were all keyed to the music of the future, the dissonance of our everyday life, so crowded with the pressures and problems of the machine age.

Because I could sing both long-hair and short-hair music, I was prepared alternately to frequent the groves of Apollo or the common hedgerow of song for the adventure of being welcome in everybody's home. My thought was that if one is simply preoccupied with the classics one sings from the head and not from the heart. The challenge of the microphone, a symbol of fear and limitation to some musical travelers, was a light that beckoned me to sing a new song to the world.

A living light to capture and proclaim with imagination the heart of a song! How capture and proclaim the heart of a song? With a personal curiosity and gusto, with a faculty of just musical appreciation? I realized I was not so interested in history nor the dusty statues in the Hall of Fame as in touching people with the living spark. That is why I never lost touch with popular songs, never became identified with a particular song. Music cannot be shackled. It must appeal to all.

By Christmas, 1930, I had been singing a whole year with Cities Service. All of us were looking forward to this first Yuletide program with enthusiasm. Together with music appropriate to the season, we had planned to present an original cantata by Rosario Bourdon, based on Virginia O'Hanlon's famous letter to the editor of the old New York *Sun*, titled "Is There A Santa Claus?" Every year the little girl's letter and the great editorial beginning: "Virginia, your little friends are wrong. They have been affected by the skepticism of a skeptical age. . . ." ascribed to Charles Dana, have been reprinted in the newspaper.

This desire of mine to do something for the children was strangely enough linked up with the Buckhout family. When I told Katherine my plans for the program, her face lit up: "Why—Virginia O'Hanlon's mother is Mother's cousin Laura!" So it was arranged that "little" Virginia O'Hanlon, now grown up and a mother herself, would come to the broadcast with the Buckhouts.

I was anticipating the stir this handsome family would create in the studio: Mr. Buckhout; his two sons, James and Clay, home from college for vacation, blond, blue-eyed, broad-shouldered, and six feet three, like their Dutch forebears who fought here in Queen Anne's War; the equally fine-looking Buckhout women, distinguished in grace and grooming; my friend Katherine, lovelier than ever. It would be like having my own family with me for the holiday.

But Mr. Doherty, president of the Cities Service Company, had other plans and suggested the postponement of ours to the following year. He had arranged a tremendous debutante ball for the coming-out of his adopted daughter Helen Lee Ames Doherty. Everyone important in Washington diplomatic and social circles, including Vice-President Curtis and Mrs. Dolly Gann, was invited to the Mayflower Hotel.

Mr. Doherty was proud of having me on the Cities Service program. For this occasion he requested Mr. Bourdon and the orchestra to carry on the broadcast in New York while the Cavaliers and I were asked to supply musical intervals in the festivities. We were told that Helen Doherty had engaged a special orchestra, whose conductor she had met during a recent visit to Spain. This was a hint to me to bring along Spanish numbers. In spite of the honor and the delightful prospect of a social whirl, I did not thrill to the invitation. For no reason that I could explain, I fought desperately against going. Something seemed to warn me, to pull me back from this alluring excursion.

The people at NBC and at the agency were stunned by my refusal. Had I suddenly gone mad to refuse a request of the sponsor? George McClelland was at a loss to understand my adamant attitude when I said to him: "I think Mr. Doherty is very selfish to ask us to sing for a small group of people in Washington when the vast radio audience is waiting to hear us." He looked at me with kindly understanding: "Missing one broadcast won't mean very much to an audience who hears you every week. But this once means a great deal to Mr. Doherty, who has been extremely ill. You will cheer his heart by going."

I could not bring myself to refuse my good friend. The next thing I knew the Cavaliers and I were entrained with the elite of New York, bound for the elaborate, million-dollar affair in the nation's capital.

I had a wonderful time at the party, dancing the languorous tangos with the handsome gallants who constantly cut in, watching Helen Lee now in the arms of the elderly Marquis MacDonald, a family friend, now whirling about with Vice-President Curtis. Frequently, during the evening, she alternated between numerous bouquets, throwing them to friends and tossing a most gorgeous rose ensemble to Dolly Gann.

At midnight the guests strolled across the promenade hall to the

Presidential dining room for a lavish supper. My escort was a mature Cities Service man who paid a great deal of attention to me. Later when the dancing was resumed, no matter who my partner was, somehow I would find him at my side when the dance was over. At dawn the saxophones and trumpets sobbed a finale, the last silver slipper clicked on marble steps, and the thousand guests departed.

"Jessica, you really ought to see something of Washington before you leave. Let me call for you an hour or two before your train, and I'll show you a few landmarks of our beautiful city."

I was constantly associated with men in my work, and it seemed the most natural thing to accept. With all this new admirer's attentions, however, I just managed to make my train back to New York. At the station was my friend Leo O'Rourke of the Cavaliers, anxiously waiting to see me safely home.

When we were seated in our Pullman chairs, he looked at me with a disturbed expression: "No matter how flattering, Jessica, don't let yourself be carried away. That's nothing for you."

I looked at him, puzzled that he should bother his head. I didn't know what he meant. I was devoted to my career, and I had no intention of falling in love. Scarcely had I arrived at Euclid Hall when a messenger boy appeared with a telegram and a huge box of long-stemmed red roses, and from that moment my admirer was hot on the trail. No matter which way I turned, I could not escape him, and very quickly we became engaged. Then a knell of warning sounded in my heart. Like Pelléas I felt, "I have been playing around the traps of Fate."

I tried to free myself from the vise of these possessive attentions without success, and with difficulty I struggled to carry on my busy schedule. I gathered my scattered resources and flung myself headlong into my work.

The General Electric Company was preparing a big show, called The Hour of Magic. It was going to take place in the newly acquired New Amsterdam Theater Roof on Forty-second Street, the home of the great Ziegfeld Follies, where stage stars like Nora Bayes, Eddie Cantor, and Will Rogers had been featured and the American girl glorified. The large stage became an enclosed radio studio, separated from the audience by a tremendous glass curtain so the broadcasting could be seen through it. On some occasions, the curtain devised by engineers to block out extraneous noise was raised for dramatic effect.

This greatest radio pageant of all time would be dedicated to General Electric's scientists and engineers who "made broadcasting possible." During an hour and a half Graham McNamee was to announce the galaxy of stars whose "genius and charm helped make broadcasting popular": Rudy Vallee, Ohman and Arden, Vincent Lopez, Phil Cook, Frank Munn, and many others, and to cap the climax, my old friend Roxy. For the gala occasion I wore a lovely white princess dress, embroidered in pearls and brilliants, and my long hair I twisted softly at my neck.

When Roxy arrived in full regalia—top hat, caped evening coat, diamond-studded cane, looking everything an impresario should, I rushed forward to greet him. He took my hand and in affectionate annoyance shook it from side to side. Then, in his quick, clipped speech, he said: "Well, little Jessie, you weren't fooling that day. You really made it."

One radio event followed another in rapid succession. A year after I had joined Cities Service, and on the thirtieth anniversary of Marconi's wireless message, NBC spanned the world by radio. In December of 1931, from New York's WEAF came a roll call of fourteen nations on four continents.

In spite of the depression the period was marked by rapid expansion, and now came the exciting news that 60 Wall Towers, the new home of Cities Service with its vast enterprises, would celebrate its completion with an official opening. As a preliminary Mr. and Mrs. Doherty invited me to tea in their penthouse apartment on top of the new building. There were many distinguished guests that afternoon; but the one who will always stand out in my memory was tall, bony, macabre Nicola Tessla, the distinguished scientist, looking like a being from another planet. Mr. Doherty soon drew him to one side, and I was permitted to listen to their discussion of plans for the approaching ceremonies. Mr. Tessla's conversation was so learned that I could grasp only a few of his ideas. Though I was preoccupied with his thick, black hair, his sallow complexion, his air of wizardry, I felt his genius.

He was the inspiration that sent me flying back to Rosario Bourdon with the idea he must write something special for the official opening.

I suggested that he compose a tone poem. He looked at me in absolute bewilderment: "How can I write music about a building on Wall Street?" I began translating it into dramatic pictures, which captured his imagination: the early morning sun gilding 60 Wall Towers, standing on the site of Captain Kidd's buried treasure, the busy thoroughfare waking up to the commerce of the day, the noise of trucks and taxis, ticker-tape, the deserted canyons at twilight, and finally the Towers magically lighted up by a taper from Arcturus, forty light years away! Within the short space of a few days, Mr. Bourdon imprisoned the kaleidoscopic pictures in a musical rhapsody, novel, eloquent, moving, and beautiful.

We broadcast from 711 Fifth Avenue. Ford Bond, a permanent member of our devoted Cities Service family, announced with even more than his usual enthusiasm the all-request program: "Song of India," "Alice Blue Gown," "Dance of the Hours," "Valse Huguette," "Songs of Home," and "The Glow Worm."

A hush fell upon the studio audience as the famous about-the-world reporter of roaring adventure, Floyd Gibbons, on-the-spot at 60 Wall Towers, joined us by remote control and recounted in his galloping, husky delivery, a new beyond-this-world adventure.

Still throbbing with the wonder of the evening, we received the applause after the broadcast. I came out of 711 alone and walked toward Central Park, my feet scarcely touching the ground. I looked up into the sapphire sky to behold Arcturus, golden and glowing, descending toward the horizon. By the time I reached Eighty-sixth Street, the heavenly torch had disappeared into the Hudson. Slowly I let myself down from the interplanetary spaces and came back to earth from the land of stars.

CHAPTER 11

LINKED WITH THE SKIES

My destiny seemed linked with the skies. We had traveled past the stars to Arcturus, and now we were going right on conquering time and space.

While Byrd was skimming across the Antarctic in his plane, searching out the unknown vastnesses of the South Pole, short-wave radio permitted us to penetrate the distance and communicate with him so many thousand miles from home. All America was vibrant with keenest interest in the exciting explorations and fervently followed the progress of the gallant expedition.

Every popular program on the networks was eager to give of its best to a special short-wave broadcast in honor of Commander Byrd. It was to be patriotic and artistically varied. Nathaniel Shilkret, celebrated for his salon arrangements, composed a musical tribute, called "Skyward." Cesare Sodero conducted his operatic group in the Lucia sextette. Buck and Wing did an amusing dialogue of North and South poles. Harold Sanford, my regular Philco director, led a quartette and chorus in a selection from Herbert's *Naughty Marietta*.

To my delighted surprise, for the occasion, I was lent to Gustav Haenschen and presented in a first air version of *Sweet Adeline* by Jerome Kern. The announcements were divided among the experts: Milton Cross, Graham McNamee, and Phillips Carlin. The thirty-five piece orchestra, the conductors, singers, comedians, announcers, engineers—the whole assembly in the WEAF studio at 195 Broadway —were taut as the arrow stretched to the bow.

Would we miss—or would we cleave the ether straight to our goal? Word was later received that we hit the mark. This was the first of a short-waved series continuing during the expeditions to Little America in the early Thirties. The wonder of it all never diminished for us, and after each broadcast we waited impatiently to learn how the program was received by the men so far from home.

Up to this time I had never been in an airplane, so without hesi-
tation I accepted an invitation from the mayor to fly to Baltimore
for a benefit concert. Since this was considered quite risky, the National Broadcasting Company heavily insured my life. Furthermore,
they instituted the rule, long since abandoned, "An artist may not fly
to an engagement, but may fly home from an engagement."

La Guardia Field had not yet opened, so we took off from Newark
airport in a small, eight-passenger Bellanca plane. For the first few
minutes I was too frightened to move. Then a thousand pictures
flashed through my mind—the intrepid figures of daring aviators.
Resolutely I turned and gazed out the window to see the shadow of
the plane moving swiftly over the earth. "Why, I am riding on the
back of a great bird," I thought. My fright disappeared and I began:

> . . . to inhale great draughts of air.
> The North and the South are mine.
> The East and the West are mine.

Meanwhile, my colleague, desperately ill, was scarcely able to
sing the concert with me that evening. I was almost ashamed of my
refreshed vitality. When the Mayor of Baltimore asked if I would like
to fly back to New York, I accepted readily, but my poor tenor
groaned.

On the homeward flight, the pilot, Captain Jack Ayres, permitted
me to sit at the dual control. He could see I would not make a pilot
in six easy lessons, for I had hardly grasped the stick when we were
"looping the loop." Captain Ayres let out a long-drawn "O-O-O-Oh"
as he righted the blue bowl of the sky. I should have known better
than to kick the needle so hard, but the exhilaration I always feel
when flying made me lightheaded.

After my next broadcast, I received a cordial wire: "Here's hoping
to meet you in the air as well as on the air soon again. Captain Jack
Ayres."

Air experiences were crowding one another in dazzling succession.
Radio, the vocal newspaper, was quick to seize anyone in the public
eye and ask him to speak into the public ear. During my first Cities
Service days, Amelia Earhart made a guest appearance with us.
Considered in terms of a "live" commercial, she was a natural. She

was vouchsafed to us in the baited atmosphere of a tremendous scoop.

I close my eyes and see her as plainly as when she stood among us in Studio 8H at 711—the lithe, slender figure, the wind-swept hair, the radiant complexion, the blue-eyed gaze that could fathom the skies, the soft-spoken congratulations.

"You sing so naturally. I can see you love it. There is no worry nor mike fright about it."

I laughed. "But you don't worry about your flying, Miss Earhart, where the dangers are far more terrifying."

"Oh, no! The time to worry is three months before a flight. Worrying while flying is just excess baggage."

I understood this wanderer from the upper air, talking so calmly about gas consumption and refueling, accustomed as she was to navigating by the stars and pondering the mysteries of the universe. In the aviatrix I saw a lesson for the singer, who must bring something of flight to song, who must think of the mechanics of singing, too, while "his thought wanders in eternity."

During these days, however, I brought a divided mind to singing. More and more, Washington was calling me back. A chain of patriotic and civic events was binding me forever to the capital. With each visit the lovely white city framed in cherry blossoms became dearer to me. But now the thought of returning was unbearable.

The mad pursuit of my admirer at the Doherty ball had not given me a moment's peace. His courtship was being conducted by long distance, and the telephone had become an instrument of torture. I could not embark on any venture without impassioned interruption. I could not practice, see my friends, go to the theater, or follow through the schedule of my busy career without the shrill ringing of the long-distance signal. Every plan died aborning, and every conversation ended in frustration and tears. The strain was beginning to weigh heavily upon my health. Looking back I wonder at my patient endurance of this possessiveness; but I was a stupid, immature girl, ignorant of how to handle the situation. Although I had made up my mind to break off this untenable condition of affairs, my suitor still continued to importune me. Washington could mean a diabolical encounter. I decided to take Nadea along.

So it was with fear and trepidation I consented to sing at the convention of the Daughters of the American Revolution. Strange how
an innocent action may set in motion a current of events flowing far
into the future of many lives! Artists are often ignorant of the behind-
the-scenes motivations of engagements, and this concert was one of
the conundrums of my professional life.

Only recently I learned from Tony Fortune, then a singer, that
he also had been approached to perform for the D.A.R. on this occasion. Apparently they rebelled at paying the concession fee of five
hundred dollars stipulated by his manager. I had been broached on
the purely patriotic aspect of giving service and gladly consented. I
was further amused to learn Tony's interpretation of my gallantry—
I was so rich I could afford to be bountiful. Whatever his disappointments in the musical world, he has been lucky in finding a way of
greater service to humanity, through medicine.

The concert in Constitution Hall went unusually well. After I had
sung a handful of arias and songs, the whole Southern delegation
stood up and cheered at my singing of "Dixie." The Daughters presented a gorgeous bouquet of red roses, and after numerous encores
I was backstage in a deserted hall.

Then in the nature of such places, the lights went quickly out, and
Nadea and I were forced to stand alone on the stone steps. Huddled
together in the doorway to escape the chilly wind, we could not catch
sight of a conveyance anywhere. The multitudinous D.A.R. had com-
mandeered the entire taxi fleet. Still it was a relief not to see my
Cities Service suitor, away on a business trip.

Suddenly out of the darkness emerged a little man in evening
clothes. It was my good friend, Commander MacNeil—"Something
told me," he said, with a twinkle in his eye, "the D.A.R. might forget
to take you back to your hotel."

Meeting with an audience in song is a communion of fellowship—
something that Utopians dream of. For the artist there is a soul-
satisfying response in the applause, while for the audience the soul-
satisfying response is identification with the artistic process. Listeners
feel in perfect equilibrium. They are moved to say, "Why, that's easy.
I can do that."

After the rapport of the D.A.R. concert, I was to enjoy an even
more rewarding experience, for Monsignor Fulton Sheen of Catholic

University had offered me the rare privilege of serving his Mass. Early next morning Nadea and I knelt on silk-cushioned *prie-dieus* before the altar, in the private miniature chapel on Cathedral Drive.

The fervid excitement I had been living through dropped from my shoulders in this quiet sanctuary, as we waited for him to begin. I leafed through my missal, my eyes falling upon the words "Come, O Lord, visit us in peace, that we may rejoice before Thee with a perfect heart." I could see that Nadea, too, was wrapped in the tranquillity of the moment.

With reverent sonority, Monsignor Sheen intoned the Confiteor. My responses followed him through the Ordinary of the Mass. Then, as he bent to give me the Mystic Bread in Holy Communion, I could hear in my soul, "Seek ye first the kingdom of God, and all things shall be added unto you."

Afterward, at breakfast, Monsignor Sheen, always an ideal host, discoursed eloquently of mutual friends, his travels abroad, and topics of the times, but at the core of his various conversation was the recurring thought that "ten men can save the city."

We were scarcely back in New York when Nadea was brought home one day seriously ill. She would have to be quiet for a long time.

I plunged more deeply than ever into work. In addition to my weekly Cities Service concerts, I was invited for a series of guest appearances on the RCA hour with Gustav Haenschen and Frank Black's singing violins. The association with these fine musicians was stimulating in its opportunity for a different instrumentation, a different interpretation, and a different repertoire.

Waiting on the thirteenth floor of 711 for the rehearsals to begin, I frequently heard outbursts of pent-up chatter, as the studio doors opened and artists poured out into the hall.

One Saturday, Gloria Swanson, ravishing in a leopard ensemble, but spent after the broadcast ordeal, emitted a loud "Phew!" as she sank on the bench beside me: "I'd rather have a child than go through that again." I longed to comfort her, but the snatching hand of the rehearsal was upon my shoulder. As I looked back regretfully, she was already disappearing in the elevator.

The anteroom to Miss Liebling's studio was likewise a beehive of coming and going performers. Here the beginner could meet the firmly launched and the current sensation. Among the fascinating swarm was mysterious Ganna Walska. The pupils admired her luxuriant chestnut hair, her exotic perfumes, her fabulous jewels, and her individually designed costumes. We were all curious about her singing, but this was one lesson we were never permitted to hear.

Imagine my astonishment at finding her in my RCA rehearsal studio, one Saturday afternoon, resplendent in dove-gray silk, her large-brimmed hat matching the fox furs on the chairs beside her. Sitting quietly in the back, I expected to hear the elusive voice, but Mme. Walska had just finished and swept off into the control room. While nursing my disappointment, a gentleman out of nowhere, perfect in manner, bent over me.

"Are you the English lady who was to meet Colonel Davis for an audition?"

I looked up at him a moment, smiling, hesitating to answer. "No," I finally said, "I'm sorry. I am not the English lady."

He vanished as suddenly as he appeared. Then he came back and in his most ingratiating way apologized: "Forgive me for not recognizing you; I should have known better. You are Jessica Dragonette."

"There's nothing to forgive," I said soothingly. "You were utterly charming."

Someone muddled the incident for the newspapers:

Colonel Davis, director of Collier's Hour, walked into a studio the other day where a girl was practicing.

"I have a rehearsal here at three o'clock," he told her.

"Oh no you haven't," the young woman replied. "I'm Jessica Dragonette. This is my studio—and you can get out."

Poor Colonel Davis never got over it. He invited me to luncheon, with the assurance he was no party to this garbled report. This was the inauspicious beginning of a friendship that lasted for many years.

It was in this same Studio H, thirteenth floor at 711, that I first came face to face with Nick Kenny, radio editor of the *Daily Mirror*. I had acted with his song-writing brother "Charley" in *The Student Prince*. Though Nick had been reviewing my programs for some time, I had not met him until he attended our broadcast. Perhaps he came out of curiosity to see in person his column's oft-repeated mention of

Thou Garbo of the air,
You keep each man your slave,
By shunning the publicity
That other artists crave.

Genuinely impressed, I took refuge in more than my usual shyness.
He held my hand in a friendly clasp, his seafaring eyes quizzically
boring into me:

"Don't you ever give anyone in the audience the come-hither? I've
been watching you for an hour. You looked neither to right nor left
—just sang your heart out for your unseen listeners."

How could he say "unseen?" After the letters that came from everywhere, easily visible were the tired farm woman lulling her babe
to sleep, the schoolchildren with their books, the grandfather nodding over his pipe, the tired workingmen turning homeward. Why,
every fireside was my audience and the whole world, my stage. And
now life itself spilled out events like a cornucopia of song.

The rhythm, the tempo of life—new, varied, original as the songs
each of these functions demanded. The movement of notes in melody, floating like iridescent clouds in a summer sky, resemble life.
So I learned of life in music and of music in life. Here was dedication in Ariadne's aria: "I am the humble handmaiden of the Genius
Creator."

The thirteenth floor was certainly lucky for me. At this time the
press department called me for an interview with the well-known
American Journal radio columnist, Harriet Mencken. The young
public relations man who escorted me to the reception room sur-
reptitiously put me on guard: "She is very peculiar and hard to
please, so watch your *p*'s and *q*'s."

It is irksome to greet a new personality in a biased atmosphere,
but with my usual impulsiveness I determined to meet the lady in
my own way. I found Harriet Mencken, now Mrs. George Bowdoin,
the antithesis of difficult—utterly simple, lovable, and interesting.
We have been friends ever since, and through the years she has interviewed me innumerable times. Always I am at a loss as to the
pressman's warning.

The seven league boots of fairyland are slow compared with arm-
chair travel by short wave. Berlin is only two inches from Des

Moines, and one short inch from London you can hear a woman's voice announcing, "Roma—Napoli."

There was romance even in American business. The Bosch Corporation was conducting a popularity poll to study the preferences of listeners so that their engineers might produce an ideal radio set. From where people lived, what they chose to hear, and how far they went for their programs, distance-getting ability could be measured. Researchers studied the artists selected by the public, noted their style, technique, and vocal range—"the high notes of Jessica Dragonette, the enthusiastic rapidity of John S. Young," the tonal beauties of Rubinoff's violin, the Irish lilt of Morton Downey, the fresh Maine rhythm of Rudy Vallee, and even Ed Wynn's unforgettable slip "gasoloon." Their popularity meant that the radio owner demanded selectivity, so he could dial his favorites without interference. From all these observations the engineers developed a tone, a clarity of reproduction never before available.

To interest the public in helping with such findings, the American Bosch Radio Corporation carried on a tremendous campaign, offering handsome trophies for the winners. The awards were twenty-four-inch gold cups to be presented on the Capitol steps in Washington by Vice-President Curtis. Partly because I was the only woman prize winner and partly because I dreaded the unexpected from my unwelcome suitor, Nadea, still suffering from illness, asked John Young to act as bodyguard. He was late for our meeting in Grand Central Station prior to enplaning. This gave me an opportunity to become acquainted with some of my other colleagues.

"It's a pleasure to meet you, Mr. Downey," I addressed Morton sedately. "I've so enjoyed your work on the air."

He shot around with, "Are you kiddin'? Or are you drunk so early in the morning?"

I was struck dumb, and hardly recovered when Rubinoff was introduced. Far from what I expected after listening to his violin, he was unshaven and sleepy-eyed.

"You're beautifully dressed," he said, taking me in from head to foot in one glance. "That's what they told me—you always wear beautiful clothes." Then tapping his chest with his forefinger, he added, "That's very important with me."

I gasped. This flight was going to be different! Fortunately, John came running to my rescue.

After the presentation of the gold cups, we drove to the White House to call on the President. Herbert Hoover, worn and harassed by depression "blues" received us courteously and revealed an unexpected humor.

"Congratulations all," he said, "but tell me, how often do you have to run for those things?"

When I answered, "Every year, Mr. President," he looked sympathetic.

"Oh, that's worse than my job. I run only every *four* years."

In a few minutes we were at the National Press Club, seated about a circular luncheon table on the floor of the large dining hall. Morton sang and Rudy and John Young spoke their thanks. When my turn came, they lifted me onto a chair so I could be seen and heard. At the conclusion of my speech, Senator Burton K. Wheeler of Montana came rushing over to me:

"You look like Dresden china over an armature of tensile steel. I'd like to draft you to make speeches throughout the country." Then fingering my gold lamé dress, he continued, "But you'd have to change that lovely costume, for I would want you to speak on going off the gold standard."

Our flight to New York was without untoward incident, but wholly in character. Morton, deathly afraid of flying, alternately clutched his religious medals and his seat belt for protection. Rudy was lost in his newspaper, and Rubinoff fell asleep. John Young and I chatted and enjoyed the scenery.

Back in the skyscraper city, I went on with the secret television experiments RCA was conducting in the Empire State Building and which continued until World War II. Mr. David Sarnoff and other officials participated while James Melton and I sang. The program was sent into the home of Owen D. Young, who called up to say he had no difficulty whatsoever recognizing us. This dubious compliment implied we were progressing, for at best the technical focus was still blurred and the image liable to distortion. Nor had the problem of adequate lighting been solved. I wondered how I was doing, for Jimmie came through like an elegant-looking Moor.

To date, the little cartoon movies were the best, but there was much to be desired in all the pictures. The engineers occupied themselves with the heavy, stationary cameras. The action remained in the subject before the lens rather than in the camera itself as it is today, directed by the master control.

Television make-up was still in the black-lips stage, so I suggested to Mr. Sarnoff that he would come through better if he were made up. When I offered to apply the black stick, he sat like a child, patiently docile to my ministrations. I have never forgotten how humbly the general took orders from his private.

Lanny Ross shared in another experiment. We were assigned as the voices of the prince and princess in *Gulliver's Travels* when the Paramount Company presented the Swift classic in technicolor. We were both occupied with air programs in New York, so the possibility of sojourning in Florida, where the movie was being made, was not feasible. Paramount, however, worked out a plan of perfect synchronization with the cartoons flashed on the screen. We sang, not to a live accompaniment in New York or Florida, but to a recording by Victor Young's orchestra in Hollywood, piped to us through head phones clamped on our ears. Thus we had no latitude, no freedom of interpretation, but like oxen to the yoke we were compelled to follow the tempo designated for the prince and princess.

In the midst of so many beginnings, the fiftieth anniversary of the opening of the Pearl Street Generating Station was like a dramatic pause. One autumn night in 1882, Mr. Edison had turned on the first electric lamp in New York City and at the same moment most of the principal stores on Fulton Street, from Nassau to the East River, were illuminated with Edison's electricity. A new industry was born. It marked the end of one era, the beginning of another.

Driving to the Hotel Waldorf-Astoria in the latest model car, my accompanist and I looked like figures from *Godey's Ladies' Book* in our fifty-year-old Worth creations of ivory satin and lace, our backswept coiffures falling in a cascade of curls. We turned to view this most modern of cities, with its ribbons of light festooned from river to river, and we were proud to salute the genius who had lighted the world. That evening, in the grand ballroom, to the accompaniment of a fine old Steinway, I sang the old songs of Bayly, Bland, and Stephen Foster. I hoped the guests would ask for it—and they did—

as an encore, "Little Grey Home in the West," Thomas Edison's favorite song.

Early that October, before the Metropolitan season began, George Engles, head of the Artists Bureau, asked me to sing for the General Electric officials in conference at the Hotel Roosevelt in New York City. A good-will gesture, no doubt, on the part of NBC. Considering myself as one of the NBC family, I was happy to comply with company policy. Frank Black's orchestra accompanied me. As I waited for the signal to begin, George Engles escorted Kirsten Flagstad into the anteroom. At that time the Artists Bureau, now divorced from NBC, were her managers.

To one who cares for loveliness, Flagstad was an idol from the first moment of her seasons here; her voice, her ability to float the musical line and to make beautiful sounds, her emission and power had evoked tears. No doubt George Engles thought her appearance would be a pre-Metropolitan scoop and surprise for the General Electric assembly. I was dying to meet Mme. Flagstad, but nobody presented me to her.

Now George Engles was inquiring, by way of distracting her from the long waiting, "Did you enjoy your supper, Mme. Flagstad?"

"Yes, indeed, the champagne was good. Maybe I shall not sing too well."

"Did you have a good summer in Europe? Do you feel rested for the big season ahead?" he continued.

"No. As a matter of fact I have a cold from traveling about so much," the diva answered.

Her friends and Mr. Engles with his associates formed a protecting wall about Mme. Flagstad, but it was very late before the program began. After my appearance, however, I went into the hall to listen to her golden voice really sing "Dich, teuer Halle." As she tossed the aria off, I could not help thinking of one of my singing teachers, who during the lesson would sit at the piano crooking his little finger.

"It takes no more physical energy than this to sing 'Dich, teuer Halle,'" he would say.

Maybe so; but no one I ever heard save Flagstad seemed to have his secret.

An eternal light burns at the Tomb of the Unknown Soldier in Arlington Cemetery, and a guard with shouldered rifle holds watch throughout the day and night. The grave is evergreen and flower-decked. "Here rests in honored glory an American soldier known but to God"—a testament of the price we paid for a peace that is not won.

Every year on Armistice Day, after one of the service chaplains prays, the President of the United States lays a wreath of flowers at the tomb, and the commander of the American Legion pays homage to the heroic dead of our country. Following the President in solemn procession, government delegates, foreign diplomats, legionnaires, service women, and visitors pass slowly down the steps beneath the half-masted flags of the states to the amphitheater close by, and the commemoration services continue.

How many times have I sung here! How many times have the deep and moving feelings almost choked the songs as my heart rose in my throat!

During Franklin Delano Roosevelt's terms in office I sang every year at Arlington, but the third time stands out in memory because he then revealed himself most endearingly human. I had just finished singing "The Star Spangled Banner." The President was standing directly behind me. In the ensuing moment, while the audience was being seated, I heard his voice *sotto voce,* "Jessica, your petticoat is showing." My face burned scarlet at the agonizing thought of my pink slip's hanging below my black velvet ensemble. I sat down among the guests of honor with all the poise I could muster. There was nothing I could do about it now. The omnipresent photographers were snapping away. They couldn't miss the offending bit of pink satin and ecru lace—the pictures still tell the story.

At the back of the amphitheater a marine trumpeter sounded taps, and I rose to sing,

> Fading light dims the sight,
> And a star gems the sky, gleaming bright,
> From afar, drawing nigh, falls the night.
> Peaceful dreams.

His trumpet muted, the marine ended taps with a dying echo. The services were over. As we left the amphitheater, Mr. Roosevelt, a catch in his voice, turned to me: "Bravely done, Jessica! I never heard you sing better."

CHAPTER 12

RADIO CITY

A switch thrown in Radio City inaugurated a new era in broadcasting. The removal of the National Broadcasting Company meant more than a change of address, more than the occupancy of the world's finest studios. Appropriately it coincided with NBC's seventh anniversary, to be celebrated in mid-November. This magnificent expression of belief in radio's future, measured out in years of concentrated efforts of pioneers, planners, scientists, builders, engineers, and artists, fulfilled an ambition, an ideal to make every silent inch of space vocal. The networks, spreading to the hinterlands from coast to coast and to the endless horizons beyond, would bring an inheritance of music, entertainment, and knowledge to every man, woman, and child.

Modern architects, changing the busy heart of the city to a center of transformed line and color, reverently placed the flying Prometheus above the surrounding lawns, golden against the clean elevation of the gray-white skyscraper. The usefulness of everyday commerce became beautiful. Maxwell Anderson, looking up at dusk, saw "a million windows facing south . . . lighting the husk of a horrible gray city, making it forever a city of dream."

But now, Death, leaping between time and space, put a swift end to one man's dream. At seventeen, George McClelland was a soldier; in his early thirties, vice-president and general manager of the National Broadcasting Company. Handling a million-dollar-a-year radio business, he was sometimes affectionately referred to as the father of network broadcasting. I had come to regard him highly as friend and adviser. Shortly after his dismissal from NBC, he was found shot in the temple, slumped over his desk with his revolver beside him. Overwhelmed by the ignominious tragedy of his demise, I could not be reconciled to my personal loss nor the untimely passing of this brilliant man, before he could be rewarded for his part in the achievement of Radio City. After singing memorial services in the early morning at the Tomb of the Unknown Soldier, on November 11, 1933, I flew back from Washington for the ceremonies in Rockefeller Center.

My heart was still heavy as I put on a floating shell-pink gown, the little shoulder cape collared with soft, black-tailed ermine. Nadea and I drove in silence through the familiar canyons of the East Fifties; turning into the Plaza, we glimpsed the full grandeur of the Radio City project. It was only then I felt my spirits soar. Like a bird, my song, too, would soon be winging the highway above the fabulous RCA building.

Already in Studio 8H on the eighth floor, an audience of specially invited guests were assembled. Merlin H. Aylesworth, president of NBC, welcomed them to the largest studio ever known. David Sarnoff from London and Sir John Reith of BBC in New York exchanged greetings and together sent messages of good will and prosperity to the rest of the world. Between speeches of Owen D. Young and General James G. Harbord, a star-studded company made music: John McCormack, Paul Whiteman, Rudy Vallee, and the Schola Cantorum Choir. Lovable Amos 'n' Andy paid a first visit to the studios. The orchestra selections and accompaniments were divided between Walter Damrosch and Frank Black, music director of NBC. After Will Rogers' congratulations from Hollywood, radio pioneers Frank Munn, Virginia Rea, the Revellers, and I were featured singers.

But Maria Jeritza was the dominating luminary of the evening. She was invited to lend luster and distinction to the radio opening. This was not a sterling grand opera performance to Mme. Jeritza, but a holiday excursion that seemed to amuse her. In her pale blue satin and pearls, she wove her perilous way through the narrow lane of the stage in front of the large orchestra, waving to her friends as she walked. She took care to drop her one-line script at her feet and sang "Say not love is a dream" from *The Count of Luxembourg* as her contribution to the evening.

Immortal Jane Cowl, darkly regal, eloquent in attitude and gesture, gave the poem *Dedication* by Burke Boyce, in a rich-throated contralto that held us enthralled:

> Man speaks afar to Man . . . His dream, his hope,
> Spurning old barriers of Space and Time,
> Roll the whole width of oceans; like Colossus
> Bestride the vastiness of mountain peaks,
> Line firesides, cities, nations, continents;
> Until the magic of a leaping spark
> Strikes off the chains of Ignorance and Fear—
> Forging a universal brotherhood . . .

Every Friday now we were regularly broadcasting the Cities Service program from this same studio 8H with a weekly audience of 1,500 people. The concerts were also short-waved to South America and Spain.

Fans from all over the United States began writing for tickets to attend our programs in the newest studios. Sometimes I had to go to extraordinary means to accommodate out-of-towners with last-minute tickets. But when someone would say, "I heard you at the Hotel Taj Mahal last week in India," or, "We listen to you regularly in Singapore and Australia," I could feel my heart expanding with ever-widening joy. I wanted to give in return my best in song.

That Christmas in Radio City, Lanny Ross and I sang our first duets for the National Tuberculosis Christmas Seal drive. We were happy to be of service and extremely gratified at the listener response. I was especially pleased to add another broadcast to the many holiday hours the radio audiences came to expect of me. More than other years that year needed the joy of music. After I sang I spoke my Christmas greeting on the air: "I wish my song might help the world to see the shining star the Wise Men followed, that joining in their pilgrimage we may banish depression and gain inspiration and peace for all." The pattern of grateful letters received was "The wish is mutual and we sing with you."

All my training had to be acquired on the run. And what is more, my artistic unfoldment, like a self-portrait, had to be accomplished stroke by brush stroke, in full view of the public. Rehearsals were scanty. They had to be attended with the music and routines well in hand in order to give the sense of flawlessness the conductors and audiences expected me to possess. How could a limited novice accomplish this, without unswerving, constant study?

Meanwhile my colleagues were oblivious to the internal drama revolving itself in my mind and heart. Unsuspecting, they found me as they had always known me, only more reticent. I gave my confidence to very few. A cloak of surface poise concealed my restless temperament and smoothed my passage through the distractions from my music. Such deviations were few. My seeming aloofness was quite naturally misinterpreted. It could mean anything imaginable. People whispered, the newspapers gossiped about "Jessica's handsome regiment," a varying circle of friends and admirers, with whom I was seen in public. Not only did they save me from unwelcome attentions, but their highly stimulating company kept me continually alert and well-informed. "The Garbo of the air" tag continued.

Why is her life "such a carefully guarded secret?" "Why doesn't she marry?"

"Well, there's the big, curly-headed blond giant." (Who, of course, was Mr. Buckhout.)

"But he is only *one* of her protectors. There is that senator, that Portuguese consul, that famous doctor—that prominent lawyer."

Even "the regiment" wondered about these tales. And each brave escort maneuvered with cautious finesse. Often they, too, asked questions: "Are you impervious to romance?" "Is this ivory-tower business a publicity gag?" "Do you expect me to wait in the stag line, while you encourage the cut-ins?"

In the Persian Room of the Hotel Plaza, an eminent surgeon-friend questioned, "You have such a wonderful career— I suppose you could never give up singing?"

Amused, I said, "Doctor, could you ever give up being a surgeon?"

The idea had never occurred to him. "You're adept at parrying thrusts," he rejoined.

He was right! Friendships always meant a great deal to me, but especially then, when Nadea was mostly confined to bed. She could not accompany me to broadcasts and other appointments. My gallants stepped in and constituted themselves a bodyguard to protect me wherever I went. I was never unattended.

The ordeal of decision concerning the persistent Washingtonian was long since past. He could never understand that I wanted to be untrammeled, free as a bird to pursue my way of song; he did not want to believe the breaking of our engagement was irrevocable. A successful man of the world, he could not abide failure. On New Year's morning, by some chance of fate, I found myself alone. Instead of going to my own parish, a strange compulsion drew me to attend High Mass at St. Patrick's Cathedral. Carefully watching the icy pavement, I did not look ahead. When I reached the top step, I saw him framed in the doorway, towering and determined. Beside myself with fear, I tried to dash past him, but he caught my arm and pinioned me: "You can't refuse to let me enter the house of God with you," he bit the words off angrily. I knew he was no one to reason with, so I didn't try; I slipped like quicksilver through his grasp and ran into the Cathedral. The choir boys in procession blocked my path of escape, so I broke their ranks, pulling them apart with desperate force, bolting out the side door and on to Madison Avenue, where I fell half fainting into a taxi. That morning I found sanctuary in St. Vincent Ferrer's church, where I knew he could never think of following me, because of his unfamiliarity with the city. Trembling through my prayers, I made an earnest supplication to be delivered from the siege—"St. Michael, the archangel, defend us in the battle."

The menacing threats and annoyances continued. Steeling myself to the inevitable, I took precautions to be guarded at every turn. Fortunately my pursuer was not aware I was no longer at Euclid Hall, but in a spacious new East Side apartment of my own designed by McClelland Barclay and Arthur Gordon Smith. This apartment soon became a magnet for artists, one of the world's greatest pianists came frequently to "practice." At his recitals the most absorbed listeners were the poet, Edgar Lee Masters, and the young song writer, Hoagy Carmichael.

The telltale signs of overwork and worry were noted in Nick Kenny's column:

> *To Jessica Dragonette*
> Your voice is like a rare old wine—
> A violin, with tone divine,
> Played by a wistful harlequin—
> But Jessica—you're much too thin!

Radio was still the stepchild of the arts. Warmed by the glowing tribute of an invitation from Olin Downes I joined in his series *The Enjoyment of Music* for the Brooklyn Institute of Arts and Sciences. I looked forward to the stimulant of singing a new repertoire with ancient instrumentation, to being associated with the great virtuosi who composed the Renaissance Quintet—Hans Barth, the harpsichord; Edwin Bachman, the quinton; Otto von Koppenhagen, the viola da gamba; Abram Borodkin, the basse viole, and particularly the celebrated violinist, Jacques Malkin, unique on the viola d'amore. Like Arnold Dolmetsch in England and the Society of Ancient Instruments in Paris, Mr. Downes and the quintet had embarked on a labor of love, bringing to life once more the music of another day, in a manner approximating its original performance.

The archaic charm of "Plaisir d'Amour," "Have You Seen But A Whyte Lillie Grow," and the five-hundred-year-old "L'Amour de Moy," sung against a background of the enchanting strains of the veiled and wistful tone color of these ancient instruments, was a satisfying innovation. Since I could not bring myself to jar the delicate atmosphere of an almost evanescent time by wearing modern evening dress, I undertook an extensive research to find a suitable costume. The Lady of the Unicorns in the fifteenth-century Cluny tapestries provided the appropriate clue, and I wore a blue velvet pearl- and gem-studded costume, lined with rose satin, over a petticoat of ivory and gold brocade; on my long flowing hair, a turban of twisted gold gauze and blue velvet, bejeweled and decorated with an upstanding blue aigrette. My costume and the ancient instruments lent a medieval aspect to the scene. The audience listened with hushed interest to the music of another day, while Godowsky and Kreisler stood up and cheered Jacques Malkin for his spectacular viola d'amore solos.

Curiosity brought many people backstage to investigate my costume. There is always a doubting Thomas in every audience, and one woman had difficulty believing the long golden hair was my own.

"Is that your real hair? Or are you wearing a wig?" Without waiting for me to reassure her, she reached forward and gave my hair a few hard pulls.

"Ouch!" I cried out. "What are you doing?"

Looking at me impishly, she replied: "I just wanted to see if the wig would come off."

On my return from a recent concert tour, Louis Biancolli kindly invited me to Carnegie Hall to hear Mitropoulos and the Philharmonic Orchestra. Oddly enough, I was seated directly in front of Olin Downes. As I greeted him, I jogged his memory, lest he had forgotten me.

"Oh, I think I remember you all right," he said amusedly. "Didn't we make ancient music together once? You look fine. How's everything going?"

Then the attractive woman with him, Mrs. Olin Downes, added, "I was there, too, enjoying it all very much. Moreover, I'm the lady who pulled your hair!"

Ethel Barrymore wisely puts the requisites for a successful career in a neat little formula, when she says, "You must maintain the complexion of a gardenia and the hide of a rhinoceros." This, like the pursuit of perfection in music, requires practice, as I learned in my pioneering.

I had been asked to open a new Atwater Kent series, emanating from the Columbia Broadcasting Company. At this time, rival networks did not exchange artists. It took a good deal of persuasion to wring a permission out of Mr. Aylesworth to accept this coveted engagement. The clinching argument was that the honor really redounded to the National Broadcasting Company and gave greater publicity to our Cities Service Program rather than to me personally. Thus my appearance on the Atwater Kent broadcast broke the precedent and augured clear sailing for other artists.

But privately it was a feather in my cap. Never before had I been included in an Atwater Kent series, which we all regarded as the acme of musical broadcasts. My thoughts went back to the great singers featured over the years: Grace Moore, Richard Bonelli, James Melton, Lucrezia Bori, Beniamino Gigli, Rosa Ponselle, and many others. And now I, too, was urged to join them.

It was pleasant to be free to rub elbows with colleagues broadcasting on other stations. Colgate-Palmolive-Peet were presenting hour operettas starring James Melton. Remembering the popularity of my old Philco series, they thought I would be a good foil playing opposite Jimmie in several presentations—*Vagabond King, Bitter*

Sweet, and *Naughty Marietta,* all under Al Goodman's happy direction. I enjoyed working with Jimmie, admired his high seriousness and musical ambitions.

On one occasion, the beauteous Risë Stevens sang with dramatic verve, then immediately departed for European study. Though the Risë Stevens of today has more polish and sophistication, nothing has been added to the beautiful voice I remember. In those Palmolive appearances no one was very excited about her outstanding talents. She had to go to Europe and South America before becoming acclaimed in her own country.

Notable among the other few guest appearances allowed by my exclusive contract were Magic Key, True Adventures, Silken Strings, Hoover Sentinels, Studebaker, and Show Boat.

From week to week there was the absorbing problem of variety entertainment for the listeners. Partly by inclination and partly because of our proximity to Latin American countries, I introduced Spanish songs on my Cities Service program, believing them to be a natural preference after our native music. This novelty so pleased the public taste that thousands of requests to include Spanish numbers came in. The Pan-American Union in Washington went so far as to call me "a good will ambassadress of song, helping to cement good neighbor relations."

Surely I have a Spanish soul, attuned to all things Iberian. Delving into the rich and colorful granary of Spanish music, I chose as surefire songs that were most strongly melodic, most exotically rhythmic —boleros, tangos, jotas, rhumbas, granadinas, malagueñas. The musical textures and designs grew more and more alluring. The strong Spanish poetry added to the fascination of the songs, and they made a vivid spot of yellow vermilion in our broadcasts. To keep this language supple, I spent a whole evening each week, conversing and writing Spanish with the distinguished Señora de Pinillos.

Besides her translations of American classics—Washington Irving, Hawthorne, Poe—into Spanish, Carmen de Pinillos was also associated with the foreign department of Metro-Goldwyn-Mayer. It was she who told me of Samuel D. Cohen's interest in my making a movie test. In an interview between a rehearsal and a broadcast, he was all politeness and admiration for my singing. Then he turned me over to the test department.

Mr. A——, the man in charge, received me cordially, but as soon as the door closed after his superior, Mr. Cohen, he went into his act. "We can't handle radio personalities," he announced pompously, and then with vehemence he added, "they just can't act. They're too stiff." With a sweeping gesture, he pointed to a large photograph on the wall. "We want people who look like Joan Crawford. We've had Nelson Eddy for three years, and we can't do anything with him. He's a dud! Besides, if we hired you, we'd not permit you to broadcast."

Mr. A—— strutted about like a rooster, jumping up and down to punctuate his crowing. What in the world was he trying to prove, I wondered, as I witnessed this comical hamming? In a few days, he sent me a scenario of *The Chocolate Soldier,* but remembering his rudeness, I could not summon the courage to go back to him.

Soon afterward I left for Florida and my first vacation in five years. Victor Grandin, the editor of *Palm Beach Life,* invited me to the première of the picture *Naughty Marietta.*

I was one of the vociferous audience who cheered a sensational new screen star—Nelson Eddy! I could not help remembering what Mr. A—— had said the day he was taking me over the hurdles, and I wondered if his face was red!

Besides, some years later *The Chocolate Soldier* was produced, also starring that "dud" Nelson Eddy and Risë Stevens. Recently, too, lunching with His Eminence, Francis Cardinal Spellman, I learned from one of his guests, Ambassador Joseph Grew, how he spent a whole day in MGM's projection room in Tokyo to choose a typical American picture and decided on Nelson Eddy and Jeanette MacDonald in *Naughty Marietta.* After the showing at our embassy in Japan, the Premier, Count Saito, thanked Grew profusely for the rare treat—it was the first and last talking picture he had ever seen; later that night he was assassinated.

A few days after arriving in Florida, I went aboard the *Masquerader* to meet John Charles Thomas on the deck of his yacht. He looked like a bronzed Viking in his matching royal blue beret and sailing jacket. His ready cordiality prompted me to tell him the Metropolitan incident of the little schoolgirl finding herself seated beside the great baritone at a performance of *Pelléas et Mélisande.* Highly amused, he gave out that wonderful Falstaffian laugh of his.

"I can see you like music," he chuckled, his eyes beaming. "Would you like to come below while I go through some new songs?"

"Would I!"

In the floating music room, Carol Hollister, seated at the piano, opened the manuscript before him.

"This is another Malotte song I picked up in California. I've sung many of them in my concerts, as you remember. I'm anxious to know what you think of this one."

In the jasmine-scented twilight, at anchor on the still, blue water, we sat entranced by John Charles's singing. This was the first rendition of that uplifting popular classic *The Lord's Prayer*.

Back in New York from my sunshine holiday, I felt the renewed zest of work. I set about eagerly to catch up with the current in broadcasting. The kilocycle directors were leaving no stone unturned to fill the long broadcasting day with whoever or whatever was of interest to the public.

The Radio Guild of the Air, devoted to presenting the best dramatic plays, reached out in all directions for suitable actors and actresses. They grasped at the good fortune of having the illustrious Mrs. Patrick Campbell to star in Pinero's *The Second Mrs. Tanqueray*. She had scarcely set foot here after leaving London when she was in rehearsal.

I studied her carefully as she stood at the microphone, queenly, her long black velvet gown accenting her dark hair and eyes. There was a great naturalness about her, and I thought I had never heard such a mellifluous speaking voice or seen such unconscious grace. Though I dared not address her then, after her second broadcast in which she recited *Humoresque*, a poem by Humbert Wolfe, her performance moved me to express my gratitude for the beauty she created. I had never expected to see Mrs. Patrick Campbell in my lifetime. I knew her only in Bernard Shaw's dramatic criticisms. Here she stepped before me from the pages in living flame.

Another revered actress lent enchantment to the studio routine and illumined the broadcasts with her immortal art. Her programs came after the Cities Service concerts on Friday nights, but I was delayed in 8H, receiving guests and giving autographs. I was only fortunate enough to hear one broadcast.

To try to describe Maude Adams is like trying to catch a butterfly. Even if one manages to hold the wings between his fingers for an instant, the butterfly escapes, leaving only silvery dust. It was natural for this sensitive artist to ask for seclusion while performing. She came to the studio like a russet Rosalind in high leather boots, peaked pillbox hat, and loose dolman coat. I watched her, as I listened in the clients' booth, acting out Babbie in *The Little Minister* without script. Tossing her bright head in magical laughter, the changing light of her face, her running, gesturing, were altogether bewitching —especially her voice, the eternal youth of her voice. I flew down the steps and impetuously crashed the barred studio. I must have frightened the gentle lady, still breathless from the ordeal of her broadcast. When she graciously gave me the requested autograph, I told her how much seeing her meant to me. She looked at me plaintively:

"Did you *really* enjoy it?" she asked.

At a preliminary rehearsal during the first months in Radio City, I noticed a lovely new photograph on Rosario Bourdon's Steinway grand. I recognized the *Barber of Seville* Rosina costume, but not the picturesque dark head. Rosario was quick to identify her as the new French coloratura, who had just auditioned for Victor Red Seal records with great success and who would sing at the Metropolitan in the fall.

Soon André Kostelanetz, the popular radio conductor, sent me tickets for his Chesterfield Hour to meet Lily Pons. He led me to Lily's dressing room in the CBS Playhouse. After I had congratulated her, consumed with a mutual curiosity, we stood back to back to ascertain which of us is taller. Lily let out in childish glee, *"Tiens! Tiens!* I am very tall! I beat you by half inch!"

Spring moved toward lilac time and once again brought me to Georgian Court for my annual participation in May Musicale. Though I worked hard and broadcast throughout the hot summer, the air-conditioned studios in Radio City made the sweltering humidity bearable. July and August attracted many more out-of-town visitors, and often by pure coincidence they heard their favorite request.

The night that Evelyn Jenkins and her mother were in the studio, I sang "You Have Taken My Heart," her brother Gordon Jenkins' first hit song. A voluntary choice on my part, it was the unexpected harbinger of a devoted friendship with the Jenkins family of Webster Groves, Missouri.

I made another friend that summer—a Dartmouth junior with his ambitions set to write. He came to the broadcast with the idea of interviewing me for the college paper. When his aunt, the noted Metropolitan soprano, Mme. Mary Mellish, introduced us, he held my gaze with his melting brown eyes.

"I've always wanted to know what a nightingale looked like—now I know!"

Smile answered smile, and we made a date for an interview. Later when he returned to college, Mme. Mellish invited me to tea to meet his parents.

His jovial father remarked: "We all love your singing, but I was curious to know what my son thought of you. What do you suppose he told me, Miss Dragonette?"

"I have no idea, but I found him most interesting." I hung on his words.

"'Oh, Father, she's adorable!'" He softened his voice to a caress and gestured as if to embrace me: "'I just wanted to put my arms about her!'"

This was the beginning of my friendship with Harry Ackerman, director of broadcasting and television on the West Coast, now vice-president of CBS. Even then the talents he has so brilliantly displayed were in evidence—I felt he would go far. Besides artistic sensitivity, he had a glowing warmth that endeared him to everyone.

That fall the Archbishop of Cleveland sent me an honored invitation to join the civic reception to open the Eucharistic Congress. During my convent days I had read of great religious conclaves at Nantes, Lyon, and Rome, but they seemed to belong to the historical past and not to everyday experience. I approached the Congress with the sense of living through a high moment of modern history.

NBC, impressed with the important role assigned me in this assembly, asked Hal Metzger and Vernon Pribble, directors of their key station WTAM, to meet me at the train and guide me through the ticklish protocol of ranking personages. The gentlemen, polite though bored, enveloped me in a protective solicitation and never left my side. This undoubtedly was an irksome "personality" coddling which they performed in the line of duty. I sympathized with their sober seriousness, but wondered what I could do about it.

Only my attempt at a rehearsal in the great hall brought Hal Metzger to life. In the midst of this lavish display of hospitality, this minute attention to the smallest detail of my pleasure, no one had thought of the possibility of an accompanist. I sat "like Patience smiling" while they tried to untangle the snarl and combed the city of Cleveland for an organist.

First, a German choirmaster from the cathedral arrived. He had never played the Garden organ before. Moreover, the keys were so rebellious to his touch, he decided the organ needed tuning.

"An orkan's like a vooman," he announced in his thick guttural accent. "You got to know how to play't, unt den sometimes it von't vork."

Still we waited while the choirmaster philosophized. Then the tuners came. After many futile attempts, they gave up the job, explaining: "It would take six months to put that old war horse in condition."

Next, three reporters burst upon the scene and, like three black cats, crossed my path.

"There *is* an organist, Miss Dragonette," one said hopefully, then quickly added, "but I *think* he may be out of town."

The second stuck to his knitting. "You've been crowned radio queen. Aren't you afraid?" he warned ruefully. "It's a jinx, you know. Every star who has received it drops out shortly after."

By the time the third reporter opened up, it sounded like a Greek chorus. "When do you expect to be through with radio?" he ventured.

The others echoed, "Yeah—when?"

Topping it all was the matter of a public tea to which I was long overdue. Mayor Benton was bravely waiting to give me the key of the city, while I lingered in the hall trying to solve the accompanist problem.

It took the impact of this ridiculous situation to rouse Hal Metzger. He rallied to my aid and stalked out, determined to bring back alive an organist. The evening edition of the Cleveland *Plain Dealer* was already on the streets. Norman Siegel, the radio editor, reported that Dragonette was sitting like a patient Griselda in the Garden—cool,

collected, charming, but as bewildered as a sweepstake ticket-
holder whose radio's breakdown blacks out the big race. Poor Mrs.
Coakley, my anxious hostess, sat quietly through the melee. Nadea
paced like a caged leopard, blowing up now and then. Finally, in
desperation, we were about to leave when Hal Metzger returned in
triumph—with an organist from the Methodist church!

"I've played this temperamental instrument before," he said re-
assuringly. Then continuing to pour oil on the troubled waters, he
went on, "Besides, I know your selections. Don't worry—we'll get
along all right." As there was no time now for a rehearsal, I gave
him almost tearful gratitude.

Mr. and Mrs. John H. Coakley, prominent Catholics, threw open
their beautiful city home to Nadea and me. Monsignor Sheen was
also their honored guest, though he was not to speak that evening.
The stay with the Coakleys was very short, but unforgettable. It was
pure joy to be accepted in the heart of this devoted family—to bask
in the mutual love and respect of parents and children—all ten of
them. The atmosphere of ease and sincerity won my affectionate
admiration. No wonder, I thought, Mrs. Coakley has received the
high distinction of a papal medal.

As we drove to the Garden back of the police escort, the whole
city seemed to be milling around us. Never have I seen such crowds.
Outside the auditorium, people were breaking the police cordon to
get a glimpse of me.

"Hello, Jessica, hi-yah?" they shouted. "Can't we see Jessica? We
want Jessica. Stand up and take a bow, dearie."

One policeman yelled back at them good-naturedly, "Gwan wid
yuz. She's busy now. Sure, an' she's peelin' pertaters." Then, putting
his hand over his mouth, he breathed into my ear, "Yer didn't cut
yer t'umb, did yuz? Yer th' only woman me wife is jealous uv."

Being Irish by contagion, I had no difficulty at all placing him as
a friendly son of St. Patrick. The wild crowds in the street delayed
our entrance. Only the police prevented my being carried on their
shoulders.

On the great stage already seated among other notables were Cardinal Hayes, Governor Martin L. Davey, Governor Alfred Smith,
Mayor Benton, the Honorable James J. Farley. I took my place among
them timidly, wearing an azure blue chiffon dress with star-shaped

brilliants and carrying an old-fashioned bouquet of forget-me-nots and pink sweetheart roses.

Between the sonorous wisdom of Al Smith and the amazing eloquence of Jim Farley, Bishop McFarlane rose to speak. I caught just the end of his introduction—"the sweetest voice in all the land." The clarion words were a call to beauty. Smiling to my new-found organist and looking out at the vast crowd for a moment I poised myself for the flight into song.

Under the magic fingers of my organist, the recalcitrant instrument poured forth undreamed-of harmony: Bach-Gounod's "Ave Maria," Handel's "Largo," Franck's "Panis Angelicus." The applause was a long rolling thunder. After the blessing of the saintly Cardinal Hayes, we dispersed, but a new crowd surged upon us at the door. The police escort was doubled, and we drove swiftly to the Coakleys' home for a supper and a reception.

In the early morning, the older children and their friends formed a guard of honor to see us on our way. Vernon Pribble and Hal Metzger, faithful to the end, also joined the throng. Today I think of my friend Hal, poet, painter, violinist, astronomer, serene on his Alfred, New York, farm, content to look through the telescope at his stars at light years' distance.

Among the waiting letters, on my return from Cleveland, I found a congratulatory note I shall always treasure—signed Bishop Spellman.

A little white program with a gold-encrusted eagle falls out of my scrapbook. "Tuesday, January 28, 1936—The White House" it reads. Immediately above are the names: Madame Guiomar Novaes, Pianist; Miss Jessica Dragonette, Soprano; Mr. Arpad Sandor, at the Piano.

This was the small folder I saw the audience perusing the night we performed for President and Mrs. Roosevelt when they entertained the Justices of the Supreme Court of the United States. The intimate after-dinner concert was held in the spacious East Room with its long French windows, polished floor, dainty chairs, and graceful flower arrangements. Here, on a slightly raised dais stood a gold piano decorated with lunettes of the Nine Muses, a Steinway showpiece from the Paris exposition, purchased by Theodore Roosevelt.

The colorful Novaes, looking like a deep gold and black Murillo, placed her hands upon the keys of the gleaming piano and played Liszt's "Tenth Hungarian Rhapsody" as never heard before. The learned Justices and their aristocratic-looking wives seemed carried away by the fire of the pianist; but, when she played the whimsical "Children's Scenes" by her composer husband, Octavio Pinto, we all sensed the artist's nostalgic longing for her own children in faraway Brazil.

Every concert is a challenge in the possibilities offered, but to find myself in joint recital with Novaes was a thrilling incentive. The White House recital was also unique in the routine of entrances: Mme. Novaes and I came upon the stage each time on the arm of a handsome naval aide in full-dress uniform.

The President, accustomed by now to seeing me frequently in Washington, beamed after each familiar song of my groups. In selecting the program I tried to reach every preference. Our good neighbors enjoyed the arias and Spanish songs best, while the Americans favored semiclassical and operetta pieces. President Roosevelt led the congratulations after the concert while the guests grouped themselves about him. I glimpsed lovely Kitty Carlisle in white, pensively leaning back against a side table with Ambassador Oswaldo Aranha and Bernard Baruch beside her.

The President was first to leave. After bidding him good night, Justice Charles Evans Hughes turned back to tell me how much the music had rested him, and for a while we sat and chatted. Mrs. Hughes, her devotion to her husband in every glance, smiled sweetly:

"The Justice won't tell you, but I will. We never miss one of your broadcasts."

"How nice of you to tell me," I answered. "I shall remember and think of you always when I sing."

Some days later, I received autographed pictures of the President and Mrs. Roosevelt framed in wood from the roof of the old White House erected in 1817 and removed in 1927. In the corner was impressed the seal of the President of the United States.

Unbelievable though it seemed, we were celebrating again—this time the tenth birthday anniversary of the National Broadcasting

Company! In breath-taking perspective, I looked back at the 1926 inaugural that week after my first broadcast. Everything had changed. The nineteen-station network had grown to a girdle of more than a hundred stations. Our banquet was taking place at the Hotel Waldorf-Astoria at Forty-ninth Street and Park Avenue. All of us in the grand ballroom, some fifteen hundred people, and countless thousands beyond its walls had contributed to the miracle of radio, to the propagation of ideas acquainting people with the scope and depth of America's intense activity. Besides research engineers whose dreams had been translated into everyday reality and function, there were artists, musicians, entertainers, educational and cultural leaders, who tamed these forces to the purposes of enlightenment and progress. NBC alone was sending out more than 17,000 hours of programs a year and 14,000,000 letters of comment were being received in return. Although radio was of recent origin, the infant industry had become a powerful young giant.

Graham McNamee, standing before the microphone as he had done at the first birthday party, introduced the international speakers of the evening, distinguished men from every walk of life, revealing what an instrument of peace and good will radio had become throughout the world. President Roosevelt and Marconi sent congratulatory messages. Lenox Lohr, president of NBC, Merlin Aylesworth, now chairman of the board of Radio-Keith-Orpheum Corporation, the Honorable Robert Jardillier, minister of communications of France, and Maurice Rambert, president of the International Broadcasting Union, were a few who spoke, along with David Sarnoff, who was celebrating, not a tenth, but a thirtieth anniversary in radio.

After dinner, Graham McNamee introduced the entertainers—all well-known radio stars. At this tenth anniversary, I was not in the balcony, on the outside looking in, but on the stage singing to the seen and unseen audience who had come to know me as a dear friend, a weekly visitor in their homes.

A young artist, just back from abroad, delivered with French chic two of the latest popular songs. Little did we dream that she was to become the "incomparable" Hildegarde.

Later, David Sarnoff in his thoughtful way wrote to all of us. To me he said, "I have always had a great admiration for your glorious talent and your participation on the program that evening was a compliment to me that I shall not soon forget."

I felt then, as now, that David Sarnoff, better than anyone else, was fulfilling the mission of Karl T. Compton's parting words: "May you discharge your responsibility with humility, faith, wisdom, and high purpose."

CHAPTER 13

MATHEMATICS: MAGIC AND MUSIC

The world listened while Sarnoff and his European guests talked with Guglielmo Marconi on his yacht *Elettra* in the waters off Genoa, Italy, and almost immediately returned their salutes via the short wave girdle of the earth that American broadcasting genius made possible. Now the machine, annihilating time and space, became the white hope helping man to understand his fellow man. Transporting the voice, transporting the flickering picture in this century, our single purpose has been to bind us more closely together; just as in other times the dreamers believed that writing, printing, and the sailing ship, making communications easier, would elevate the human spirit.

As radio approached the technical perfection its engineers were achieving with networks covering the globe, Europe was already a seething caldron of unrest. American newscasters, their ear to the ground, with portable transmitters ever ready on the spot, made America the only really informed nation in the world. Following the tenth anniversary celebration, however, greetings in the universal language of music came from Vienna, Paris, Rome, London, Warsaw, Stockholm, Berlin, Budapest, Brussels, Amsterdam, and Tokyo. The instrument of peace and good will was now a living reality—one world, the dream of the ages, seemed imminent.

The American people could stand with the crowd keeping vigil outside Buckingham Palace to receive word of George V's death and hear soon after this tragic news the proclamation declaring the beloved Prince of Wales, the new king. Any American listening in could hear the royal heralds on the Friary Court balcony of St. James's Palace.

The pageant moving swiftly forward, Edward renounced his birthright for "the woman I love." All America was at the radio to take to heart the never-to-be-forgotten, simple, dignified words beginning, "At long last . . ."

Civil War in Spain, Mussolini's swift conquest of Ethiopia, from Addis Ababa the farewell of Emperor Haile Selassie and Hitler's hysterical voice inciting the Nazis, came in a matter of minutes via the magic waves. Newsrooms of the world-wide networks brought us first-hand history more quickly and fully than the newspapers could print the events.

Religion, Wisdom, Art—these were the verities. But what of the artist in such a time? What could he contribute to the security of the people of his nation and time? For me the answer was music and becoming a better artist, to help build an island of peace in a troubled universe.

Meanwhile the living language of music was also undergoing a change. A new idiom was being spoken in the arrangements of the large orchestras. André Kostelanetz was attracting attention mainly because of the styling of his orchestrations by a group of young musicians blazing trails in musical presentation. They used fresh original effects—combining instruments and instrumentation in a novel and interesting way: they were evolving the American musical expression, principally in the field of jazz. Most of the ideas were born in Joseph Schillinger's studio, where a new system of musical composition was being taught.

Radio arrangers were pressed—they had to turn out quantities of work in a short time. To these denizens of the music libraries, burners of the midnight oil, Joseph Schillinger was a heaven-sent miracle, a gold mine. The arrangers and mercantile composers could not wait for inspiration, nor could they afford to be geniuses. They had to produce quickly and compose music to suit any purpose on short notice. The Schillinger system taught them how to accomplish this feat. In time more than 500 students found their way to Schillinger's studio to discover what scientists and artists had been searching for since time began—to learn that "the processes of art creation" were

not "a gift from heaven" and the work only of "genius [but] . . . to
discover the mathematical basis of 'divine inspiration'"—the synthe-
sis of music and art through mathematical principles.

Could anyone learn to compose or to produce art? Yes, according
to Schillinger, "anyone with intelligence and an ordinary school education who is willing to work hard and who has the capacity to
learn . . . with the adoption of an engineering technique, the entire
approach to musical patterns becomes mathematical."

It was a perfect tie-up: music for the machine in the machine
age, music for wholesale entertainment in the promotion of sales.
Approximately 200 NBC advertisers were spending in the neighborhood of $32,000,000 on broadcasting in 1936.

To George Gershwin—who traveled to Paris for study with Ravel
and whom Ravel dismissed with a wave of his hand: "*Mon vieux,*
you write such charming little things. Keep on as you are and let it
go at that"—Schillinger was a savior. He helped the popular American through the most ambitious undertaking of his life, *Porgy and
Bess.* I remember how glowingly Gershwin talked of Schillinger
when I met him in Florida, while he was finishing the score. Schillinger
wholly revived his inspiration.

Gershwin made me think how curiously small the world is. I had
always been interested in jazz. This penchant goes back to my Philco
days when Frank Black was making arrangements of popular music
for the first Palmolive Hour. I had a number of George Gershwin
and Duke Ellington records. Later I went frequently to the Capitol
or the Paramount to hear what the jazz-boys were doing—Tommy
Dorsey, Gene Krupa, Benny Goodman, and other favorites. Their
virtuosity on the trombone, drums, and clarinet fascinated me. Just
as Wagner had extended the use of the instruments in the brass
choir, these men were doing the same thing in a different field. However, the ever-recurring similar eight measures of music went
against the grain.

When I met Schillinger I was curious to know why a composer
of so-called serious music was so interested in jazz. He told me:
"When I was in Russia, I not only had a jazz band, but I lectured on
jazz and the music of the future." He spoke of "jazz as the music of
the masses, of its revolutionary role in rejuvenating music," of what
he called, in American journalese, "hearts and dollars."

It made sense! His jazz band was a hybrid group of three saxo-
phones, three brass, four rhythm instruments, two violins, and an
oboe. The composers he played were chiefly George Gershwin and
Irving Berlin in Frank Black arrangements. One year later, in
America, he was teaching George Gershwin, and later Van Cleave,
Benny Goodman, Paul Lavalle, Mark Warnow, Oscar Levant, Glenn
Miller, George Leeman, among many others.

Schillinger could write music in the style of any composer, past
and present. Beside his Houdini-like ability at opening musical locks,
what appealed to me most strongly was his preoccupation with the
tempo and idiom of the present. Abandoning yesterday's world, he
could grasp not only the meaning of today's world, but also invent a
language to express it. He was fond of telling us how much at home
he felt in America: "I feel my correct tempo for the first time in my
life."

Nadea and I were so mesmerized by Schillinger's genius that we
wanted to share him with all our friends. Most of them found his
engineering principles as applied to music and art too high flown.
Yet they flocked around the piano like fascinated children when he
would spin a melody out of their names and telephone numbers. Or
playing the keyboard with one hand, he would improvise an accompaniment with the other hand drawn over the strings of the piano.
Some of our musician friends, however, not driven to accept him by
force of circumstance and being impervious to new ideas, received
his theories with revulsion and horror. To them he was an iconoclast,
desecrating the sacred tradition of music.

There was nothing of the fussy pedant about Schillinger. To us he
was a dear, warm friend, a gentle and lovable human being full of
goodness and childlike wonder. Schillinger confined to his teaching
schedule and I to my singing schedule found little free time; however, Nadea and I were always delighted at what was in store for
us when he would call on the telephone: "I want to introduce you
to a new gastronomic experience." This became a round of the most
unusual restaurants in and near New York where we became acquainted with only the rarest of foods.

When a few good friends foregathered, Schillinger would display
his sense of humor and his incomparable mimicry. He would amuse
us by the hour with imitations of famous conductors. All these were

excruciatingly funny; but his portrayal of Glazounov, his former teacher, made us hysterical with laughter. Sometimes he would caricature a buxom soprano, a bass-baritone, or a high tenor. In perfect pantomime he would mimic them with open mouth as though he were singing. And we were convulsed with what we heard though he did not utter a sound!

One evening, reading the New York *World-Telegram*, I found a full column story on the editorial page concerning one David Eugene Smith, professor emeritus of mathematics, Columbia University, Persian scholar and author. The saga of this extraordinary man so moved me that I began inquiring among my friends if anyone knew him. Among the first I approached was Mirza Mahmoud Khan Saghaphi, formerly page to the mad Shah Nasser-ed-Din, later first delegate plenipotentiary, chargé d'affaires, consul general of Persia. The Prince's face lighted up at the mention of his name: "I have known Dr. Smith for years. He has one of the finest collections of Persian art, and I like his translation of Omar Khayyám better than Fitz-Gerald's."

Before I could reconcile myself to the belief that Dr. Smith was not a fictitious character, Mahmoud brought an invitation to meet him at luncheon.

David Eugene Smith received us in his charming home with all the hospitality of an Eastern potentate. He showed us his fabulous collection of Korans, glass, jewelry, paintings, and *objets d'art*. Then proudly offering me his arm, he led us to the dining room. We sat around a large table to a sumptuous meal of diverse courses, heavy with condiment, many of them Persian dishes. Besides our host and Prince Saghaphi, there were the publishers Viola and David McFarlane, godchildren of Dr. Smith, Rabbi Bernstein, a member of the Bahai Church, and the wide-eyed Dragonette sisters. Presiding over such a heterogeneous gathering appealed to Dr. Smith's universal approach to life. He was interested in any dedication that was inspired by the highest sincerity. He firmly believed that "everyone is in a small way the image of God." It was like sitting at the feet of a master, hearing him discourse on "the power of thought, the magic of the mind."

Schillinger flashed through my head. What would result from the meeting of these geniuses? No two men, I thought, have more in common—a very Damon and Pythias of matching intellect. Schillinger, though much younger than the aging Dr. Smith, was elated at the prospect of rubbing minds with a colleague. At last he could speak out freely to one who would understand him.

When Nadea and I escorted Dr. Smith to Schillinger's studio, the amenities of introduction were hardly over when Schillinger moved toward a table laden with scrolls, wood blocks, and mathematical paraphernalia, so eager was he to unburden his brilliant mind to his distinguished visitor. But Dr. Smith seemed suddenly weary. He was not even listening to Schillinger's magical merchandise. Looking out the window, he sighed: "You have a fine view here, Professor."

Poor Schillinger opened a scroll: "I have divided the parallelogram differently. . . ."—but it was of no use. Dr. Smith interrupted him: "Where will you spend the summer, Professor? I shall go to Persia again. I go every year."

Nadea and I sat by, utterly frustrated at the complete absence of accord between these geniuses. It is one of the disappointments of my life that nothing came of this important meeting of two great men. The genius mathematician who could appreciate the perfect rhythm of mathematical expressions, the perfect symmetry, the perfect geometric picture—like the façade of the Parthenon—could not see this perfect example of the power of thought—the magic of Schillinger's mind.

"Euclid alone has looked on beauty bare." Schillinger composed poetry in like symmetry, made designs, mixed colors, even applying his universal principles of engineering to music, stagecraft, moving pictures, and modern machinery. William Paley, president of CBS, spent much time in Schillinger's studio reviewing this aspect of his work. But most of the magic of his mind died with him in 1942. He left, however, two gigantic masterworks: *A Mathematical Basis of the Arts* and *The Schillinger System of Musical Composition.*

It was unfortunate the learned Dr. Smith's imagination could not follow Schillinger in his Jules Verne-like flights. Yet in Schillinger's estimation no soaring of the imagination could equal the real wonder of the real reality.

In August, Dr. Smith sailed for Persia and Schillinger went mountain climbing. He wrote from California:

Dear Sisters:

—"but angels are so few"—it depends entirely on the altitude. For instance, at the altitude of 7,000 feet, everyone is apt to become an angel. Living in and above the clouds actually transforms one into what I call Angelus Alpinas. I had ten glorious days of mountain climbing on Mount Rainier.

That August, neither on the sea nor in the mountains with geniuses, I was on my way to Cleveland to broadcast the Cities Service program from Radioland, as part of the Great Lakes Exposition. This was the first time the program had been broadcast anywhere except from the National Broadcasting Company's studios in New York. But tonight the entire Cities Service concert was being given in Cleveland on the stage before more than 13,000 guests, in the magnificent setting of the exposition. Not too far from us, outside the auditorium was Billy Rose's famous aquacade featuring the Olympic champion swimmer Eleanor Holm. To commemorate this festivity, Rosario Bourdon wrote an original march as a "Salute to Ohio."

Cleveland held many enchanting memories of the previous year, when I sang at the Eucharistic Congress. Unfortunately, our stay was limited, but I tried to fit in everything the hospitable Clevelanders had arranged. I was scarcely out of the airplane before they rode me through the broad avenues of the city beside the lake to greet the mobs of exposition sight-seers—then to a reception at the city hall to be given an admiral's cap.

Rehearsal was in the imminent distance, yet I could not disappoint my audiences in the hospitals. Many had written "you are an important part in our pattern of life. Do come to see us during your visit." These patients listened to me regularly on the air and would be disappointed not to see me in person. The songs had pulled their heart strings. I had to go and visit them in the wards—singing and talking awhile at each bed.

It is true I always "dressed" my songs at broadcasts in Radio City, but now I was singing where people knew me only as a *voice*, yet had never seen me as a *person*. I could not bear to mar the impression they had formed. Moreover, I would be the only spot of color on the vast stage with the large orchestra and the quartet.

Hattie Carnegie designed a ravishing blue gown (my twenty-sixth to date) for "Alice Blue Gown" and for the first half of the program

in which I also sang Victor Herbert selections and "Beautiful Ohio."
For the aria "Te souvient-il du lumineux voyage" from Massenet's
Thais I wore a pale pink tulle gown with dainty silver paillettes in
a most unusual design.

Thousands of visitors from the state and from all over America
heard us in the auditorium that evening as well as millions over the
radio. Women eager to see my gowns at close range crowded backstage. Boys tried to run off with my fan while I was busy giving autographs. A tiremaker from Akron said: "I enjoy you on the air but I
was afraid to come. Radio stars can be so disappointing, but here's
a secret. I'm glad I did!"

One lady from Dearborn brought her parrot Laura to see me "in
person." Quite frequently radio listeners wrote me how much their
pets also enjoyed my singing. "My cat Mittens always curls up in my
lap when the Cities Service program begins." "Rags is just as quiet
as I am, with his ears cocked to the radio for you." But for a pet to be
brought to see me was most unusual, and I must say that Laura be-
haved very well during the program. "Every time you sing 'Annie
Laurie,'" said the parrot's owner, "Laura thinks you are singing to
her."

I expected a song from Laura in return or at least a few words,
but she was silent as a sphinx. Though her impatient mistress coaxed
and coaxed, Laura cowered on the bottom of her cage, alternately
eying me and the backstage crowd. When we all despaired of hearing the parrot speak and her annoyed mistress was carrying her
down the steps, every head turned at the sound of an eerie "Jessica—
Jessica—I love you—" with loud sounds of kisses and "Ha! Ha! Ha!"
Better late than never, Laura had found her tongue.

Next morning at the Horticultural Gardens, in a lovely flower ceremony, a special pink and blue gladiola was named Jessica Dragonette.
I had namesakes in the animal kingdom throughout the country—
particularly prize heifers. Having a flower named after me was definitely more exciting, and everybody was so kind I could not help
thinking aloud to Nadea as we boarded our plane: "Isn't it wonderful
that in so many cities, towns, villages, and even on farms all over the
world, but particularly here in America, there are appreciative people, who are friendly and outgoing?"

With each personal appearance I became less and less "a mystery lady," my life less and less "a carefully guarded secret." I found these colorful excursions into centers of contact with the people stimulating—and the friendships I made along the way among the treasures of my life. People found me pretty much the average American girl, getting along in the American way, by hard work and study. They liked me for refusing the siren call of Europe and my eager enthusiasm for music in spite of world-shaking history. I was still full of visions—radio visions.

Recently singing at the glamorous first Cinderella Ball in Detroit, the highlight of the social season there, at the invitation of William J. Scripps, Jr., I remembered an earlier visit when WWJ opened their handsome new studios. The Detroit *News*-owned station was one of the oldest and finest in the country, owing its being and much of its distinction to the foresight of William J. Scripps, Sr. For over seven years my Cities Service program went over the WWJ network every Friday evening. Detroiters were curious and the station invited me to participate in their opening ceremonies.

As Nadea and I boarded the parlor car to Detroit, we came upon John Charles Thomas and his accompanist, Carol Hollister. I hesitated for a minute before addressing John Charles. The little Continental mustache he was wearing confused me; it so changed his appearance I wasn't quite sure it was he. Carol must have said something funny then; there was no mistaking his laugh.

"Look who's here!" I exclaimed to Nadea, delighted as I always am to see my dear friend.

"Hot-diggety!" was John Charles's snorting retort, with that swaggering gesture of his arm. He twinkled, "Where are you going this time, Blondie?"

"Oh, I'm about my radio business," I said, falling into his mood. "WWJ in Detroit is having a sixteenth birthday. I'm going to sing."

"Too bad," he answered. "You'll have to miss the opening Ford concert. You're slipping—I thought you never missed a John Charles Thomas concert."

"Maybe I can manage both," I reassured him.

We reached Detroit Sunday morning, and after breakfast together, Herschel Hart, radio editor of the Detroit *News*, joined us. While

Nadea and I went to Mass, John Charles looked over a new boat. Boats were his hobby—he was always looking at one.

"Why don't you come along? You might decide you want to be a skipper yourself. Nothing like it to take your mind off singing." I was flattered that he thought I could afford anything so halcyon. "On second thought," he laughed, screwing up his eyes and showing the deep dimple in his cheek, "I don't think you'd better come. Remember how you got me out of that River House joint?"

He was thinking of the day, after trying out a boat on the East River in New York City, we pulled up to the pier at River House. As we got into the elevator to go up to the street level, the operator looked at us suspiciously.

"Please, I don't know you?" he inquired. John Charles Thomas' representative came boldly forward. "This is Miss Jessica Dragonette."

"Yes, I know," smiled the elevator man, "but—"

"And this is Mr. John Charles Thomas," our companion announced.

"Never heard of him," said the man. "Where did yez want to go?"

John Charles got a great kick out of telling the story on himself. His down-to-earth sense of humor endeared him to all his friends. It strikingly contrasted with his stage personality communicating luminous Renoir-like palette colors to his audience every instant.

I was honored to be associated at the dedicatory program with two of the foremost actors of the Broadway theater and the movies—Ethel Barrymore and Walter Hampden—appearing in an abridged version of *The Servant in the House*. They rode this old war horse for all it was worth, wringing out of it undreamed-of beauty and depth with their sure artistry. Here, again, was the dramatic interlude with which I longed to vary a concert program.

Detroiters flocked to the studio to see in person the voice they knew so well. Every Friday night they were accustomed to hearing me and my songs were their requests: Chaminade's "Summer," Kern's "I Dream Too Much," Thomas' "Connais-tu le pays?" "Only a Rose," and "Sympathy."

After the rehearsal there was a letter waiting for me at the hotel. It was signed "Servite Sisters per Sister Annunziata":

We are twenty-four little Servite Sisters, who have never missed one of your broadcasts in over seven years. We love your singing and we would love to see you broadcast at WWJ tonight. Our rules will not permit this. They cannot, however, stop us from wishing to see you—

I was curiously touched by this ardent community and their remarkable Mother Superior who wrote the letter; so between the rehearsal and the broadcast, I drove to the end of the city to see them. As they met me at the door, Sister Annunziata announced: "Yesterday we said nothing on earth is perfect."

"The imperfection in this case," said another Sister, "is our inability to make our gratitude known to you, dear little friend."

The younger Sisters fluttered about, like fleet-footed angels, bearing simple refreshments: ice cream in ginger-ale and homemade cookies.

"Oh, this is sinful food, Sister," I admonished playfully. "I am singing tonight so I shall have to abstain. Besides, if I ate it I might not get myself into the fairylike frock I brought along especially for the opening."

The Sisters went into surprised peals of laughter: "Sinful? But why?"

"Shall I tell you, Sisters?"

"Yes, yes," they cried.

"Well, then, come close." I began to whisper: "It's food that would be two minutes in the mouth, two hours in the tummy, and a lifetime on the hips."

The Sisters laughed as though they had never heard anything like this before. They detained me until the last moment, and I just had time to get myself into that fairylike frock of pale rose and silver and drive to the broadcast.

The next day I received another letter: "You have always been a 'real' person to us, but since your visit and our having seen you—it is so different."

In all these ten years of broadcasting, punctuated by one vacation midway, I wanted above everything "humbly to give pleasure" with my songs. To appeal to the intellect and the imagination of my listeners, yes, but above all to their hearts. Since I was in no way a complete artist and much of my study was interrupted by continual performance, I felt I should have some help in program preparation and repertoire. While I had personally chosen vocal selections from a wide repertory range, some outside aid and inspiration would bring out the best for my audiences. I also wanted to improve my technique. I was ever on the lookout for an illumination to feed the sustained effort I was engaged in—giving an identity to the new radio industry's expression.

One day, as I sat in the crowded anteroom to Miss Liebling's studio she opened the door: "Come in, Jessica. I know you're very busy, so I'll take you first."

I slunk down in my coat collar and sheepishly looked at the waiting pupils. As I followed Miss Liebling I cast a dejected look over my shoulder: "Don't hate me, please!"

Inside the door, we went to work on some Brahms songs. When we were finished, I said: "Are the Lieder all right? I don't feel I can work them up to the perfection of the French and Spanish songs. Don't you think I should go to a Lieder coach? You have such a large class—you cannot possibly give me the time I require."

Miss Liebling was reluctant to encourage me, for she understood my sensitive nature better than I knew. And with that great intuition of hers, she wanted to save me from the jarring clash of alien temperaments.

"You know I understand the Lieder very well," she said quietly. "Why should you want to go to anyone else with these songs? I really don't think you'll add anything. Coaching I can understand, but teaching? You have learned your singing here."

So great was my ingrained pursuit of perfection—the reckless hazarding of gains for a thimbleful of knowledge wherever it was to be found goading me forward in the unfoldment of the singing art—that she could not hold me back. Art, I was convinced, like architecture had to be built. The artist is not born full-blown from the head of Jove. After my lesson, I went immediately to Arpad Sandor for help with the Lieder, and later, for a time, I studied with the distinguished composer and teacher Frank La Forge.

On returning from an appearance in *Faust,* with the Chicago Opera Company, Jean Tennyson and her inventor husband, Camille Dreyfus, came to Radio City to hear me sing. Jean was a pupil of

Miss Liebling's. Though I had never met her in the studio, Miss Liebling conveyed charming messages from her, so I sent her tickets to a broadcast. At supper afterward we talked of her studies with Mary Garden. "She is in Europe now and when she returns, I'll have you meet her, Jessica," said Jean.

Though I had no contact with Mary Garden in any way, I unconsciously gravitated to the repertoire she found so congenial—principally Massenet and Debussy, whose music I explored strictly from choice, never aware of the Garden resemblance. I had not meditated upon the Garden career, as Glenn Dillard Gunn of the Washington *Times-Herald,* recently felt my concert programs indicated. After accepting Jean's offer with much anticipation, to date, my wish has not been realized!

Jean also told me that when she was learning some Debussy songs on the Riviera, Mary Garden told her: "Debussy's music is like the gently falling autumn leaves—red and yellow that gather quickly and then scatter." Perhaps, but I think of his music in Shelley's description:

> O wild West Wind, thou breath of Autumn's being,
> Thou, from whose unseen presence the leaves dead
> Are driven, like ghosts from an enchanter fleeing,
> Yellow, and black, and pale, and hectic red. . . .

One evening, at the home of Jean and Dr. Dreyfus, John Charles Thomas entertained us not with his singing, but with extraordinary card tricks. He must have practiced for years, for so skillful was his legerdemain that standing quite close to him at the piano we could not see how he got "the cards into the sealed envelope."

After taking leave of our cordial hosts that night, we came upon one of the waiters who had been serving us at supper, standing by the elevator door. He looked on me as just another blonde—his hero worship was all for John Charles.

"Mr. Thomas," he said, "I always hear you when I can. But when you sing your concert on Sunday, I shall be on duty. Would you sing a few measures for me now?"

John Charles burst into "Home on the Range" and after a pat on the shoulder and a resounding good night, we went down in the lift. He was twinkling and chuckling again: "How was that, Jessie? I guess we're even now!"

During this period, the motion picture studios were constantly after me to give up broadcasting and spend some time in Hollywood. Since I had embarked on a pioneering job that was not yet finished, I did not feel I could do this. After all, when Hollywood allowed its stars to broadcast, it did not suggest that they abandon the movies. Why should I abandon radio?

But finally Lou Diamond, vice-president of the Paramount Company, talked me into doing a scene in a picture which would not necessitate my going to Hollywood or interrupt my broadcasting. It would be a mistake, he thought, to desert the microphone. He was a frequent visitor not only to my weekly broadcasts but also to May Musicale at Georgian Court each spring; and he was likely to turn up in any personal appearance audience from New York to Chicago. "Jessica darlin'," he would say, "I wouldn't tell you to do anything that would hurt you in any way. But I think you belong in *The Big Broadcast of 1936*. We'll shoot your scenes in Long Island, and if you don't like the sequence when it's made, we'll just take it out. How about it?" It was impossible to refuse him.

Lou Diamond's secretary failed to notify me that the Hollywood staff of *The Big Broadcast* would expect to see me on a certain day. I arrived home from a brief week end in Atlantic City to find waiting for me in my apartment the director, Norman Taurog, and his two assistants; Lou Diamond; Ralph Ranger, Leo and Stasia Robbin, Paramount song writers. Of course, I was surprised, to say the least. I apologized for keeping them waiting.

Norman Taurog said good-naturedly: "Well, now that you're here, let's do some work. I'd like to go through your wardrobe and see what you have that might be good for the picture."

I might have been the best-dressed woman in radio, but I had nothing that met with Mr. Taurog's approval. Nothing gray "and gray photographs very well."

The coiffure was next. I could sit on my hair, but it wouldn't do —it would have to be cut. I knew 1,000 songs, but I would sing "Alice Blue Gown" and a song by Robbin and Ranger called "Through the Doorway of Dreams." This was six-thirty in the evening, though according to Mr. Taurog's schedule I would have exactly one day to have a new dress made, to weep over cutting my long hair, learn a new song, be made up by Eddie Senz, and be on the set at nine o'clock in the morning on Long Island. Mr. Taurog gave all the orders expertly while the two assistants took voluminous notes and clucked assent.

In the fever pitch of our concentration, the city had become aggressively noisy. We grew conscious of crowds moving, shouting, cars racing, fire bells, police and ambulance sirens. Unable to imagine what was happening, we turned on the radio: a man had been standing on the ledge of the seventeenth floor of the Hotel Gotham for over fourteen hours, threatening to jump. A policeman stood by, feeding him cigarettes and talking to distract him. Everybody at the conference was impelled to go out and join the gaping crowds. Nadea said: "I'm afraid to go for fear he'll jump." And just as we turned into Fifth Avenue from Fifty-seventh Street, we saw him plunge, flinging himself to death.

I thought it was to the poets we were indebted for transforming women from what they were to what they are! No, it's to Hollywood! The dress was made, the hair was cut, the song was learned, the make-up was perfect, the set was beautiful, Mr. Taurog was pleased. But I asked to have the scene cut out of *The Big Broadcast!* Why? I can only quote from a letter I later received: "Please never leave radio for the movies, although I would hardly blame you if you did —it must be very tempting. I can't imagine radio without you. After seeing *The Big Broadcast of 1936* you went way way up in my estimation because you withdrew from it. . . ."

Until 1934 most large network dramas originated in New York or Chicago, but when one of the earliest and most successful of these shows, Louella Parsons' *Hollywood Hotel,* jumped from thirty-ninth to tenth place in a Crosley rating for popularity, it showed that Hollywood drama and personalities were good radio possibilities. Today Hollywood is second only to New York as a production center.

At first the Hollywood stars were not quite at home on the air; Joan Crawford and Jean Arthur, willing enough, suffered from mike fright. Once when Patsy Kelly appeared on Phil Baker's Gulf program, she fainted just before it was time to go on the air. The producer had a heart attack, but Patsy recovered and the program went on without a hitch.

Mae West, doing a guest appearance for Chase and Sanborn under the outstanding producer Dwight Cooke, read her lines straight at rehearsal in the Adam and Eve playlet, but let herself go on the actual broadcast with full Westian implications. The FCC offered a stern rebuke, and the general public loudly protested. Cecil B. DeMille of the Lux Radio Theatre alone seemed to be able to quell the early Hollywood hysteria. Thus Hollywood and its stars were taking an ever-increasing part in radio drama. With all of this going on, it was incredible that I could not put my point across with the agency men to induce them to make use of this popular trend for one twelfth of our otherwise musical program.

By this time Cities Service was beginning to see that every guest appearance I made was redounding to their benefit, so I had no difficulty whatsoever in securing permission to appear on the Alka-Seltzer program in Chicago. I was pleased to share a program for the first time with the unique Alec Templeton and take part in his ingenious music-comics, which have since become so widely acclaimed. His fancy hit upon William Tell—I felt that my past was still catching up with me. What would Fräulein Klaus of Georgian Court have made of it? That was just it—no one was supposed to make anything of it—we were tearing off into the wildest farcical burlesque. The madder we became, the more his imagination flowered. It was a lark to be associated with anyone having such a spontaneous gift of improvisation. I had difficulty coming back to the mood of "The Maids of Cadiz" and Tchaikovsky's "Love's Own Waltz."

After rehearsal the Earl Zimmermans entertained us at the Casino Club with a group of their intimate friends, among them the appealing Spanish-eyed Lolita Armour, then Mrs. Jack Mitchell. Alec joined us and was happy as a child over having champagne. Intermittently raising his glass and singing an original toast for each of us individually, he was like an irrepressible boy forever bubbling over with music.

At the next Cities Service broadcast there was a candid cameraman sitting in the front row, and every time I took a high note I could hear the little click of the shutter—I shuddered to think what the picture would be like with the gaping cavern of a mouth. I soon found out. In a few days there was a new magazine on the newsstands. It had a two-page spread of "National Bedtime Characters at Work . . . inhabitants of a new era of fame—a species of unseen celebrities whose fame and future depend on intimacy in countless homes." In the circle of candid shots were Walter Winchell, Jack Benny, Rudy Vallee, Frank Black, Gypsy Rose Lee, Dorothy Thompson, Helen Hayes, and Jessica Dragonette. Under my picture the caption read: "This is a rare candid camera shot of the 100% radio built personality. She hates having her picture taken with her mouth open." The periodical? This was the first issue of *Life* magazine!

It was difficult to fit in all the benefit requests that came to me, but who could refuse the invitation of 425 cadets from West Point to sing at their military ball benefit for Holy Trinity Chapel?

To a man we unanimously voted for you as radio queen. You can't refuse, and each of us expects to dance with you. So don't disappoint us. We are enclosing a long list of our favorite songs for you to choose from when you come. Won't you please help us to

"CARRY ON
FOR GOD AND COUNTRY."

From the high-voltage tension of the studio in Rockefeller Center, I drove westward to the Hotel Astor. As I appeared in the doorway of the ballroom and the captain of the corps announced my arrival, the cadets and their beautiful partners stopped dancing, sent up a cheer, and began singing the "Army Alma Mater":

> Let Duty be well performed
> Honor be e'er untarned
> Country be ever armed
> West Point by thee.

As soon as the echoes of their lusty voices died away, two cadets escorted me to the stage. I lifted my eyes to the surrounding boxes full of officers and guests of the military, and before me on the polished ballroom floor stood the graceful girls in their flower-hued dresses and their gray-blue clad partners. I sang songs for them from the long list they sent me, and after resounding applause they came to claim their dances.

Suddenly, in the midst of so much gray-blue, a handsome stranger in full evening black and white tapped my escort on the shoulder and at once began addressing me in French. "Mademoiselle, I am Count Roger de Palluel. I have listened to you with such pleasure—

I had to see for myself whether your name and voice matched your personality. I am happy they do. I know you speak French because I have heard you sing it without flaw."

If he had any thought of dancing, there was a solid blue wall advancing that made any such idea impossible, but not before I learned we both knew Eunice Howard, the pianist, now Mrs. Chester Dane. Through a clairvoyant vista, I glimpsed our future friendship that happily continues to this day.

A little gray souvenir, a dance card bound with a gold-tasseled cord, was signed by all the cadets: "The echo of your sweet voice lingers not in our ears but in our hearts."

Enshrined in a niche of my mind is the special day I lunched with Robert de Veyrac, designer, and Antoine de Saint-Exupéry in the New York studio of Bernard Lamotte, the painter. Bernard had promised me some good sole with white wine sauce—he would prepare it himself—and some French conversation with real Frenchmen which he thought I badly needed. Bernard was eager to have me speak more colloquially—more "argot." He complained I spoke French "*trop académiquement.*"

Several latecomers joined us at table, and after another interval, in answer to the studio bell, Bernard let in a large, broad-shouldered man dressed in rich brown. All eyes turned to him as he entered, and I was caught by his soul searching glance. Remarking his dark head, I observed the bruises on his chin. He found a place at the far end of the table and at once started a lively conversation with his friends.

"Jessica," Bernard explained, "this is Comte Antoine de Saint-Exupéry, a famous French flyer who also writes books."

"Oh, yes," I replied quickly. "I have read his *Vol de Nuit* and love it."

Saint-Exupéry's brown eyes smiled. He was obviously pleased "The little blonde American has read my—*comment dit-on en anglais —Night-Flight?* That is very nice indeed."

Bernard was likewise pleased that his only American guest felt at home among his countrymen. "He was lost for a very long time and almost died of thirst," Bernard was explaining, in his French-translated English.

"Yes, yes, I know," I murmured softly so the others could not hear.

"He was a prisoner of the Libyan desert sands. Evidently the marks on his chin are the battle scars."

"You surprise me, Jessica, I didn't know you knew him."

"Only by his books," I said.

After luncheon, Saint-Exupéry asked for a pencil, and taking a knife he patiently shaved off the lead into a fine powder. "Mademoiselle Jessica, I have a collection of hand prints. I would like to add yours. Would you allow me?"

"Surely; with pleasure," I answered. He spread the pulverized lead over my open hand and pressed it against the white sheet of paper. The imprint was clear, and Saint-Exupéry described what the shape of the fingers and the lines of the palm revealed to him.

"Now that we have it," he said, "we will want to preserve it." And with an earnest, musicianlike gesture he blew a fixative over the picture. "Will you please sign it for me," he asked.

"Gladly," I eagerly assented. "I shall feel honored to be in your collection."

The sunny afternoon was flushed with sunset when we left Bernard's studio. As I took my leave, Saint-Exupéry came forward to say *au revoir*. "Fair exchange—as you say in English." And opening his *Wind, Sand and Stars,* he signed his name on the fly leaf and put the book in my hands.

O poet soul, great patriot lost in the skies, I open your volume treasured through the years, and hear your voice as I read: "Only the Spirit, if it breathe upon the clay, can create man."

CHAPTER 14

THE GREAT MISUNDERSTANDING

Scarcely a day passes that I do not receive letters from air friends all over the world, asking the same insistent and persistent questions: "Why don't we hear you on the radio?" "Don't you like to sing for us any more?" "Are you so rich you don't want to be bothered?" "Have you retired from public life?" "We can never forget the way you sang 'Breath of April,' Mimi's 'Addio,' 'Estrellita,' 'Alice Blue Gown.' It doesn't seem natural not to hear you."

I always answer truthfully, "Of course I want to sing for you." "So rich, how could I be?" "A bother? My singing was never a bother, but bone, muscle, and breath of me."

Reference is made by air friends to various books that authoritatively dismiss my "case" with a few lines of summary:

"After a financial disagreement with her sponsors, Miss Dragonette retired from radio," according to Lloyd Morris in *Not So Long Ago*.

"Her absence from radio is one of the big puzzles of the industry to listeners . . . to commercial sponsors and broadcasters, however, there is no mystery at all. Miss Dragonette has set a price of $2,500 per week on her services. . . ." according to Francis Chase, Jr. in *Sound and Fury*.

Some of these questions and statements have never been answered —they are equally puzzling to me. *I have not retired. I was not replaced. I left Cities Service of my own volition. I did not ask for more money or put a fixed price on my singing. I never had financial disagreements with sponsors.*

As I have already pointed out, when I starred in the Philco series in which I did the light operas and overnight changed to a concert program—Cities Service—a great part of the radio audience still longed to hear me in a dramatized spot from their favorite operettas. During the seven years with Cities Service, singing everything from grand opera to popular songs, I pleaded with them to cater to my audience by including a scene around a principal light opera song —the whole bit not to take more than three or four minutes. But this request was never granted.

I really loved the Cities Service program. I loved my associates, especially Rosario Bourdon for the example and inspiration his high musical caliber provided. His devotion to a harmonious whole increased my own enthusiasm. Since we had no budget for program expense, he usually paid orchestra overtime rehearsals out of his own pocket. He often gave me an extra piano rehearsal when we were working out some new musical event to enhance the program. In these circumstances I could not bring myself to burden him further with operatic copyright fees or special orchestrations for my songs, though I felt they were essential; so I paid for them myself.

Up to this time Hollywood was still testing radio. Now they were invading it, presenting their stars more and more frequently in scenes from the latest popular motion pictures—a quite natural, if tardy, awakening on the part of the West Coast studios. The cut and dried, neat two or three minutes' sequence was ideally suitable, and the scenes could be interspersed in a musical program with immense effect. That Hollywood was now doing it emboldened me to harp on the theme of this trend for our Cities Service presentation. At the weekly meetings I kept suggesting: "Why not dramatize the commercials? There must be plenty of romance in oil and pipelines. Acting it out makes it so much more human and effective." I talked until I was weary, but my words still fell on deaf ears.

My personal and guest appearances continued to be greatly limited and were dearly bought with endless conferences—any decision concerning the program brought protracted, dead-end discussions. But I did succeed in making four light-opera appearances for Palmolive.

During one of these rehearsals, Tom Revere of the Benton and Bowles agency asked me if there would ever be a possibility of doing a broadcast series for one of their clients. Though delighted that they wanted me, I hesitated in my answer, "Yes, but I don't think I would be happy in the future doing just one type of program." He seemed exhilarated at the prospect of inaugurating a movement away from the hidebound routine of radio.

"By golly," he said, "you've got something there. At least it's never been done and that's what we're looking for—originality. Boiled down, what would it mean?"

"Exciting programs in a series of five revolving broadcasts, including a light opera, a play with music, an original radio presentation, a condensed grand opera, a straight concert."

His curiosity aroused, Tom Revere led me on: "I remember your Philco series, the most outstanding light operas ever put on the air. They were believable and different. Let's talk about this some more?"

This was decidedly heartening reaction as against Cities Service's lethargic complacency in a time when change in radio expression was long overdue. If only I could have persuaded them to swim with the tide in one twelfth of the program, I would have felt we were not merely treading water.

Many times, as we sat about the conference table at our weekly program meetings, I repeated earnestly: "Gentlemen, however charming our program is, we must not coast on our laurels. If we want to keep our top rating we must work hard not to lapse into a deep, dull rut." Then, looking up at the blank faces, I realized I was casting my pearls before agency men. Before me loomed a long vista of stereotyped programs in which I would become more and more limited to formula.

Encouraged by Tom Revere's receptivity, I now went back to our Cities Service discussions resolved to take a new approach. We had a valuable asset in Frank Parker; here was another likely spot that would lend itself to dramatic effect.

Frank Parker was wonderful to work with. Our duets had caused quite a sensation; they were a rare experience in which the words of the song became the most subtle romance. Really living the story, we seemed to give each other the spark that electrified whatever we were singing. Since Frank was a definite drawing card, I felt he deserved more compensation than just his Revellers Quartet salary. This would have protected us from the possibility of his being lured elsewhere, but I was waved off with the usual budgetary excuses, and before long Frank left us for the Jack Benny program. Here was a time that Benny could be induced to be extravagant instead of penurious—and it paid off!

On one occasion, however, I was successful. At my contract renewal time, I persuaded Mr. Aylesworth to change his mind about replacing Rosario Bourdon.

"Why would you want to change such a fine music director, Mr. Aylesworth?" I asked. "You would have a hard time replacing him."

"A change is good, Jessica," he replied with his quick, smiling ebullience. "You know—sometimes just a little thing like walking around the block or wearing a mustache is good."

"Some things are not so simply solved," I said thoughtfully. "It takes more than a mustache to make a distinguished musician."

Rosario Bourdon remained our director until after I left the program, but I never forgot what Merlin Aylesworth said about change.

Meanwhile Nadea, guileless as to business intrigue, felt that I was giving my life to a lost cause—a situation where everybody's hands were tied. The solution really rested with me, had I not been too preoccupied and naïve to see it clearly as I do now, looking back. I am sure that had I gone over the heads of both George Engles and the agency man to Alton Jones, he would have personally seen to it that something was done.

Watching my consuming devotion to my work, Nadea tried her utmost to free me from this blind obsession lest I wreck my health. Although never my manager, she was closely associated with me as secretary and gave a good part of her life to my care and well-being.

Close to renewal time, re-reading my 1936 contract with Cities Service, she was startled by the omission of their option on my services for 1937. She pondered this—she could not believe it was an oversight. In any case, it did give her an opportunity of considering a change of program if I so desired, since the omission of the option left me free to seek other sponsors.

Frankly puzzled, Nadea failed to bring the matter promptly to my attention. It was likewise a delicate situation to handle with NBC. They professed to be delighted with my services, yet I learned that the Artists Bureau head, George Engles, who also acted as my NBC agent, was constantly auditioning other singers for my radio spot. The omission of the option could mean an undercover change of heart on the part of both NBC and Cities Service. In such huge organizations with many diversified aims, one was forever walking on eggs. Nadea worried about me constantly, hoping for a solution to the impasse.

George Engles, at this time a vice-president of NBC, joined the Artists Bureau in the early Thirties. This marked him as no Johnnie-come-lately to radio; however, we never felt he was "with it"—his career having matured in the concert field where he had managed established artists like Paderewski and Schumann-Heink. Perhaps because his department inherited my long-term contract, he took me for granted and evinced no enthusiastic interest to go to bat for me.

At contract renewal time, he would usually escort me to the door of the president's office. After a cordial greeting from Merlin Aylesworth, they would depart, leaving me with Alton Jones, Cities Service president, to work out our business arrangements. I remember the first time this occurred. Alone with Alton Jones, I did not know what to expect from such an important conference. If only George Engles had coached me how to conduct the interview!

"They have auditioned other voices for me—I must admit they sing well," Mr. Jones began tentatively, studying the effect of his words.

"Naturally there are many people who sing as well as I do. I doubt if they have my taste and experience," I ventured timidly.

"Oh, we like you very much," Mr. Jones hastened to reassure me.

Frightened at what might lie in ambush, I summoned what logic I could: "If I came to Wall Street, I would sit at your feet and learn, for I know nothing about business. But I do know something about music and what your audience wants to hear. The point of beginning is whether you like me and want me to continue on the program."

I remember that after this conference I was ill for several days lest I had said the wrong things to this outstanding Wall Street financier. A new contract was signed, and after the next broadcast Mr. Jones called me to tell me how much he enjoyed my singing.

It is understandable that a valuable client like Cities Service should take precedence with George Engles over an individual artist, but one did not expect to find an attitude of indifference and *laissez faire* from one's own representative.

The petroleum company was one of the clients brought to NBC by brilliant, dynamic Merlin Aylesworth, whose task it was in his early presidency days not only to help make broadcasting popular, but to seek clients for its support. He was, and still is, on the board of Cities Service. In the thick of the advertising agencies' advent into radio, NBC in turn bestowed the Cities Service account on the Lord and Thomas agency, presumably as a good-will gesture toward their chief, Albert Lasker, a powerful advertising tycoon. The slightest wishes of Cities Service were therefore paramount to every other consideration.

So close indeed was the bond between NBC and its oldest client that the idea of suggesting me on a different program was not only unthinkable but impossible for George Engles. And had I gone to him with Palmolive's offer, he would have lulled me with faint-hearted promises into accepting the *status quo*. There was no way of breaking the deadlock except by bold action on my part. It never occurred to me to seek outside advice, for I was accustomed to acting independently. From the beginning my training at NBC had encouraged this bent, since we were all involved in a pioneering job.

On the other hand, with the omission of the option in the 1937 contract, I was free to listen to the ardent wooing of Palmolive. There would be no long-drawn-out negotiations they assured me: the contract was ready and waiting for me to sign. It included the new revolving program cycle with which Tom Revere was so taken and an arbitrary salary of $2,500 a broadcast that they themselves stipulated. Moreover, Palmolive would give me a more extensive network, while Cities Service had abandoned its coast stations, a disappointment to devoted listeners in Los Angeles, San Francisco, Portland, and Seattle who had to get me by way of Denver or by short wave.

Now that the decision to change my sponsor was imminent and unavoidable, I hesitated. A terrified sense of foreboding and portent that I construed as natural timidity oppressed me. Had I become so rigid, so crystallized that I could not change? Had the climate in which I was working so choked my exploratory impulses that I was rendered immobile? Had I become the very antithesis of what an artist should be in heart and mind, supple enough to snare fugitive beauty in the gossamer thread of song?

Was it better to please Cities Service in a narrow canvas or to accept the challenge from Palmolive that could mean triumph—or failure? Should I leave my beloved and gifted associates for the untried? My outward actions in no way betrayed the inward turmoil of my thoughts.

Finally, after a few weeks of deliberation, I decided to take the plunge, whatever the outcome. Nothing that I could gain by remaining steadfast and stationary could ever compensate for a lack of flexibility. Even if I lost everything, the self-discipline of a new beginning was worth the risk. I was thrilled at the prospect of having my own program, trying out a variety of entertainment that had never been done in radio. I set another goal for myself beyond the blue horizon. "To seek, to strive, to find, and not to yield."

Reviewing my seven years with Cities Service, I saw them pass like a day. So possessed with the music had I been that I was oblivious of the passage of time. Nor could my brain admit any possible deception around me. During the years of broadcasting many programs, every executive of NBC had at some time attended with family, sponsors, or clients. Since they were manifestly cordial, it never occurred to me I was not among friends. Nor could I foresee a time when I should not be welcome freely to discuss any problems that might arise. True, I had never gone to them to make a nuisance of myself. Besides, in the setup, George Engles was directly concerned with my activities. I had never suspected for a moment the contemplated program would not be emanating from NBC. Therefore, knowing the value of well-timed announcement, I gave ready consent to the request of Palmolive not to divulge prematurely their plans.

One Cities Service broadcast day Nadea announced quite simply to George Engles: "Jessica will not be available for a Cities Service renewal."

He received the news with startled amazement: "Why, what do you mean? What about our option?"

"You have no option in the contract, Mr. Engles," Nadea replied.

"Oh, you're mistaken. We always have an option."

He summoned his secretary to bring the Dragonette contract from the files. He opened the folder, spreading the pages on his desk; and, running his pencil down the printed lines, he stopped short at a paragraph. It was not only unbelievable but downright embarrassing to find the option missing.

"This is definitely an oversight, Mrs. Loftus," George Engles gasped, and picking up the telephone he summoned Mr. S—— from Studio 8H, where our Cities Service rehearsal was in progress. "Why doesn't Jessica want to continue?" he went on.

"She feels this is the moment to do something different again in radio," answered Nadea quietly.

Mr. Engles looked up childlike and guileless. "There's no reason why she can't do all those things on the Cities Service program."

Nadea was flabbergasted. "But Mr. Engles, Jessica has only been asking for seven years!" Then she added, "She is not just accepting any contract from any sponsor, but one who will allow her to do a unique type of program. Besides, Jessica insisted upon conditions that would allow her to give Cities Service more notice than her contract requires. This absolves you, Mr. Engles, from the obligation of instigating a change for her. Which, don't you remember, you told me you could not do?"

Momentarily the shift of responsibility placated him. But complete consternation broke through the iron stolidity of Mr. S——, as he stood listening. It had taken six years to penetrate his placid imperviousness. As agency representative of his client Cities Service, leaving out the option was an unpardonable oversight on his part. At his utter bewilderment, Nadea began to think that Cities Service's failure to catch the omission was due to routine—my contract, long-termed and in the main unvarying from year to year, could not have been closely examined.

"Why should Jessica want to leave a program that is going so smoothly?" he asked. "You never should break up a winning team, I can't believe she'd be fool enough." Then, turning to Nadea, he added vehemently, "I'm supposed to protect my client, y'know. Why didn't you speak up about that option earlier?"

Genuinely sympathetic over their dilemma, Nadea volunteered, "How could I know it wasn't intentional? There are always rumors. . . . Gentlemen, what can I do to make it easier for you?"

Both men jumped at her offer and said in one breath: "Go to see Sheldon Coons, vice-president of Lord and Thomas!"

The unsuspecting Nadea was being used as a catspaw to pull their chestnuts out of the fire. George Engles was up to his old tricks. In radio, as in farce, every trick is legitimate, if you can get away with it. Our hands were tied, while theirs were free. Broadcasting that day, I needed Nadea's help, but she dropped everything and foolishly went to the assistance of the gentlemen in distress.

Neither of us had ever met Sheldon Coons. Tall, dark and dour, he received Nadea with smooth Oriental deference. He salaamed and proceeded to give her the greatest encomiums and admiration for my singing.

Before she could tell the purpose of her visit he said: "Whatever offers have been made to Miss Dragonette, Cities Service will top them. And anything she wishes to do on the program, Cities Service will gladly consider." Nadea was rooted to the spot in dumb amazement. No doubt George Engles had already apprised Mr. Coons by telephone of what to expect.

"But, Mr. Coons," she stammered, "Jessica has been pleading for little things for so long. Why this sudden turnabout? It was not a question of money, but an ideal program."

Then taking another tack, Mr. Coons apologized for having been ignorant of program problems. With every persuasion at his command, he urged that Jessica Dragonette remain with Cities Service.

Nadea, hard put to it, summoned her last remnants of strength and barely managed to say: "It is too late to turn back, Mr. Coons. A contract has already been signed."

Mr. Coons' whole manner changed. He revealed his hand, showing he was conversant not only with the new plans, but also with the new sponsor, Palmolive. This was a blow to Nadea, since we had been sworn to secrecy by the Benton and Bowles agency. Only now a pattern seems to emerge. For years I have felt like a pursued Liza, tantalized by the question of the "Closed Doors." It is possible that even then, as today, Sheldon Coons may have been part of a consulting board for NBC. Not long ago I learned that at that time he had close business relations with both Cities Service and Palmolive. Therefore, I have never understood why Mr. Coons was interested in intensifying rather than mediating the issue between these two companies, as it is obvious that a conference of all parties to the controversy would surely have resulted in an easy solution to the difficulty and might have entirely averted the "great misunderstanding."

"The whole Lord and Thomas organization are tensely awaiting the outcome of this conference over Dragonette," he added, trying to arouse her sympathy. "What's more, they are counting on my ability to convince you that Jessica cannot, must not, leave Cities Service."

The die was cast in the signing of the new contract. Nadea could not retract. Yet Mr. Coons' belated revelations were difficult to plumb.

Nadea barely recovered her composure when he veered again: "Suppose the new program fails? Suppose the promised changes you dream about cannot be realized?"

"Jessica has faced that possibility. She is prepared for failure rather than retreat."

The interview was over. Mr. Coons drew himself up to his full height and walked to the door with my collapsing sister. There, with sinister impact, he flung the gauntlet, the cabalistic words: "Good day, Mrs. Loftus. *We shall see what we shall see!*"

Nadea, worn and white, arrived home with barely enough time to prepare for the broadcast. She told me nothing then, but I felt a pall in the air. That evening, as I sang "Sweet Mystery of Life" and Mimi's "Addio" from *La Bohème*, I could feel the old sense of foreboding. Years later my sister told me that with every throb of the music and loudest when the orchestra played, Mr. Coons' words were beating themselves in her brain: *"We shall see what we shall see!"*

After the program I gave many autographs, welcoming my friends as usual, among them the R. A. McClelland family, fans of long standing who had driven all the way from Indiana. Despondently they told me they had arrived one minute too late for the broadcast and were closed out. They stood in the hall, their ears pressed to the heavy doors to catch any outfiltering strains of the music. Their disappointment added to my distress. I knew the strict rule of locking the studio five minutes before a broadcast and how important it is. Still I felt an exception should have been made. How heartless and callous that these faithful friends who had driven so far should not have been admitted. The barring of the doors inauspiciously sealed the culminating events of the day.

Mr. McClelland, much moved at my concern, tried to comfort me as we said our good-night farewells: "I have made an electrical organ in appreciation for all the songs you have given us. In a few days it will be on its way to you, and when your fingers move over the mother-of-pearl keys to make musical accompaniment to your singing, I hope you will think of the McClelland family far away who love you very much."

Neither Nadea nor I slept that night, but talked and walked the floors until by morning we knew that some Machiavellian hand had set mischief in motion. To save face, NBC and Cities Service took advantage by jumping the gun and going to press first. My unlisted telephone rang constantly. The newspapers were all asking why

Cities Service was dispensing with me and why NBC had sent this nonsensical statement to the press.

Apparently Nadea's conferences with both George Engles and Sheldon Coons were variously interpreted; these inaccuracies, like contaminating pollen, fastened in many minds and someone of importance made the most of publicity license. I could not explain my position, having been sworn to secrecy by Benton and Bowles. We were astounded. We knew nothing about any release. Nor were we prepared in any way to meet the unexpected blow. In that all-consuming race to beat the rival sponsor and punish me, they tried to destroy all that I had been building for more than a decade.

Burke Miller of the NBC press department called me first: "What's the low-down on this bombshell that has just come out of press—we're all dumbfounded!"

"What do you mean?" I asked innocently.

"How can you be so composed?" he hurried on with annoyance. "Haven't you seen the release?"

"No, I haven't—what does it say?"

"It says Cities Service is letting you go because the public wants new talent"—he broke off—"How can you take this lying down?"

"I can't talk now," I replied. "Why don't you wait to hear my future plans?"

But the tentacles had fastened. My silence convinced him more firmly of the truth of the release.

"You certainly are a trouper," he commented sadly. "I congratulate you on the way you take it on the chin."

I was outraged at this treatment. I immediately tried to contact George Engles; Lenox Lohr, president of NBC; John Royal, vice-president; Alton Jones, president of Cities Service; but every door was closed to me. No one would so much as give me an appointment nor even speak to me on the telephone.

Years later I was told that once Nadea gave George Engles the news about not taking up my Cities Service option, he called a special meeting of the NBC executives. He told them Nadea had gone directly to Cities Service and asked for so much money they simply could not meet the demand and, therefore, decided not to sign me for the following year. Furthermore, "pulling a fast one," she had bulldozed Palmolive into tying me up quickly, in order to cover the fact that Cities Service was letting me go.

The obvious next step would be to make Palmolive feel exceedingly stupid in paying double the amount I was currently receiving. Mr. Coons and Mr. Engles might well have sat back at this juncture with the thought that having sown the wind they would inevitably reap the whirlwind.

By her foolish, generous gesture in going to Mr. Coons, Nadea had put the instruments of revenge in his hands. He would thwart the new program idea at every turn by convincing Tom Revere that he had gone overboard, involving his client in unnecessary extravagance by paying a single artist such a high salary, then surrounding her with an expensive production. Tom Revere began to feel a lessening enthusiasm over what he had considered a grand coup, for now he was made to believe that it was in reality a bad bargain.

All this is at long last clear to me; then it was shrouded in mystery because I could not conceive such diabolical plotting. There was not another major performer in radio who had not changed sponsors—often as much as half-a-dozen times—Ed Wynn, Jack Benny, Kate Smith, Jack Pearl, Rudy Vallee. Why should I have caused such a tempest? Every renewed effort to reach someone in authority at NBC came to naught. The doors were never opened.

Meanwhile the radio editors over the country consigned the release to the wastebasket. Fans and fan clubs threatened to boycott radio and Cities Service unless I returned. Later they demonstrated their loyalty in a different way: in Minneapolis 15,000 people ignored a taxi strike and a blizzard to hear me sing, and an audience of 150,000 attended a concert at Grant Park when I appeared as soloist.

After auditioning so many artists for the coveted Cities Service spot, it was ironical that George Engles should have been found empty-handed at the crucial moment. As a last resort, he chose one of his sustaining program singers whose contract had been languishing for five years. In his feverish urge to shift the responsibility for having been caught napping and to discredit me in the public eye, the incongruity of the following press release had never occurred to him: "Some extensive surveys and one of the most thorough coincidental checks of the radio audience ever made by a sponsor had indicated a desire for new personalities. . . ."

The ridiculousness of this false pronouncement was further emphasized; only a few weeks prior John Royal had come to me in Studio 8H and announced: "Do you know according to the most recent surveys, that 66,000,000 people listen to you?" As they say on Broadway, "Who's kidding who?"

Since I could not reach Mr. Jones, I wrote him about the resentment of my radio listeners and newspaper friends. In my innocence I even offered to introduce the new singer as my friend and announce I was changing my sponsor in order to give more varied entertainment. This, I claimed, would make for good will toward Cities Service, assuaging the rancor kicked up among listeners. Mr. Jones implicitly believed I had made the change for monetary reasons, yet he saw the advantage of my gesture. He took occasion to soothe my embarrassment and distress over the NBC press release with the indifferent comment, "As I read the announcement in the light of your feeling, I agree that it is not in good taste."

Later, however, he rallied more strongly:

In order that there may be no question in the public mind about how the Company feels as to your leaving the program, I shall personally see to it that suitable announcement is made at such time as is appropriate, expressing the deep regret of the Company at your leaving, and wishing you every success in your new broader field of endeavor. I shall also take steps to see that suitable arrangements are made so that your adieu to your audience may be under the most pleasant auspices, and that the introduction of Miss —— will be as you would like to have it.

There was vindication in Mr. Jones's letter, but nothing could make up for his not seeing me personally. I do not blame him in the light of all that later became revealed. My thrust is: until that time when *he* had business to discuss, he always managed to confer with me.

I had worked ten years for NBC and seven for Cities Service. It broke my heart to realize that every supposed friend had deserted me and fallen into the trap of intrigue. The tumult and the shouting continued unabated, during which time I never gave an explanation to the press, so sure was I that I would be cleared of the great misunderstanding which had arisen between NBC and me. No attempt to clear it up was ever made.

The press department took a logically intelligent position, when they were called in after the rumpus of the "release." One member of the staff pointed out how impractical it was to discredit an outstanding artist, who alone with Kate Smith had maintained the feminine lead in popularity. He voiced the wishes of the 30,000 workers of Cities Service. At my leave-taking they presented me with a seven-sided plaque for

seven years of loyal and distinguished service—seven years of devotion to the interests of Cities Service—seven years marked by ever new heights of broadcasting artistry—as a tribute to warm and friendly associations and in sincere appreciation of the work of a truly great artist. . . .

With her flaming sense of the injustice that had been done, Nadea thought it was a case for suit against the offending parties, but with my incurable optimism I firmly believed the situation would be cleared, that in due course NBC would realize I was not leaving them; they could also profit from the valuable asset of my new program, designed to carry radio entertainment to further heights.

One shock was hardly allayed when another followed: I learned that the Palmolive programs would emanate from CBS! Was this the reason Benton and Bowles swore me to secrecy? Or, in reprisal for my action, did NBC refuse to give them time? Try and try again as I have repeatedly, the answers to these questions remain a mystery.

So perfect was the propaganda plan to disparage me that the fabrications exist to this day in radio and agency circles. Recently, I talked to one NBC executive whom I knew well in the old days and asked his help in securing source material. He was clearly antagonistic. Holding his hand up like a traffic cop, he almost forbade me to refer to the incident of my leaving NBC. I sat quietly patient while he recounted his version of the tale. In essence it hewed to the error line.

"You began to believe your own publicity," he stated coldly.

"What publicity?" I asked in astonishment. "The washed-out drivel about me? Come now, if I were a Hollywood star, the ballyhoo might encourage a swelled head."

Suddenly he was struck with the absurdity of the idea. "Well, anyway," he said, "if you are writing anything controversial, be sure you do not hint, infer, nor insinuate anything detrimental to NBC."

I assured him that such was not my purpose, that it would be nice to set the record straight once and for all. Only then did he listen to my side of the story. When I had finished, he was speechless.

Powerful indeed is the empire of habit. Leaving the microphones of NBC, I felt the nostalgic homesickness of a loyal citizen departing from his native land. The psychosomatic result of all this appalling disillusionment was a shattering illness that confined me to bed. For the first time in my career, I was forced to cancel an engagement of utmost importance—the opening of the new Palmolive Beauty Box Series.

Propped up on my pillows, I listened to Lanny Ross graciously pinch-hitting for me, singing like a gay troubadour, and wishing me an early return. Baskets and bouquets of flowers from all parts of the country transformed my home into a bower of roses, pink, red, yellow, and creamy white. These lovely messengers brought not only a measure of healing with them, a respite from heartache; they were a cloud of witnesses to the affectionate devotion of countless air friends. I was no longer alone nor forsaken. I had been dwelling in the dust, but they were waiting to hear me. Now I must awake and sing!

CHAPTER 15

"BEAUTIFUL DREAMER"

In a daze I entered the CBS Playhouse No. 2 on Forty-fifth Street. It was not quite ready for broadcasting, having been recently reconverted from a Broadway theater. The engineers were still improvising with its suitability for radioed sound. It was Tuesday already, and I was barely acquainted with the tentative line-up of the music and the rough script. On the Sunday before, Kenneth MacGregor, my new director on the Beauty Box Theater, whisked the scenario away after a brief run-through, as it had to be worked over by the writers. Likewise, Al Goodman, our musical director, gave me a teetering idea of the possible order of the musical numbers of the score in hand. "Since the show will be only a half hour instead of an hour, we can't hope to do very much," he said.

Although I was conversant with most of the light operas we were likely to present, I was not prepared to be completely illogical concerning their musical sequence. In reviewing *The Merry Widow* score with Al Goodman, for example, he found nothing at all strange about transposing the Merry Widow's entrance song, "I haven't been in Paris long," making it the finale of the operetta. Of course, this threw the whole story out of joint, if we were to have any semblance of the original. When I balked at this incongruity, he didn't take it kindly.

"You're the only prima donna we have ever catered to," he said condescendingly. "This is definitely against agency policy." Intent on rescuing the character from disintegration, I let this conundrum pass without comment.

The Tuesday rehearsal was supposed to be the "first dress." The orchestra was assembled in the middle of the stage, the chorus on one side, the actors and singers on the other; and milling around were the announcer Jean Paul King, the conductor, director, CBS contact man, the Benton and Bowles account executive, and the busy engineers. In the dark cavern of the theater, beyond the stage, sat an indistinguishable group of people.

Everyone received me cordially: "Why, you don't look ill; you look fresh as a daisy. Are you sure you weren't playing possum?"

It was consoling to know I didn't look as if I were wearing my heart on my sleeve, for what was going on in that hidden chamber of my being was no one's affair. There were countless interruptions in the "dress" rehearsal. The orchestra occupying the center of the stage, with its sectional microphones, was constantly being rearranged; the actors and singers almost in the wings on one side and the chorus directly opposite made for confusing traffic around the mikes. Raising and lowering of the microphones to accommodate, first, the speaking level of the actors, then the level of the wider range of the singing personnel, created almost insurmountable problems. Further confusion ensued because I was the only one who spoke and sang. After the rehearsal run-through we discovered we had a full hour's show. Then right and left the slashing of the script began.

Up to this minute I didn't have a leading-man singer for the Wednesday show. I had only a leading-man actor in the person of Richard Kollmar. The unruddered sailing almost unnerved me—the constant manipulation of the draperies in the theater, the disparaging remarks of the engineers: "This theater is a jinx; no good for broadcasting. We've done everything to deaden the overtone; it still isn't right."

The whole cluttered-up atmosphere made me feel faint. I longed for my old studio 8H in Radio City—that bare, clean ocean liner, presided over by the able, conscientious, supreme Frank Williams. He was testing every second during the program. His ear, acute as a sea captain's eye, was aware of the least atmospheric variation, of extraneous noise that might blemish the clear sound. With Williams we had long since done away with that abominable "mixing" practice. We broadcast the large orchestra of forty-five men, singers, and quartet through one microphone. There was no other way the listeners could receive the music with even sharpness and purity.

I never saw or talked to the writers of our Palmolive shows, but now the directors were cutting the script, which was bad from start to finish. For the past ten years I had been experimenting with a form, a form of its own for this young art—this child of the century; its heart, I was convinced, was somewhere between the tautness of the short story and the clarity of the movie scenario.

The agency boys, who were also feeling their way, had evidently sold me a bill of goods, and it gradually dawned on me they were more interested in publicity than good entertainment per se. Not a word that I said about the five-pointed program series was understood. My "sweet talk" was misinterpreted as a quality of voice the sponsor found enchanting in the acting lines of *New Moon*—a prebroadcast transcription. If it was so attractive to the client, they reasoned, why beat their brains out with what I wanted?

They were buying a personality with a great following. Therefore, the positive original mind I brought to the situation made me suspect and was overshadowed by coverage in the papers, by my picture on the front of the *Daily News*—that good "over six million circulation."

My fervor was dissipated instead of utilized to good advantage; my high-keyed affectable romanticism, congenial to the immediacy of radio, was lost on them; and my impetus could reach no other positive congenial mind. They missed completely the impact of my dedication: that radio might have something of its own. Was this, then, the endeavor, the ideal program for which I had fought and died?

They stood about, staring at me as if I were some lost, bewildered child. They eyed one another for reassurance in their idiotic procedures; they went searching into tradition. They listened to other broadcasts and reacted with copycat antics. Even here they were trying to keep up with the Joneses! They looked for precedent right and left—for any possible excuse, and finally settled for the operettas in condensed form—an old form that rattled around like little buildings on a grand scale, an obsolete form completely unsuitable to radio.

I tried to imagine myself an oyster in this system of irritations; the future would tell whether I could raise a pearl. What I had done so far in radio had invited imitation. In this venture upon which I had staked so much, I could see nothing ahead but a dead end!

In the five-minute orchestra break, I sat apart disconsolate, among the *longueurs* of trial and error. Somebody in the control room back of me said: "Who's the blonde?" And it set in motion in my head all that somebody said, the crazy merry-go-round of gossip:

"Is that Dragonette? How does she feel on this new program? Kind of pretty. Is it true she was replaced by Cities Service? She was really a fool to leave the spot where the audience knew just where to find her. Fool? Whadda ya mean? Who's a fool to grab a fast $2,500 per? Nice goin' at that. She started as a school kid at $25 a broadcast. She's the only one so far who's made radio. And, of course, radio's made her. It's been her proving ground. She doesn't seem commercial, but yuh never can tell. Why'n't she get in the Met, instead of spendin' all her time in radio? She could uv gone 'round the country, too, and cleaned up. Why should she hide her light under a radio bushel all this time? It's the biggest crap game in the world. D'you think she really likes this program? For my money it doesn't seem to give her enough scope. I dunno. It's the comedian wanting to play Hamlet, I guess. Why the hell does she bother? I wouldn't if I had the money she's made. I'd get married and forget it. Her voice is certainly beautiful. Too virginal, I think. Maybe I'm prejudiced because she's been a headache to a lotta nice boys. So-and-so is crazy about her; when she refused to marry him, he suggested they live together. She threw him out, he told me, her eyes blazing like a wild tigress's. She flung the words after him: 'I'm no public playground, thank you.' She doesn't seem so high and mighty. Talks soft as a kitten. But then you never can tell about women. So-and-so has tried to break her down for years, to catch her unaware. She sounds human enough when she sings, but when you meet her—always that starched apron approach. However you take it, NBC's farewell to her was kinda shabby. Yeh, but don't forget that fast 2,500 berries."

Suddenly there was a flutter of entrance. The account executive got up, and Al Goodman was all smiles to meet a dashing, young, ruddy-complexioned man. He was coming up the stage steps, followed by Paul Lewis and Austin Wilder of the Columbia Concerts Bureau, their publicity woman, Constance Hope, and a secretary. I soon learned he was to be my singer-leading man. A tenor from the Metropolitan Opera and lately an idol in Vienna, he was natural and likable; things brightened considerably for me. He was an American, a graduate of Yale—Charles Kullman.

I found Charles a responsive and willing colleague. Yet it was apparent that his beautiful, brilliant voice had been trained to opera projection and there would not be time to make a shift to the unprojected technique suitable to radio presentation. The engineers tried their best with the single overhanging mike in the front of the stage. But this was soon abandoned because it set up a kind of marathon race back to the microphones so he would be in place for the sequence of the speaking lines and the duets we sang together.

It is amusing now, to consider how little care was taken to match Kullman's singing voice with a comparable speaking one in an actor; or why he was never asked to speak his own lines, which I know he can do very well. Consequently, one week he would sing to the spoken lines of a decidedly English actor or another week sing to the spoken baritone pitch of Richard Kollmar. It didn't seem to bother the script writers; our operetta series was only one of the many "shows" they had to turn out quickly for their agency. The same was true of the director. It was all part of the period pressure.

The writers were compelled to follow the course of least resistance. Lulled into an illusion of creating they would string words together to introduce a song, and as relief and scene endings they interspersed copious door slams. I made up a rhyme about them:

> Eenie meenie miney more
> When in doubt you slam a door!

This fake procedure gave me the jitters, and I wrote a whole portfolio of letters to Tom Revere complaining about the door slams, the hard-to-swallow, lumbering, down-to-earth explanations of the simplest actions. Did they think listeners had no imagination at all? But the sparks from my long experience were snuffed out. Many times, Tom Revere didn't even bother to answer the letters.

Meanwhile, the actors were focused on their theatrical ambitions; the singers, Charles Kullman, later Robert Weede, Thomas L. Thomas, and Jan Peerce, had other fish to fry; they were opera bound. Their excursions into radio were by courtesy of managers to increase their popularity. There was an element of inconsistency in confining these operatic voices to operettas alone, especially those with limited singing roles. They would have shown brilliantly to advantage in the five-pointed series we thought we were going to have. Sometimes my heart ached for them as well as myself.

"It is too late to kick when one has let himself be shackled," as Montaigne points out. Looking back I wonder how, in the midst of this heartbreaking disappointment, the pressure, the absurd crowding around the mike, the break in the rhythm of the personality playing opposite me, I could manage to forget everything when I stood before the instrument to broadcast and become the character I was playing. It is true I said my accustomed dedication just as I had always done before performing, inspired by my school-days' portrayal of *The Little Juggler:* "Dear Lord, I offer this *divertissement* for Your pleasure." Away from the microphone, however, I was bogged down. With the best intentions in the world as far as radio art was concerned, I was retrogressing rather than progressing. No one knew how to handle this expensive array of craft and talent, nor how to give a keel to his gigantic sailing fantasy.

For the Easter program, the agency decided Kullman and I should do a concert, singing operatic selections and songs appropriate to the season—the *Thais* "Meditation," Bach-Gounod "Ave Maria," "Connais-tu le pays?" Walter's "Prize Song," and Bizet's "Agnus Dei."

Kenneth MacGregor was called off this program as director and Herschel Williams, who knew absolutely nothing about music, was unleashed upon us to frisk about with utter nonsense. At the last dress rehearsal, on Wednesday afternoon, he decided it would be a good idea to sing the arias in English, since the audience was not foreign. The American public had only been listening to all kinds of music for ten years; even if they didn't understand every word of the arias, they knew their operas as well as anybody. But to Herschel Williams, up from the deep South with playwright ambitions, radio was a detour. He was too handsome for comparison with the bull in the china closet, but his touch upon the program had the same effect. Outside of "timing," he was decidedly *de trop* on such a program. He stormed about theatrically like a ham impresario, screwing up his face, awkwardly forming the drawling words on his petulant lips, expending himself in small change.

Because I was a successful singer, I would never again have the opportunity of experimenting with radio forms. This privilege would be saved for others. Three years later, my ambitions were fulfilled in Orson Welles, Norman Corwin, and Arch Oboler, while I was repeating myself on the Ford Hour.

The day Herschel Williams took over as director there was more fuss and last-minute change than ever. Instead of concentrating on the right setup, he had a tantrum. Then when he read the indifferent radio reviews next day, he looked for a peg on which to hang his peeve. Nadea was adjacent to him in the control room at the first rehearsal. It was helpful to me to have someone there who knew my voice, for I was among strange engineers and I was unaccustomed to the low mike setup in use. The sound men found her helpful, too, and all was congenial until Mr. Williams became vehemently temperamental. With a dramatic gesture he ordered her out of the control room.

This new threat to peace of mind was alarming; for he complained about Nadea, not only to the Benton and Bowles agency, but to the CBS representative as well, that her presence inhibited his working effectively. However, I took the situation more seriously than it warranted, for, when I arrived at the next rehearsal, the director was neither Herschel Williams nor Kenneth MacGregor, but Donald Cope! MacGregor, though not the expert director he is today, at that time had a broad base of experience. He was quick, sympathetic, and clever. When I frantically inquired of the agency why he had been removed after we were rolling, they did not even bother to answer.

All these years I have wondered about the unsolved mystery, and buttonholing MacGregor the other day, I decided to ask him point-blank. "Maybe you can tell me now, Mac, why you were removed from the Palmolive Beauty Box."

"I dunno." He shot a quizzical look at me. "If you didn't ask for my removal, then it was just simple agency policy." He shot his hands into the air.

"Simple as—? How could I ask for you to be removed, at the same time I was begging Tom Revere to send you back?"

"I dunno." He gave me that canny Scotch look again. "After all, remember how you asked to have me removed from Cities Service when I was first assigned to the program?"

"I asked to have you removed?" I questioned. "Well, this beats everything." Here it was all over again, I was thinking—the double talk and passing the buck!

"Well, that's what Mr. S—— told me, and I've hated you for it for fifteen years."

"If that's true, how do you account for my fighting so hard to get you back after you left Cities Service, that you were reassigned to us? Remember my speaking into the mike: 'You see, Mr. MacGregor, we couldn't get along without you.'"

"I've never forgotten how beautifully you handled the whole thing," Mac said, "with your everlasting politeness."

I looked at him in resigned numbness. "Well, one thing at a time, let's get back to Palmolive. Maybe you'll believe me if I show you the letter I sent to Tom Revere."

"I do believe you now," he conceded, "and I'm sorry I never spoke out about it before." And bending down, he kissed me affectionately on the cheek. "Forgive me, please forgive me."

Tom Revere continued to ignore my request for Kenneth Mac-Gregor as director, and Don Cope led us further through the mirror maze of bad scripts. My bare, alert senses were screaming at the cold-blooded tactics of the agency, it was no use to complain—they reserved the right to do as they deemed best. I was a resistance of one, crying in the wilderness, but I persevered in creating an atmosphere, working to make every word, every song count in the narrative, rejecting the extraneous, seizing the spontaneous moment to intensify the dramatic effect. Out of the thunder of this inordinate time, and at the cost of no little pain, we gradually found our way by a new map, and the half hour operetta versions became faceted little gems: *Merry Widow, Countess Maritza, Count of Luxembourg, Land of Smiles, Rogue Song, Pink Lady, Mme. Pompadour, Rio Rita, Student Prince, Irene, New Moon, Blue Paradise, Vagabond King, Red Mill, Princess Pat, Sweethearts, Prince of Pilsen, Sari, Waltz Dream, Three Musketeers, My Maryland, Chocolate Soldier, Dream Girl, Dearest Enemy, Blossom Time, Naughty Marietta, Only Girl, Maytime, Eileen, Lady in Ermine, Bitter Sweet, Robin Hood, Mlle. Modiste.* The critics and audiences alike enjoyed and praised them. Ben Gross of the *Daily News*, dean of radio critics, regularly rated us "***out of any editor's supply of twinklers." Fans wrote that their wish of hearing the musical productions was coming true.

Beyond the two original programs and the Easter concert concession, the five-pointed series was never mentioned again. Moreover, the agency acted as if they had never heard of it. The multitudinous fan mail was construed as proof positive of the wisdom of their choice to stick to the operetta format; regardless of my contract and the three-year exclusive clause they exacted of me, they were relentless in their determination to remain on the single track.

Many listeners asked for an hour's program because they missed the arias, classical, Spanish, and sacred songs they were accustomed to hearing me sing. But it was no use. While the letters were tabulated and resealed, they were only important because they measured listener response to the program. I felt my own heart under the press with them. This was the first time my mail had been opened by alien hands. These letters were dear to me, and it seemed a violation of intimate confidences. Like X-ray reports, they told me the throbbing inside story of countless American homes in remote places —and everywhere. They told me how much people depended on me for beauty, inspiration, faith, and friendship, after their work was done, during family illness, rearing of children, and almost every activity of daily living.

I contained my high-voltage current as best I could through this stormy, frustrating passage. Sometimes I had forcibly to cast out the program worry from my mind, and I tried to walk it off. One afternoon, Leonardo of the faithful regiment took me to Central Park. We roamed until we were tired, then turned into the children's playground for a little rest. I unconsciously went to the seesaw. Leonardo, over six feet tall, played at sitting on the opposite end of the board, while I teetered on the other. It was dusk, and the evening star and Jupiter were already in the heavens. The noisy city lay in the deep, dim distance beyond the high, wired wall. I sat there, soothed by the hushed surrounding of the amethyst evening.

Leonardo's voice broke the spell: "Angelita, don't you think we'd better go? It's getting late."

Leonardo's gentleness was always surprising, for it did not match his athletic appearance. He had known me a long time, and having dedications of his own, he fancied himself half slave, half guardian, and signed himself "*Su esclavo.*" One of the many interests we had in common was Spanish, and for that Iberian world we had renamed each other.

Obediently I rose and followed him to the gate. When we reached it, we found it locked! This was a nice fix. Doomed for the night, in the children's playground in Central Park! Leonardo, long and slim, a fullback at Yale, couldn't wiggle his snake hips through the open wedge of the twin-doored gate. What to do? They would be sending an alarm out for me soon, and it would certainly be embarrassing to be caught in this predicament. I peered through the high-wire fence into the distance, and at a transection of the park I could see the traffic cop. Maybe Leonardo could act like a cheer leader; he began calling out: "Hi-Hay! Yeh-heh—heh, ho there!" It wasn't easy, for yelling was not Leonardo's forte—he was no Metropolitan basso. Finally the policeman heard the noises, tracked them down, and found us.

I was shamefaced, as he put his key in the lock and released us from the closed garden. After a hasty thank-you, I tried to run away —but nothing doing. He had to make his report. That is how the newspapers got a morning headline:

OF ALL PLACES

Jessica Dragonette and a tall companion were locked in the playground in Central Park last night. What will the press agents think of next?

Meanwhile the silent group around Charles Kullman began talking to me, whenever a respite in the rehearsal afforded them an opportunity. The music hiatus was a change of gear, in which I looked forward to chatting with Constance Hope. She was warm and amusing, a mistress of small talk.

Paul Lewis, generally quiet, became boisterously alive once, as he patted his hand up under Kullman's chin. "Better look to that, old man. That sag won't be good for the movies. See how trim the little lady is."

Charles retorted good-naturedly: "Oh, come on, I'm still a very young man, but I'll see what I can do."

Austin Wilder was more gentle spoken, yet insistent: "With your large following, Miss Dragonette, you would have a ready-made audience in forty-eight states. You ought to do a tour, and Columbia Concerts Bureau are the ones who can best plan it for you."

Meanwhile the "Great Love Stories" appealed to Benton and Bowles, and in their releases they used the parallel I suggested between the greatest teller of tales, Scheherazade, and myself, as mistress of ceremonies of the Beauty Box operettas. The public was the Sultan and the twist of the dial, the fateful sword.

In the hope of further expanding the idea, in the first weeks of Palmolive, the Benton and Bowles publicity office sent a beautiful, dark girl to see me. Helen Strauss hardly sat down in my apartment when she began to feel ill. I saw her sensitive face grow pale and I hastily brought her a glass of claret before we went on with the interview. As she lay quietly on the couch in the living room, she began to reminisce slowly:

"I have seen you before, Jessica. Once when you were walking on Fifth Avenue, all dressed in gray, and I thought you looked more beautiful than when you are dressed in those four hundred-dollar singing gowns. I was with Rosalind Green and as we passed, Ros said: 'There goes a completely dedicated person. That's Jessica Dragonette.'"

"I'm happy you mentioned Rosalind Green," I replied. "We both made our auditions for the Coca-Cola girl in 1927. Her beautiful speaking voice would have won her the part, but the sponsors wanted someone to sing as well as act. I've always treasured what Rosalind said to me that day: 'Jessica, I'm so happy you're to be Vivian. I don't think I could feel this way if it were anybody else.'"

Palmolive was only one of the fourteen Benton and Bowles programs their busy city editor, Helen Strauss, publicized. Though she was unacquainted with the overcharged goings-on about us, she was nevertheless under the same prevailing pressures that finally broke her health, and she had to leave shortly after we were under way. Once she asked me to go with her to Brooks, the costumer, to select appropriate operetta costumes in which to be photographed for her forthcoming releases on our "Great Love Stories" presentations. What scenes and actors these costumes evoked! I could see the faces on all the flyleaves of my light opera scores: Fritzi Scheff, Donald Brian, Fred Stone, Ina Claire, Edward Johnson, Mitzi Hajos, and many others.

Helen Strauss worked hard under stress, yet there was not visible about her the general frenzy—she was cool, calm, apart—like a Chinese goddess. We became friends and at the musicale at Georgian Court, that May, we made plans to meet her friend Mary Chase, who was working on a charming fantasy that turned out to be *Harvey*. But there was never time and the next thing we knew, Helen had gone away to regain her strength. During her convalescence she turned to her own writing and her own love story. She is now the wife of the actor, Fred Cotton.

That year on St. Valentine's Day, I was voted America's Radio Sweetheart, and a valentine company sent me a six-by-four-foot valentine, the largest ever designed. The Western Union Telegraph Company also sent a singing boy with a special message from all the employees: "Happy Birthday to our Sweetheart, Jessica Dragonette." Along with thousands of other greetings, Jack Benny another Valentine's Day child, sent me some original lines:

> Roses are red, violets are blue,
> February has me and you.

But strangest of all messages was:

My valentine to you still carries the same wish for an early return to NBC.

> Sincerely yours,
> George Engles

As the months went torturously by and it became evident that the agency had no mind to fulfill their contractual obligations, I listened more and more to the suave, persuasively polite Austin Wilder. He was impressing me with the Columbia Concerts Bureau. "Won't you let me come to see you at your home so we can talk without interruption? I want to acquaint you with the functioning of our organization; we can do a lot for you."

Nadea was receptive to the concertizing idea, consumed as she was with the burning desire to set me free of this exasperating "eating my heart out." During his visit, Austin Wilder gave us the Columbia Concerts Bureau layout: the Schang division managing Lily Pons and others; Evans and Salter, Lawrence Tibbett, Helen Jepson, Nino Martini; Haensel and Jones division, Guiomar Novaes, Richard Crooks, and others; all worked together as a pool. So being managed by one division was in most aspects like having the advantage of all the other departments. This statement, of course, proved to be an exaggeration, for each group was really in competition with the other, in much the same way as Lever Brothers, with Lux, Rinso, and Swan.

"Mrs. Loftus, let me take you to see Mr. Parmelee," Austin Wilder suggested. "He is the manager for Haensel and Jones division." Nadea immediately accepted the plan. Her basic honesty and generosity, her indifference to details, often obscured her caution and discriminate judgment. Not suspicious by nature, she was apt to accept too readily face values. In this, we are fundamentally alike and therefore unqualified for business. What radio was to me, I was to her—a consuming preoccupation. Without a guiding hand, such a combination was doomed for commercial defeat, and a strong guiding hand is what we did not have.

> O for a Muse of Fire, that would ascend
> The brightest heaven of invention
> A kingdom for a stage, princes to act,
> And monarchs to behold the swelling scene!

If even a thought can generate a wave which has its eternal influence, one speculates whether the Bard's wish, reverberating through the ether for three hundred years, whether the substance of his dream has not become incarnate in our time through the miracle of radio. From early morning, between my rehearsals and broadcast on May 12, 1937, I was constantly at the radio to hear the coronation ceremonies of Their Majesties, the King and Queen of England and the British Empire. I felt particularly proud to be broadcasting, listening, being a part of radio on Coronation Day. How we had grown from the early nineteen-station network!

The far-flung fantastic vision I saw long ago as a child was even more incredulous in its reality than I had imagined. On Coronation Day, Their Majesties were the King and Queen of the hearts and minds of the whole world. Listening in, we could hear the global hustle around us; everyone else was also listening, conscious of the two tremendous forces joined in this most dramatic, historical event: centuries-old pageantry and modern broadcasting.

In our program that evening I joined the general rejoicing of my air friends in Canada and the rest of the British Empire. They responded to our broadcast with a warmth that was the ultimate in neighborly affection. "Your words serve to bind even closer the ties of friendship between us."

Letters from listeners in far places reach us like the rays that travel miles from a star in the firmament, making a pathway of light between us. I always try to answer because I feel in music we share "the secret places of the soul." From Lincoln, Nebraska, after the *Irene* broadcast that summer, I received a letter from Stephen Cartwright, news commentator for the Central States Broadcasting System. Being deaf and blind, he heard me only through the vibrations felt when he placed his hands over the loud-speaker. "For a long time your voice has echoed in the soundless night of my existence," he wrote. Later he revealed the whole story—the extraordinary story so full of adventure and triumph that I could not keep it to myself.

Floyd Gibbons was concurrently doing his "Your True Adventure" series. "Here is a natural for you, Floyd," I said, handing him Cartwright's letter.

After reading it, he stood there speechless, with tears in his eyes:

"If I send for Cartwright, Jessica," he said, the reporter coming back to himself, "will you re-enact your part in his story for us?"

"Yes, Floyd. I would be glad to pay tribute to such a valiant soldier."

It was arranged to have Cartwright come from Nebraska, and Floyd Gibbons and I helped him tell the story that kept the radio audience sitting on the edge of their chairs.

Cartwright's injury was the tragic aftermath of an explosion in Siberia during World War I. He was an engineering student then, and after he was discharged from the Army, he returned home to California and resumed his studies. A few years later, visiting a friend at Long Beach, Steve turned on the radio after lunch. He was just in time to hear the introduction of my song "Alice Blue Gown." When I finished, Steve turned off the radio and said to his companion: "This song was perfect. I wouldn't like to spoil it by hearing anything else."

It was the last song he ever heard that way. Later in the day, Steve sat on the beach after an hour's swim. As he turned to his friend for a cigarette, something suddenly snapped—and he went blind and deaf. For weeks he lay in that dark and soundless void until one day an angel of mercy, passing through the ward of the hospital, began writing something in his hand. She was trying to penetrate his isolation. At first he did not understand, but slowly into his lonely mind seeped the light and life of communication. Mary Louise Plantner, a social worker, taught him to see and hear, through Braille and lip reading, and helped him fight the miraculous battle over his almost unsurmountable handicaps. Living a normal life again, he treasured through the years the memory of the last song he heard that day on the beach.

With a tremor in his voice, Floyd was telling me: "Jessica, if you will sing 'Alice Blue Gown' and allow Steve to put his hand on your throat, he will be able to hear you."

The three of us stood together around the microphone as I sang. The studio audience was in tears, and afterward many people asked me how I had the courage to do such a thing. "I kept thinking," I said, "of that angel of mercy, Mary Louise Plantner."

Listeners within three hundred miles of Pittsburgh had organized more than a thousand Jessica Dragonette Clubs and were eager to have me sing at the Allegheny County Fair in September, so they could "take a look at the many-time 'Radio Queen.'" The summer had been excruciatingly hot everywhere, and Pittsburgh was no exception until the night of the concert, when the temperature dropped to the thirties. Seventy-five thousand people turned out in spite of the cold, but while I sang my heart out in a program of arias and songs, in a décolletage of lilies of the valley and white organza, I wondered if I could weather the elements. I had to be in fine fettle for the broadcasts of the current week.

There is nothing quite so colorful as a state fair; one is part of a gigantic exposition of the industries and accomplishments of the vicinity. I was asked to do everything from piloting a fire engine to milking a cow; and I did my best to oblige!

The Cornplanter Indians staged their famous tobacco dance and when I sang the "Indian Love Call" for them, Chief Strong Fox was quite taken with my thoughtfulness. Afterward I asked for his autograph which he painstakingly wrote out for me. A crowd stood about waiting for him to ask for mine in return, but in his imperturbable way he just looked after me, as I said good-by, with the great dignity of his people.

We were in rehearsal for *Princess Pat* when I got back, and soon after that performance, my friend Harry Ackerman, now the white-haired boy of Young and Rubicam, asked me to "guest" on his Summer Stars series with Oscar Bradley's Orchestra and Harry Von Zell as master of ceremonies. It was stimulating fun to work with a comedian, sing straight songs, and do a dramatic scene from Noel Coward's *Conversation Piece* with Burford Hampden. Pete Barnum directed the show, and Young and Rubicam went to much trouble in giving me a graceful presentation, even to paying five hundred dollars copyright fee for the five-minute Coward scene.

On the dreary shores of Flushing Meadows, where workmen were breaking ground and officials were dedicating the first lonely building of the New York World's Fair, at the request of Grover Whalen's committee, I sang "America" and the "Star-Spangled Banner." Two years later I came back for a dinner with the Ford summer hour cast from Dearborn, Michigan, and found myself in a fairyland of modern palaces, gardens, and colored foundations, illuminated by night with elaborate displays of fireworks. The wonder of it increased with each visit, especially those under the magical guidance of Joseph Schillinger with his bride Frances.

My health was ever Nadea's concern. She had lived through our mother's illness, then her own inherited debility. Though I was never sickly, it was only by the strictest care and discipline that I was able to maintain the even keel of well-being. I was frail, highstrung, and did things with full throttle. Nadea had the nagging hallucination that I was doing too much and would break under the strain of work. These worries, together with what she referred to as my "fire-horse temperament" had her forever on tenterhooks. She insisted that after three years of constant broadcasting I should take a vacation.

I did not relish the anticipation of broaching the subject to Tom Revere. The operetta formula was going very well; he would not take kindly to interrupting a successful series even for a much-needed vacation, but finally I wrote to him.

Meanwhile, impressed with the agent attention accorded Charles Kullman, I began to listen more sympathetically to Austin Wilder's persistent sales talk about Columbia Concerts Bureau. "We are doing very well for Nelson Eddy; we could do the same for you. Even if you don't contemplate a tour at once, why not lay the groundwork for one?" The right way would emerge, for I had placed my life and my singing in that circle outside myself; they were in God's hands.

Tom Revere was long answering my letter, and when he did write, he completely ignored the vacation. After nine months, the program abruptly closed. Just like that, cold and unceremonious! There was nothing beyond the words, "We and our client have decided to discontinue the Beauty Box Theatre after the show of ——." Neither Tom Revere nor Esty Stowell explained nor came to say good-by. It was hinted that my asking for a vacation precipitated the closing, that the show was too expensive and unnecessary to continue since the sponsor had already benefited from the publicity of the "change." Later the agency lost the account and Tom Revere left Benton and Bowles, but the real cause no one seems to remember.

Radio had reached a peak, I reasoned, and was in a phase of repeating itself; besides, the dramatic trend I had so long foreseen was in full swing—even Cities Service, now cut to a half-hour program, was dramatizing the commercial. Musical shows were receding from the scene; rapidly changing world events were bringing an overnight interest in news—a good time to take a leave of absence and sing for my audience face to face.

CHAPTER 16

"FROM THE MOUNTAINS TO THE PRAIRIES"

I stood at the microphone after my last Palmolive broadcast to say farewell to my air friends. "I shall be leaving radio for a while for the long-deferred pleasure of seeing you, face to face, in your own communities; and I look forward to greeting personally the many, many air friends I have made through the years."

My cheerful words, however, did not ring true to the ears of the American public, accustomed to my slightest inflection. They seemed to sense something spurious in my tone, an atmosphere of a peculiar tint, and they promptly sent an avalanche of letters in the tens of thousands to the stations, protesting my absence from the air, and threatening to boycott the radio if I did not return.

Nothing was done to clear the mystery for them, and the whispering campaign went right on, dogging my every step. It was to the discordant music of this contretemps I set out on my first concert tour.

The wisest choice, Austin Wilder had pointed out, among the Columbia Concerts departments, was the Haensel and Jones division. "Jones" was added solely for euphony's sake. It had been formed some years before solely to handle a young American tenor, extremely successful first in Europe, then in America—Richard Crooks. Because of this earlier success, Wilder saw, on the part of Mr. Haensel, a possible like enthusiasm for another rising American singer. But Mr. Haensel, now in his ripe years and ill, could not be expected to have his former vigorous fervor for another incipient concert career. He had likewise a disdain of radio and radio artists. They had been the thorn in the side of the concert business for the last ten years.

"First, the radio wrecks the concert business," he was thinking aloud, "and now they want to reap the benefit of its prestige."

Buried deeply under the artistic veneer of this veteran concert manager was an inherent contempt for the vulgar commercial step-sister of the entertainment family. He had guided the opera and concert stars of the past; they were known quantities. In taking me under management, he wasn't quite sure of what he had let in under the wire.

He accepted the "golden guppy" from that horrible radio fish bowl on the gamble that the inconsequential little one might hatch out a colossus at the box office. Meanwhile, lost in my dreams of perfection and thrilled over the preparation for a new expression, I did not recognize the exploitation scheme until I was well launched in my first season and found myself booked in the largest auditoriums in the country. Where was the radio queen now? Among the other pawns on the chessboard, being manipulated about wherever the master player saw fit to speed us. I lacked only a Barnum to give the exploitation taste on a grand scale. In that first season, I never remember singing to an audience of less than 3,000 people.

My first concert on November 22, St. Cecilia's Day, in the time-hallowed Academy of Music in Philadelphia, I treasure with affection. It was a benefit for the children's wing of St. Mary's Hospital. The dressing room that was mine for the evening, the stage manager told me, had been used by the great Caruso. From the opening Handel aria, with organ accompaniment, written to Dryden's words:

> But oh what art can teach
> What human voice can reach
> The sacred organs praise,
> Notes that wing their heavenly ways
> To join the choirs above. . . .

through the Bellini and Massenet arias, the Lieder, miscellaneous and Irish songs, it was sheer joy of singing. Each song, a cry of the heart, "break for the gone gold unspent." Far from the static crystallization of limit and prescribed time, I breasted the full flowing tide of music.

A trainload of friends traveled from New York to join the large concert audience; and flowers and gifts from air friends all over the

United States and Canada greeted me. But, though my notices were
exceptional, the Columbia Concerts Bureau still considered me circus
fodder and was only delighted over the name "Princess of Song,"
given me by the music critic of the Philadelphia *Inquirer*, Linton
Martin, and they used it in all my future billing.

Since this was an initial concert I wanted it, in every way, to be a
dedication to music, so besides my songs, I also made the offering of
my concert fee; half of it went back to St. Mary's Hospital and half
toward the new stage in the Casino Building at Georgian Court.

Arpad Sandor was with me; he had played for every well-known
singer and instrumentalist from the time when, as a very young man,
he had come to this country with Louis Graveure. This was to be
the start of a long musical association.

However successful the debut, Nadea was not to be dissuaded
from the notion that I needed a rest. She insisted we take a vacation
and soon. She feared the crescendo of happenings on taut, hyper-
controlled nerves might lead to a breakdown. We made plans, therefore, to spend some time in California before going to Hawaii for a
concert.

"I don't want you to wake up one day and blame me for not taking
care of you," she warned. "Remember the clothespin story?"

The clothespin story was about a girl with a very broad nose who
hated her mother all through life, blaming her for this unchiseled
feature. "She could have done something about it," she would say to
people, who remonstrated with her for this lack of filial devotion. "I
hate her. It's her fault! If she couldn't think of anything else, she
could have put a clothespin on my nose. It would have made it slim,
but *no!* She let me live my whole life with this monstrosity, when
a little homely clothespin could have saved my face."

Gayelord Hauser, the famous dietitian and author of *Look
Younger, Live Longer*, saw us off on the *Matsonia*, rechristened
Lurline. He had been our exciting host during our weeks in California and with his breezy generous manner left no stone unturned,
revealing the West Coast paradise to us.

I had met Gayelord Hauser through my neighbors, George and
Madeline Sack. Reluctantly I accepted an invitation from them to
hear him lecture. I was skeptical lest I be bored with just another
diet faddist. Since I have always believed that singing is half sport

and half art, I did not have to be told that health is the cornerstone of a singing career; that good food, adequate sleep, fresh air, sunshine, and exercise are essential. The singer's body has to be cared for, like the athlete's, and I was accustomed to eating what they eat at the training table—lean meats, leafy greens, vegetables, and raw fruits. However, Hauser's easy stage manner, his obvious vitality and fitness, impressed me so much I went right out, began drinking my vegetables, and raised my glass in a toast to "Here's How—ser!"

It was amusing to hear him introduce me to people.

"She's pretty," he would say. Then waving his hand, "You'll never believe it," he would add, "but she *eats* b-e-e-e-a-u-t-i-f-u-l-l-y."

We had many good times at parties in his Sunrise Hill home on Angelo Drive. One evening he invited me to the Ballet Russe de Monte Carlo at the Philharmonic in Los Angeles; afterward he entertained the entire ballet company. It was strange to see the lovely ballerinas unmasked from their *Coq d'Or, Scheherazade, El Sombrero de Tres Picos,* and *Giselle* settings. They sat about like obedient Degas', wide-eyed at the parade of Hollywood stars who came and went. Walt Disney resembled an El Greco as he sat on the floor looking up at Mrs. Disney, a double for Norma Shearer. Irene Rich preceded Adrian, with whom she came to the party. Everyone gasped to see her looking so beautiful in a white-fringed gown. I had never seen her before, and as I gaped a woman whispered to me back of her fan: "Pray, dear, you look that way when you're her age!"

Like that daub of white paint the artist uses to accent a vivid color on the canvas, Adrian entered, bearing a large white cage on his shoulders; standing in the middle of the gay, luxuriant guests, he opened the door and let out four white doves. Suddenly there was silence, while these heavenly creatures circled the chandelier and floated softly about; all the while Adrian stood like some hypnotic fancier. After this brief spreading of wings, he lured them back into the cage. The interlude had all the flair of a *pièce de résistance,* a true ballet scene even to the startled attitudes of the ballerinas. The party was a farewell to California, for we were sailing the next day for Hawaii where I would sing a concert as well as continue my vacation in Honolulu.

Gayelord Hauser stood on the pier in Los Angeles, waving his scarf until we were out of sight. Then Nadea and I sat on the deck and saw the whole ribbon of our joyous California days unravel before us on the northward stretch up to San Francisco. As we should not sail to Honolulu until the next evening, we tried to see as much of this unusual city as possible. My friend Vera Edmondson, a transplanted Australian, eagerly introduced us to the cable cars; Gump's, that Pandora's box of wonders; the Presidio, where I found a friend of my early Liebling studio days, Louise Wright, the light opera singer, now the wife of Lieutenant Colonel Alexander George. I shopped fast and furiously at I. Magnin's. This was my first long journey, and I had not yet learned the streamlined packing that much airplane travel was later to teach me. Among the dresses I bought was a charming chiffon print of *Snow White and the Seven Dwarfs*, the currently acclaimed technicolor film.

We left San Francisco just as the sun was setting over the Golden Gate, and looking at the backdrop of the high-bluffed picturesque city, spangled and gleaming in the red and yellow glow of evening, I thought how all the descriptions of San Francisco beggared the living reality I was beholding.

We had supper in our *lanai*, watching the flying fish sporting after the passing ships. The blue Pacific looked calm, and the prospect of four lazy days at sea after the rushed years was too incredible to contemplate. Our first night out of San Francisco we retired early. We wanted to make every moment of this ocean voyage count in stored-up energy, to give our best in the coming Honolulu concert.

We had no sooner turned out the lights when a great roll of thunder sounded and everything in the stateroom—trunks, chairs, toilet articles, suitcases—was violently flung about; we ourselves were thrown out of our beds. My accompanist, Hélène Tardivel Byers, who occupied the adjoining room, banged frantically on the door. In the rolling and pitching of the ship, both Nadea and Hélène were seized with acute *mal de mer*, and I spent the night administering between them.

For three days the storm raged, and not a soul left the staterooms. A solitary man and I were apparently the only good sailors on board, the only ones who walked the top deck and occupied the steamer chairs. He was James Simpson, president of Marshall Field's in Chicago. He looked vigorous enough, but apparently his doctor had ordered him to rest in Hawaii. His party were keeping to their rooms during the rough passage. I recognized him as the father of a college friend of Leonardo's, but I did not disclose my identity as we walked and chattered.

"Are there any celebrated people on board?" he asked me.

"Celebrated? I think you are, sir."

"Oh, I mean singers or actresses."

"Indeed, I wouldn't know; but perhaps if you ask the captain—"

We kept up our daily mileage around the deck, and then, one glorious half day out from the islands, the ship came to life with people everywhere. Mr. Simpson and I bent over the deck rail to observe the purple and green patches appearing in the tropical waters, and as we resumed our walk again, a couple addressed me:

"Aren't you Jessica Dragonette? We attended one of your broadcasts in Radio City and we thought we heard you singing in the saloon under our stateroom."

"Oh, I hope I didn't disturb you."

"No indeed, you consoled us and took our mind off other things."

"That's it," smiled Mr. Simpson, looking like the cat that swallowed the canary, "I knew who you were all the time. My secretary told me, and we've been having lots of fun, because Mrs. Simpson is a Jessica, too. You might just as well face it—it's out of the bag—and we're all coming to hear you in Honolulu."

The enchantment of arrival in the islands has been described by many writers, the swift passing of Diamond Head, the first sight of pink stucco, Nuuanu Pali, the flaming trees, the diving boys, the band playing, the girls in hula costumes, the women in *holakus*, the *leis*, the languorous singing to the ukuleles and guitars; but no one can describe the unforgettable burst of wonder to my delighted heart. It was romantic to be lured into the ambience of a different pattern of life where fascinating ancient custom has been assimilated into a modern way of living; and there are the climate, the gorgeous colors, the hospitable people, the warm friendships to cherish through a lifetime.

George Moody was one of the first among the people I met. A Texan, he was a jewelry designer with Paul Flato, married a Rice of the first five missionary families of Hawaii, and is now a permanent pillar of island society. Moody admired my Tibetan necklace, made of turquoise, lapis, and coral inlaid bone and my Persian dancing-girl earrings. He wanted Doris Duke to see them, but unfortunately she was in Persia at the moment. However, shouldn't we like to see the beautiful house Drew Baker, the architect, was building for her on Kaalawai? Drew could talk architecture, and I could talk music. He said he didn't understand a note of it, and I said I would send him a book that would show him how music notes were comparable to the lava stones in the foundation of the wall we were sitting beside. He would come to recognize music, too, in the soft rhythm of the sea accompanying our talk.

Before we left the islands, friends invited us to a *luau*, that day-long ceremony of cooking on river stones covered with seaweed and buried underground: roast pig, potatoes, corn, and vegetables. Thirty of us sat at table in a *lanai* decorated with palm branches and *ti* leaves, to a meal of endless courses of delicious Hawaiian food. I tasted squid for the first time and was horrified to find out it was really octopus. I also learned the proper way to eat poi, that lavender library paste concoction, with the forefingers dipped in the gruel, rolled, and carried to the mouth. We sat feasting while a Hawaiian comedian entertained us with the famous "Cock-eyed Mayor of Kaunakakai."

We met Commander Heard and his stunning wife, Midge Vanderbilt, that evening. The next day, they invited us to tea to meet their charming children—a little daughter of incomparable beauty, a heavenly flower in this paradise of flowers, and a slightly older handsome son.

The Honolulu audience received my program of arias, French, Spanish, and American songs with marked pleasure, and after each encore, they would place a *lei* around my neck and make me raise my hand and promise to come back. When I sang my last "*Aloha Oe*," I was so laden with necklaces of carnations, tuberoses, *pikaki*, *mauna loa* flowers, I could hardly stand up.

There wasn't enough time to learn to play the ukulele as Godfrey did nor the Hawaiian guitar; but I did study Hawaiian songs with the natives, and from the finest dancer Iolani Luahine, daughter of the court dancer to Queen Liliuokalani, I learned to do the authentic hula—that lovely dance, born out of the native rhythms of tree and sea, in which the hands tell a story to the rhythmic patterns of the feet. The untouched natural quality of the vanishing Hawaiian is impossible to describe. It is a far remove from the hard-boiled, self-conscious existence of the large city.

After being entertained at Schofield Barracks, our army base there, we lunched with another first family, the Rosses, overlooking Pearl Harbor. When I admired the picturesque little Japanese fishing boats, my hostess remarked: *"They sail so far from the shore, and we don't know where they go."* This was only four years before our Pacific Fleet was demolished in the very vicinity in which we were dining.

In the blaze of noon, I went to see the monument to Amelia Earhart, a simple slab of marble on the Nuuvanu Pali Road, high above the blue-green sea. On her South Pacific journey, Amelia Earhart had stopped in Honolulu. With sober demeanor, they were telling me quietly that at the time of her visit the natives could hear the Kahuna drum beats that always presage danger. The Hawaiian people do not believe in erecting a monument to a living person—this had been planned by American officials—and during the ceremony when the slab fell, they were certain that Amelia Earhart would never fly the South Pacific again.

I knew Station KGU only through the letters of its managing director Henry C. Putnam, who had been writing me that they got my Cities Service program regularly with good reception via short wave. Later when the Clipper service began between California and the islands, he sent me the first *lei* of gardenias out of Honolulu. Afterward these became contraband. Once I sent him a recording of the whole program, including the *Aloha Oe*. Harry, the young Chinese on the KGU staff, found it difficult to believe the song was ever sung outside the territory of Hawaii. He beamed as he listened: "Gee! That makes a guy feel good."

Nadea and I held close every last minute in Honolulu; the singing beneath our windows at twilight in the Royal Hawaiian; the early morning hours before dawn in our *lanai*, looking at the Southern Cross; and now, heavy with *leis*, once again we were boarding the *Lurline*. George and Constance Moody saw us off; Commander and Mrs. Heard wired us; and all our Hawaiian friends told us to be sure to throw our *leis* in the ocean as we passed Diamond Head. This would insure our return to the enchanted isles.

Aloha! That all-embracing word, farewell; we had a wonderful time; come again—*aloha nui nui* meaning even more aloha, God speed, kept ringing in our rhyming thoughts after the last pinpoint vestige of verdant island had vanished from our sight—*aloha nui nui!*

When we docked in California, the worst of the spring floods was over; yet the aftermath of damaged rails and washed-out roadbeds made travel precariously dangerous. My mail was waiting in Beverly Hills when we arrived. I picked up a wire from Rosario Bourdon—sent several weeks earlier. I could hardly believe what I was reading: "I have resigned from Cities Service." One year after I left the program, Rosario Bourdon was also gone. He had been with Cities Service three and a half years longer than I. It wasn't like Rosario to resign; he had always told me "he wanted to die in harness." The feeling of desolation his wire communicated to me was deeper than sympathy at the humiliation of a friend and beloved maestro. It was a sense of loss for radio. One did not pluck such men, like golden apples, from the trees.

Rumor had it that in the conference rooms another chess game had been played. The Cities Service Orchestra under Bourdon was an assemblage of the finest musicians; why not make it the basis for the proposed NBC Symphony Orchestra under Arturo Toscanini? As a house orchestra, committed to working a thirty-hour week, they could be assigned to the now reduced Cities Service half-hour program with Frank Black, NBC music director, as the new conductor —a perfect tie-up with costs kept to a minimum.

One cries out against the element of offense in the prescribed world of business; the lack of grace and dignity in dealing with an outstanding artist like Rosario Bourdon. One does not try to skin a star like an onion to find out what is inside. Indeed one cannot! He was given a casual, oral dismissal at rehearsal on the broadcast day, and told his services were no longer required. The merest shred of good manners would have dictated a written statement and reasonable notice. Concurrently with his dismissal was circulated a hint that he had taken to drinking. This stigma was the easiest excuse to fabricate. In Rosario's case, nothing could have been farther from the truth.

Through the kindness of those exquisite friends, Marie and Henry Hotchner of California, who rerouted my tour, I was able to avoid the flood-devastated areas on the West Coast, and arrive in time for my next concert in Tucson, Arizona. I was delighted to see my brother Fred, his wife, and above all the children, Anne and Tony. But an unusual air of tension, a chilly stillness that precedes a storm, pervaded the atmosphere into which I descended from the train. The faces of the people who met me were strained and sad. I asked Fred why the cloud over this dazzling desert city.

"They are waiting for General John J. Pershing to die. His coffin is in that train there; newspapermen are waiting to speed the final word to their home offices."

The idea was suffocating to me, and I began inwardly praying not to be sucked into the general morass of negative thinking. When I arrived at the Arizona Inn, there was a phone call from the *Arizona Daily Star:* would I mind coming to the newspaper office to be interviewed, as no reporter could be spared from the Pershing vigil?

The darkest gloom hung over the editorial rooms. The city editor told me of his friendship with Pershing and how awful he felt over the inevitable demise. Next, the editor-in-chief, William Matthews, came out to greet me.

"Although you are my favorite singer," he said, "Mrs. Matthews and I will not be able to hear you at the Temple of Music and Art tomorrow. We don't dare leave the general's bedside."

Usually contained and reticent, I found myself at the explosion point. "Everyone here seems to be helping the general to die. Aren't any of his friends helping him to live? He's a soldier, used to fighting. I don't think he wants to die." Mr. Matthews looked up startled at this unexpected outburst; but before he could speak, I cut in: "I hope you and Mrs. Matthews will come to my concert. I mean to dedicate my singing as a healing prayer for the general. I'm sure he'll not die during the concert." Genuinely moved by my earnestness, Mr. Matthews and his wife did come and stayed for the whole concert.

At five o'clock the next morning, I was on my way to Seattle, Washington, and as the train sped to its destination, I turned on the radio in the club car to hear, "crisis passed; great improvement in General Pershing's condition." I could hardly contain myself until we reached the next stop. Then I wired Mr. Matthews four words: "I told you so." By the time I reached Seattle, I heard from him.

"The general steadily improving, Pershing family grateful. Signed: William Matthews." More things are wrought by prayer than this world dreams of.

The Japanese current gives Seattle, Washington, a mild climate, though in latitude it is parallel to Bangor, Maine. The journey from California through the dark green virgin forests of the Northwest country, past Mount Rainier, and finally to the unusual city itself was a treat for my effete Eastern eyes.

Basil Cameron was the symphony's current season conductor. He was giving a concert for the 6,000 high-school students of the city when I arrived, and I was asked to attend and give a few words of greeting. The children were highly disappointed not to hear me sing that afternoon; and, when Dr. Cameron had scarcely finished his last selection, they pounced on me from everywhere in the vast, barnlike auditorium and imprisoned me among them so that I was unable to give the autographs they were seeking. I had to be rescued from this dangerous onslaught by newspapermen who came tearing down from the balcony. They had gotten their "picture" and were free to devote themselves to unloosing me from the children's grasp. Dr. Cameron was very provoked at what he called their bad manners. They listened politely to his reprimands and then went merrily on doing just what they pleased.

Meanwhile John Charles Thomas wired me from Fargo: "Hope to arrive in time for concert." He had already been marooned for two days in the great snowdrifts of North Dakota and he never did arrive until the day after the concert. The manager of the hotel, Mr. Howe, amused at these hourly telegrams of suspense, took matters into his own hands and set out with horse and buggy to fetch John Charles. On his return to the hotel with the prize, there was much fun and commotion in the street. I should have liked to have remained asleep in the early morning; there was nothing to do but get up and join the rejoicing over the safe arrival of our friend.

After an hour's singing, John Charles asked Marius, the Olympia's famous French chef, to prepare a gourmet luncheon for us—a soufflé of chiffon consistency, crisp green salad, and strawberries à la Marius with a sauce that defies description. This was a memory for John Charles to carry to Victoria, B. C., where he would sing a concert that evening, and for me to carry to Minneapolis, where I would be going in a few days. So delighted was Marius with my singing in French that he has never forgotten it, and at Christmas and Easter I never fail to receive a culinary masterpiece. He is the best chef I have encountered in all my travels.

The concert reviews referred to the climax of the Seattle Symphony season—acclaimed me not only for voice, but also for genuine individuality of interpretation, intelligence, and taste in music. I mention this because together with these reviews, large audiences, and high fees for the foregoing concerts, when I returned to California, I received the following wire from Haensel and Jones: "With current bill including Honolulu—Tucson—Seattle commissions deducted net of Seattle check is $127."

Unforgettable is the souvenir of singing under the baton of Mitropoulos. I was a prim miss on this first concert tour, prepared for my prescribed portion of the program: "Un Bel Di Vedremo" from Puccini's *Madama Butterfly;* "Connais-tu le pays," from Thomas' *Mignon;* a group of concert songs, and one encore, Schubert's "Serenade."

Mr. Mitropoulos looked askance at this American youngster as I mounted the stage. The rehearsal went beautifully until we came to the encore, for which I had no conductor's score, but a marked vocal copy to follow. Something went wrong in this relatively simple accompaniment but I was oblivious, lost in the pleasure of singing with such a thrilling musician. I felt the lightning strike when the maestro threw the music on the floor, scolded the musicians, glared at me, and walked out of the rehearsal. I didn't know what to do. I wanted no wedge between us for the evening performance. Mrs. Scott, manager of the symphony, rushed upon the platform, attempting to restore order. After a few moments I went to Mitropoulos and apologized.

"I am sorry, Maestro," I said forlornly. "I have come from California and my orchestrations have come from New York. There has been no time to look them over."

Mitropoulos frowned at me. "Next time," he said, "put them in your brief case and carry them in your own hand." He seemed appeased, however, with my apology, and I went back to my hotel to rest my frazzled nerves.

At five o'clock in the afternoon, Mrs. Scott roused me out of sleep and told me to go to the nearest music store and purchase some extra music as 15,000 people had bought tickets for the concert despite bad weather and a taxi strike. They would undoubtedly want more than one encore.

"Who will play for me?" I asked.

"Why, Mitropoulos himself," answered Mrs. Scott.

"But will he want to?" I said falteringly. "Besides there will be no time to rehearse."

"It isn't necessary," she hastened to reassure me. "Mitropoulos is a dream pianist." Remembering the morning's skirmish, I was relieved at this.

Upon the apron of the stage that rose from the pit that evening Mitropoulos seated himself at the centered Steinway. He looked for all the world like a nineteenth-century, French drawing-room picture. He accompanied me with a flair that enchanted and, though there were eight encores, I never knew for which of us was intended the rich applause.

In spite of the whispering campaign that preceded me—"She can't be heard outside a telephone booth"—James Davies, music critic of the Minneapolis *Tribune,* wrote: "I was suspicious that her voice would not carry through the huge auditorium, but this was an error. She was heard everywhere and accomplished her aim by singing naturally and simply."

Beside the music page I was also reviewed on the sports page of the Rochester *Democrat* and *Chronicle.* The headline read:

TENNIS BOYS (PERRY AND VINES) SHOULD INCLUDE JESSICA IN THEIR ACT; HER HIGH C DRAWS 'EM.

Only a tennis toss from the armory across the street, Jessica Dragonette, celebrated concert singer, appeared before a "standing room only" audience. One could have dragged a net down through the reserved seat section at the armory and few, if any, would have been trapped.

American audiences are the same in small towns as in the cities. Frequently more real culture is found in the hidden places, and a genuine love of art and music in those farthest from New York City. Singing fifteen concerts in one month in Oklahoma, in the cities of Bartlesville, Ardmore, Chickasha, Ada, Tulsa, I was enchanted to find even children under fourteen years of age a large part of the responsive subscription audiences.

In Edinburg, Texas, a jewel town in the gleaming girdle of the Rio Grande cities, I sang an unusual first concert under the Cultural Arts College auspices. The press conferences with newspapermen and women were stimulatingly active. They not only asked me questions, but also sang for me, "The Eyes of Texas Are Upon You." This certainly made me feel I was on the spot. The pioneer in me responded strongly to this new community where so much was happening—Americans from other parts of the United States were the vital ingredients shaping a life into what it was to be. I felt a great working eagerness germinating here, to build the kind of country they really wanted. I had the feeling of standing on the edge of an important beginning, finding myself among these happy, friendly, serious people. One day the volcanic fertile valley would be another California: the ebony trees, the grapefruit, the huge Persian limes, the flowers, all inspired me to rename the city—*Eden*-burg.

"Don't wire—shoot!" Mrs. Niles Robertson told me the sign read over the Harlan County telegraph office. I looked surprised at the soft-voiced schoolteacher among the delegation come to Lexington, Kentucky, to drive me the long journey through the mountains to Hazard, where I would give a concert the next evening.

"Why the name Hazard?" I asked the choral director who engaged me.

"You'll find out," smiled Miss Kesheimer. "It is really a bone-of-contention town."

It was strictly a mining village, and everyone was in some way connected with King Coal. The choral director, an extraordinary woman, had kept music alive during the twenty years she had lived in Harlan County by giving piano lessons to the miners' children. As a young girl, she and her railroad-engineer father had stopped once in Harlan, where she remained to do a pioneering job. Not a scintilla of good taste was forfeited, singing for this interested audience. They had heard me on the air for a long time. I was not only an old friend, but they were acquainted with my music.

"Oh, I'm going to that," they would tell me when I asked them if they were coming to the concert. They stopped to talk to me on the street; they asked me to be photographed individually with almost everyone in Hazard; and, giving me a miner's cap, they even said I could go down in the mine with them if I wanted to. This I refused flatly, remembering: "It is bad luck for a woman to go down in the mine."

Sandor fell ill en route and could not go on to Hazard with me. At the last moment, Karl Kritz, a director of the Berlin Opera who had recently escaped from Nazi Germany, pinch-hit for him. Our rehearsals were on railroad trains without benefit of piano. Kritz was a trouper and sportsman in every sense of the word.

Before going to New Orleans we traveled northward to Houston, and, as I received the fresh impressions of local communities everywhere, I was able to reaffirm first hand what I had come to know, that Americans are a most music-loving people, possessing a wide compass of varying tastes. Formerly self-conscious about music they have, largely through the influence of radio, come of age and characteristically demand the best. Likewise the American artist is understood and feels at home at last in his own country. Many times the local management asked me to give radio reviews, to call attention to the concert in hand. This gave me an opportunity really to visit with the people.

Loving clothes as I do, I always feel closer to the women when I am being interviewed by a fashion commentator. WFAA's Gail Northe looked very chic as I sat opposite her in the radio studio for our chat; back of her a line of women's-page editors were taking notes.

"You're looking very smart, Jessica," she said with a rising inflection, "in that purple wool suit you're wearing. What is the embroidery around the neck and on the lapels? Is that something our grandmothers wore, now in fashion again? It's passementerie, isn't it?"

"Yes, thank you," I answered, trying to catch her jauntiness, "but you look stunning yourself, Gail Northe, in that draped turban with flowing scarf, like a vision coming across the desert. Tell me, would you call it Bedouin?"

"No," she said, with a sad wobble to her flexible voice, "it's Lilly Daché!"

My touring continued into the summer, and late in August, Minnie

Guggenheimer persuaded me to appear in a Lewisohn Stadium concert for the benefit of the summer-music fund. Willem van Hoogstraten conducted and Harold Bauer, the celebrated pianist, shared the program with me. Together we succeeded in drawing a crowd of 22,000 people to the amphitheater. All New York including His Honor the Mayor, Fiorello H. La Guardia, turned out.

After my portion of the concert I had to leave to catch a late train to Chicago; I went to bid good-by to Bauer and told him how sorry I was not to be able to remain to hear him. He graciously congratulated me, then with a note of bitterness in his voice he added, "Audiences don't always clamor like this," he said. "Remember to hold on just the same and ride the waves!"

I thought a good deal about what Harold Bauer said, at my Chicago concert two days later, when I sang to the largest audience of my wildest dreams, 150,000 people!

North and South, East, West, and back and forth sometimes, I went singing in this tour of our American continent. Duluth, Minnesota, stands out because I visited this city of hills in a January of eighteen below zero. Everything was frozen; from doorways and eaves hung huge icicles easily three feet in diameter widening to six or eight feet. The whole apple-cheeked population were gravitating to the largest ski jump in the country, participating and watching. I stood among them for a moment to view the winter-wonderland spectacle; storing away in memory the Minnesota landmark, evergreens and birches side by side on the white snow beneath the clear blue sky, and the moon coming up over Lake Superior.

Surely no one would venture out for a concert these frigid nights. But they did come, braving the frozen ground and petrifying cold; and afterward gave a reception for me in a hall decorated with live evergreen trees. In air rich with the odor of fresh balsam, we gathered before the open fireplace to talk and visit. The quiet friendliness of the townspeople brought my heart to my mouth.

As I left the next forenoon, there was a great hullabaloo in the hotel. The men had left their places around the lobby stove and were talking and gesticulating excitedly. A bear had wandered in from the woods to warm himself! He was, no doubt, hungry, too.

"We got 'im. Yessir! When you come back again, Miss," one of the men told me, "you'll find his hide up there on the wall!"

I kept right on going up to the Christmas interval, and afterward I set out again, singing well into the summer of the next year. In all this while I never lost touch with the radio, for that would be losing touch with the world. I kept informed about the war of nerves issuing from Germany and the flood tide of momentous events that seemed too fast for the winged words of the kilocycles. Along with other Americans, I heard the voices of Hitler, Neville Chamberlain, Edouard Daladier, Mussolini, and Eduard Beneš. Perhaps for the first time, during these racking days it dawned on people how really close we are to London, Prague, Rome, Warsaw, and Munich. Radio, the free competitive American institution, made every move of this terrible time known to us.

Now I was back singing my third summer concert "under the stars" in Washington Park, Milwaukee, in the magnificent Blatz music shell. Grace Moore was chosen to open the series, and I was scheduled for late August. However, Grace had to cancel because of laryngitis, and I was summoned at the last moment. What a scramble to be ready with orchestrations, alternate plane and train tickets in case of bad weather, and clothes on short notice! But all this keyed-up tension and three-ring-circus existence is part of a singing career. I returned to Washington Park, where 30,000, 40,000, and 50,000 people came each season to hear me; but this concert was to be different, Sigfrid Prager, the conductor, explained at rehearsal. I was to be inducted as an honorary member into the local chapter of the National Musical Fraternity, Sigma Alpha Iota; besides, we were to have a royal audience with us. Norwegian Crown Prince Olaf and Princess Martha would attend the concert that evening with G. B. Skogmo, Norwegian Consul; Governor J. A. O. Preus; Mayor Daniel Hoan; and Mr. and Mrs. Rudolf Hokanson, Norwegian citizens of Milwaukee.

I added Solveig's song from *Peer Gynt* to the encores in honor of the royal couple; they beamed with evident pleasure. But when the audience called out for "Alice Blue Gown" and I asked them to join in the chorus, we were all surprised to observe Their Highnesses singing every word along with us. The little American song had found its way to Norwegian hearts.

The handsome royal couple could not have been more gracious when I met them afterward in the warm evening. I offered my fan to Princess Martha asking her to do me the honor of keeping it. She acquiesced easily; and, before I left Milwaukee, Prince Olaf himself presented me with two photographs both autographed by Their Highnesses.

After a Toronto concert and participation in the official opening of Canadian television, I went to Philadelphia to sing in Robin Hood Dell under the distinguished conductor Sir Ernest MacMillan. On my return to New York I did several broadcasts in rapid succession, one with Raymond Paige's "99 Men and a Girl" program. In the arrangements of this colorful conductor I could recognize the fine hand of a Schillinger disciple. "Magic Key" for RCA under Frank Black came next. And then a request from Bob Ripley to appear on his "Believe-It-or-Not" series. Bob had in mind a unique incident in my career that he was eager to dramatize.

The story hinged about Shirley Swinn, a young Canadian nurse who dreamed about becoming paralyzed and then being cured by my singing of "Ave Maria." The dreamed-of tragedy actually happened three weeks later, and Shirley lay unconscious in a Toronto hospital. Her nurse, in turn, wired me asking if I would sing the "Ave Maria" at a given time via the air, and she would put a radio in Shirley's room. When the singing was over, the girl awakened and said she had heard the "Ave Maria" clearly and felt better. Before long she was completely well and told her story to Bob Ripley.

Ripley's twist was to have Shirley in one studio and me in another and not have us come face to face until a certain moment in the actual broadcast. He realized this might be hazardous, but he risked the chance for dramatic effect. Fortunately for me, Shirley would not see me until after I had sung the "Ave Maria." By this time the touching denouement had me worried.

We were all simply stunned when a calm Shirley looked at me and smiled: "Thank you, Jessica, for being the instrument." She went on quietly, "You look just as I imagined you when I heard you singing the 'Ave Maria' that healed me."

During my absence from radio, when sometimes in a matter of ten days I would have sung personally to more than 300,000 people, I still felt the pull of fans calling me back to the microphone. They said no matter how many concerts I sang, I would always be far away from some of them; but when I sang on the air I was with all of them at the same time. They were storming the stations for my return and now in the current *Radio Guide* poll all of them intended to vote me Star of Stars as a testimonial of proof to the incredulous broadcasters. It was a heated race, apparently, and the *Guide* poll caused disparaging editorials all over the country. Newspapers and fans alike complained the polls were fixed and that press agents had been buying up coupons in the hope of electing unknowns to prominent positions. Curtis Mitchell, vice-president and editorial director of *Radio Guide,* felt he should answer the "nasty crack" at his magazine and the poll. He spoke out to his discreditors:

To attempt to explain fanatical devotion to her [Jessica Dragonette] by thousands and hundreds of thousands of people throughout the country would be to attempt to explain relativity. Frankly, I myself don't understand it, but I've talked to those folks who do adore her, who spend their money traveling thousands of miles to hear her sing a few songs, who correspond with other Dragonette fans, and I know they are legion . . . In the devoted following there is something both mystical and cockeyed.

CHAPTER 17

POSTSCRIPT TO DISENCHANTMENT

NBC had arranged a special salute in celebration of my return to their management. It hadn't been easy for Dan Tuthill, a live wire in the sales department, to make the lion lie down with the lamb. Coming to see me at my home, he had a hard time convincing me that NBC had anything good up their sleeve for this prodigal daughter; to instill confidence he emphasized our long acquaintance. Though he had been in sales almost since the beginning of NBC, and we knew each other, we had never before been associated in any program business.

"Your selection as Star of Stars has stirred up much broadcaster interest," he told me. "I would like to negotiate some radio programs for you, but it would be awkward unless you are under our banner."

So eager was I to seal up the two-year breach between us and to go back on the air for the sake of my clamorous fans that I let Dan talk me into signing for a short term with NBC.

It was like wading in an area of floating mines to be back. On the calm surface nothing had changed. Malcolm, the doorman at the RCA Building, was there to receive me, his great height reminding me of Raeburn's picture of The McNab.

"I saw your car the minute you turned into Forty-ninth Street, Miss Jessica," he purred with his quiet Scotch inflection. "Seeing you again makes me feel good. You belong here—seems like old times."

Malcolm's words were comforting; I had so long partaken of the life of the building, I could not enter it indifferently. I passed the crowded lobby in front of the information booth where I had purchased the first tour-ticket that day when the NBC press searched the city, then finding me under the hairdresser's dryer, they rushed my damp hair up under my hat, and insisted I pose for the ticket-buying picture. Page boys and elevator men smiled recognition as I entered the lift to the third floor.

Dan Tuthill was waiting for me outside of Studio 3B. We had half an hour before the Dragonette Salute broadcast, arranged for my return. I expressed pleasure over the chosen studio. All the studios were known to me, and their idiosyncrasies were almost personable. But Dan's mind was on business.

"I know you are doing a great many concerts," he interrupted, "but we are equipped to handle those for you. The NBC Artists Bureau control the Community Concert Series all over the country."

Was he implying I sign up with their concerts bureau, which in essence meant resigning with George Engles?

"Don't look so startled," he went on persuasively. "It's much better to let us handle your complete professional activities." Then, changing his tone, he said suspiciously, "By the way, I hear you didn't get such good notices in Toronto."

No doubt this misinformation emanated from the very Artists Bureau he was persuading me to rejoin. I was tempted to fling out Grace Moore's classic remark, "Don't you know I've made my career on bad notices?" But I kept my peace, and with a modicum of modesty I produced the Toronto clipping, every line exuding praise for the Massey Hall concert.

Just then a page boy appeared in the doorway. "Ten minutes, Miss Dragonette," and I answered the call-to-arms.

A surge of happy remembrance welled up in me as I sang my first number—Irving Berlin's "I Poured My Heart Into A Song," with Harold Sanford, my old Philco conductor. He felt the rushes of tenderness moving along the current of the songs—all requests for this program.

Brilliant sparks reached out to Graham McNamee who was announcing me: "On the autumn day in 1926, a young unknown slipped before a microphone; on that occasion Harold Sanford was there, and we are pleased to have him again on this home-coming to Miss Dragonette." My mind flashed back to that day in the Telephone Building when his buoyant laughter helped me through my first broadcast. Now I felt the same warmth between us once more. Had my mind been able also to flash forward, I would have known I was never to see him again.

Lenox Lohr in a personal word of cordial welcome was saying: "It gives me pleasure to be part of this program tonight, because it brings Jessica Dragonette back to her radio listeners after her long concert tour. Just as many of you did, I heard her for the first time on Cities Service and came to look forward to her performances which have been among the highlights of radio."

After more songs with the orchestra and male chorus, Orrin Dunlap, Jr., former radio editor of *The New York Times*, added a reminiscent salute: "To the first exclusively long-term commercial artist of NBC, the first to introduce many firsts in radio. For myself, I can say with pleasure, 'Welcome back to radio.'"

George Engles, smiling in happy approval, sat in the front row with the assembled studio audience, and was the first to congratulate me. Who could fail to be touched with this sincere effort to right old wrongs? I certainly was, and yet I could summon no genuine confidence in all around me. Though there were copious evidences of good faith, my intuition told me this was a futile attempt at recapture of a life that was. Suddenly the place stifled me. I saw it in the past, as part of my childhood dreams. The magic of former days had gone stale; my youthful innocence had transformed a hard commercial world into an enchanted place, but now I was completely disillusioned.

Surviving my visit to the haunted building, I sighed relief when the Salute was over. Why had I stooped to compromise? I took the disappointing attempt at appeasement into the night and purged it in a drench of moonlight. My thoughts were voices throbbing in my temples, sad voices, "—there are tracks on the driven snow," they were whispering, and "gone is the first fine careless rapture."

Still inwardly chafing, I listened to Dan Tuthill's pleasure at how well everything went off. "Let me tell you, Jessica, it wasn't easy getting you guys together." Now he modulated to a change of key. "We're having increasing union troubles. It may become too difficult to broadcast at all, with the ever-inhibiting restrictions of that *Caesar* Petrillo."

I listened with fretful patience to his words. This was the tough commercial shell that surrounded the inner core of my dedication. The selling was his part to perform. I had all I could do to follow the will-o'-the-wisp, perfection. What time-wasters, I thought, these eternal break-ins of business, dimming the inner growth of the artist's life.

There was a whole season of concerts to be sung through before the NBC contract would be in full effect—great bodies move slowly, and each concert, each song, each moment of singing was important to me. I could not approach even the daily practice without the white heat of eager anticipation. Let the morning session go badly, and I was sickened for the day.

Dan Tuthill felt my behavior in these compulsions needed coaching: "It's a commercial world, and you've got to play the game on the outside, no matter what your inner convictions are. Learn to soft-pedal the highbrow stuff."

"The audience understands me," I answered, close to tears.

Feeling his words hit home, he went on: "This irresistible charm, beauty, personality, never reported engaged or in love, while a large company of the most attractive New York bachelors escort you everywhere is fine; but to agency men and broadcasters it looks phony. Is it true, they ask me, she'll kiss, but won't go further? What makes you tick, anyway?"

Furious at his brashness, I hurled at him, "I've been too busy ticking to find out!"

He looked me straight in the eye, watching for the glint that would betray me, and I looked him back in silence. I was not obliged to explain to anyone what I was thinking: "Whither shall I go from Thy Face?" Even if I could have explained, he would never have understood—that I love the company of men, but since my unhappy engagement I had vowed I would never marry; that I care—care about everything in my life.

Dan's manner softened. He promised to keep me in touch with the radio picture, and while I was on the road, he hoped I would think about a complete management by NBC.

"Don't knock yourself out with those concerts," he said with genuine kindness. "Take it from an old soldier, nobody really cares much."

He had something there, but it wasn't the whole story. One's ideals are one's own; I was used to the belief that we can't expect others to glorify us for holding on to them.

Now I went into feverish preparation for a new kind of appearance, two concerts, two nights in succession. This was something different—a common custom in Australia, but unheard of in America. The Omaha *World-Herald* would sponsor the concerts as their contribution to the Twenty-Second Convention of the Nebraska Music Teachers Association, 3,500 strong, who would meet in Omaha.

Besides the two concerts, would I not join the forum on the previous day and give a talk on program building? Violet Martens, a vocal coach of Chicago, would speak as well as the pianist, E. Robert Schmitz. The idea was absolutely frightening. While my musical feeling and knowledge had successively grown and broadened with each concert, I couldn't see myself ready to talk. "Thank you," I wrote back to the newspaper, "I don't lecture. I only sing."

But they would not be put off. They wrote again, "Surely, out of your vast experience in radio and concert, you can find something to say on program building." They also included in the letter some program suggestions of their own: "Sing only light things that people know—"

The element of incongruity between a request to lecture to music teachers of the state and singing "light things that people know" teased my imagination. It became the touchstone that set me to work on the talk. Since there are no song Baedekers, I had to dig out the material from remembered experience. I worried not so much over the two different concert programs as I did over the lecture. It made me ill and forced me for two days to go to bed, where I wrote the promised talk.

I saw the city unwrap itself from the long folds of yellow mounds, and on the platform to receive Nadea and me was a committee of newspapermen, teachers, and citizens, including Mayor Butler of Omaha. He was a jolly man, and we had scarcely exchanged greetings when, fingering his watch chain, he chuckled knowingly, "I'm a bachelor—so far!"

Interviews ensued; then luncheon with the teachers, among whom I found a fellow student of Estelle Liebling in her Berlin days with Nicklass-Kempner; she was Mary Munchoff. Afterward I visited St. Mary's Academy, because the nuns sent two messengers who insisted "the Sisters of Mercy have first claim on you. We also want a write-up for our school paper. Mary, the editor in chief, will take it." I started off with fillips about current this and that, feeling my way with the young editor; but she was not to be dissuaded from her reportorial convictions. Later she sent me the interview and these are her impressions verbatim: "Dragonette, symphony of refinement and culture. Her ideals illumine her personality. The Sisters' training has left its indelible mark. Miss Dragonette says the habit of study and self-discipline they fostered has been invaluable in her singing career."

Surely, we could squeeze in a visit to remarkable Boys Town and Father Flanagan, a teacher hostess was urging. No, it wasn't far. And yes, you will be back in time for the lecture.

August Borglum, brother of the American sculptor, Gutzon Borglum, was already introducing me when I arrived. I went directly to the lectern on the small platform erected in the ballroom of the Hotel Fontenelle and began to speak. As I raised my eyes to look out over the audience during the talk, I noticed a black-veiled head bobbing up and down in the last row. The impression remained in the margin of my thoughts. When the forum was over, and the teachers flattered me by asking questions, I turned to see Mother Annunziata, my little Servite friend from Detroit, in the crowd around me. She was now teaching in Omaha at Holy Cross School.

"You see what my prayers have done," she said plaintively. "They have brought me to Omaha to hear you in person. Tomorrow night and the night after I shall sit in the wings on the stage while you sing your concerts. I have permission to do so."

No words were needed; my bewildered expression conveyed my surprise to the conjured Mother Annunziata. As for her prayers, she was unquestionably telling the truth, for she is now back in Detroit again, where I first met her, at St. Juliana's School.

The irony of my apprehensive stage fright over addressing the teachers was set off by the reporter reviewing the session. "That was a good spiel and interesting too. But of course you didn't write it. Who 'ghosted' for you?"

"Thanks, I'm glad you liked it," I answered with relief. "This is my first offense."

"Really! Well, what I liked best was what you said about popular songs framing the music for a nation, that part about 'there is no essential difference between the lullaby of a medieval mother and that of a twentieth-century Manhattan mother; the serenade of a troubadour to his lady or an American college boy's "Of Thee I Sing, Baby." '"

"I was cooking with gas then?" I said playfully.

"That's right!"

"That's right," I repeated. "It's the constant interchange of the musical idea transmuting, perfecting, adapting the current material that finally evolves as the art song."

These concerts were given in a barnlike auditorium that holds 7,000 people. I was not quite sure whether my physical personality could carry to the back of the hall, much less the intimate recital songs, without benefit of microphones. There was justification of all I did in the eager way the audiences received the two completely different programs of music, extending over a wide gamut of recital songs to modern opera arias. Into a palpable silence, I sang Paul Nordhoff's "This Is the Shape of the Leaf." The burst of applause afterward was eloquent thanks for bringing the unhackneyed to this appreciative audience, rather than the same old familiar chestnuts.

The tribute is all for American audiences; it is of them I sing, because I know them.

People came back to meet me from the surrounding cities and towns of Nebraska, and as I said my last good night and requested a pencil for a late autograph seeker, Austin Wilder stretched out his hand.

"What are you doing here?" I asked in astonishment.

"I'm on my way to Chicago for business and thought I would stop off to hear you. Remarkably well done," he said. "Why, your voice is as big as Moore's in a hall."

We had a friendly supper together, but it wasn't until our return to New York that I understood the real purpose of his visit. Columbia Concerts had never been able to collect the fee for the Gary concert. Whatever the loss to me, they were only concerned about their commission and had sent Wilder to pick up the Omaha check so they could deduct the Gary and Omaha commissions before turning the remainder over to me. Strange ways of the concert world! The artist busy with music is uninterested in and usually neglects business procedure.

I had performed on the 25th, 26th, 27th of October; and now on the 28th, we left Nebraska for another turn in Wisconsin, where I would sing a concert on the 30th, then all the way back to Philadelphia for "college night" at the Automobile Show on the first of November. I could never have made this engagement on time without the assistance of my friend Richard Horsman, who measured out the minutes in small doses, allotting them wisely, without stepping on anybody's toes.

Back in New York I found myself as busy as on the road. Mayor La Guardia himself called for me to sing on Armistice Day at the Eternal Light Shrine in Madison Square. "How do you manage to look so youthful with all the work you do?" he asked as I hopped in the car. "This is a good thing you're doing for us—Rose Bampton has also consented to sing."

The Mayor didn't know the half of it, for I was off the next day to make a recording of "Is There A Santa Claus?" with Rosario Bourdon at the RCA Victor Recording Studios. Immediately afterward, I went to Washington to sing at the semicentennial of the Catholic University of America. I shuttled back at the request of Mrs. Her-

210 Faith Is a Song

bert Hoover to broadcast for the Girl Scouts program with Morton Downey. For the rest of the month I had nothing to do but prepare for my coming Boston concert at Jordan Hall on the twenty-second.

This was my first Boston appearance, and I was excited over it. The nearest I had come to singing in the American Athens was in the charming environs of Melrose, Quincy, and Framingham.

That year Franklin Delano Roosevelt had anticipated the real Thanksgiving by a week. After the Jordan Hall concert, I was pleasantly surprised to learn that Archbishop Spellman with a bevy of nieces had attended the concert and His Excellency was beneficently inviting me to Thanksgiving dinner with the family in his father's home in Whitman, Massachusetts. Regretfully I had to decline since I had already invited for Thanksgiving dinner in New York the Portuguese Consul, Dr. João de Aragao Barros; Dr. Martin Higgins, and Dr. Edward Dowd, both of the Catholic University, all of whom had journeyed to Boston for the concert.

It was already snowing as João and I said our Thanksgiving Day prayers in the quaint little Church of Our Lady of Victory. He was pleased as we descended the steep steps. "I am glad we did that, Jessica; life without religion is like a flower without perfume," he said.

Now we raced back to Christ Church to have another look at the beautiful stained-glass windows. Then we crossed the Common once more to see the delightful old houses with the purple glass on Beacon Hill. The joy of discovering Boston would spread out over the years ahead.

I sat with ears at attention during the fascinating train journey to New York, drinking in the distinguished conversation of our guests: Martin Higgins, a young San Franciscan, one of the four living Byzantine scholars of the world, now teaching Latin and Greek; Dr. Dowd, handsome, brilliant, and Bostonian, teaching philosophy and literature; and Dr. Barros, diplomat, moving eloquently among many subjects.

I had known the two clergymen for some time, but Barros only lately. I had seen a good deal of him when he was stationed in New York; recently he had been transferred. He told me he liked Boston better than New York because it reminded him of London—then throwing me a knowing glance, "there is just one thing lacking."

Nadea's atavism ran to ancient Greece and Byzantium, while mine ran to things Mediterranean. The star-pointed conversation had all "that trick of thought that falls in well with mine." Besides, in addition to wisdom and serenity, Barros had wit and beauty. His gray eyes, handsome brows, chiseled features were the more striking because of his black hair, and his sudden smile was unforgettable. The two priests roared with laughter when, discoursing on ancient things, Barros quipped:

"An authoress called me at the embassy the other day. 'Dr. Barros,' she began, 'I am writing on Portugal. Can you tell me exactly how old Portugal is?' 'Oh, no one knows that, Madame,' I answered." Then laughing, Barros continued, "'But I think it would be entirely safe to say that Portugal was in existence before Adam and Eve.'"

When we arrived in New York, and Barros was looking to the baggage, Dr. Higgins cornered me. "Jessica," he said seriously, "you could do much worse than marry Dr. Barros. He is utterly charming, and I can see he's in love with you. It is not good for man or woman to be alone."

I smiled enigmatically at his kind admonition; I had not gone so far toward Barros in my thoughts. I still felt there could be no division with my music, this precious gift entrusted to my care.

It was wonderful to be home for a while after so much travel, and I was enjoying the gravitational pull in João's direction. I would be in New York less than a fortnight before starting west and south again. During the extra day of Barros' visit, we went to the opera to hear the exquisite Bidu Sayao in *Manon;* then to the theater to see the new Brazilian bombshell, Carmen Miranda. Barros was greatly amused over her title "bombshell." Now it was time for good-by.

As we stood at the gate in the Grand Central Station, waiting for *The Puritan* to be announced, Barros turned to me: "*Saudades,* Jessica, *saudades.* I expect to leave for Portugal in the spring. Will you think about coming, too? *Saudades.*"

João had taught me his often repeated lovely word. He would look at me and smile, "Whole volumes have been written on it, Jessica." Then, attempting to clarify it for me, he gave me the Spanish equivalent, "*Soledades* is what the Spanish troubadours said in leave-taking, but it is not quite the same. *Soledades* lacks the nostalgic admixture of endearing emotions."

The Puritan to Boston gave a shush-shush, and Barros mounted the platform. When the train left the station, his voice was swallowed up in the noise and the smoke. As he waved good-by, I could distinguish two words his lips were forming, "Spring! *Saudades!*"

Between whiles, when I was not chasing a train or plane to some far place of singing, I pursued my vocal studies. Now my education took a new turn with H. Maurice Jacquet, a specialist in French repertoire. Jacquet was not only a vocal coach, but a distinguished conductor and composer as well. The great Verdi himself, an intimate friend of his father's, took him as a boy of three to the rehearsals of *Falstaff* in Paris. So vivid were his impressions that even today Jacquet recalls every observation. At nine he was a protégé of Massenet, and at seventeen acclaimed for conducting *Louise*. Together with his outstanding musical activities, which took him all over the world, he was the first to publish the then so-called ultramoderns, the now familiar *Les Six*, among them Milhaud, Poulenc, Auric, and Honegger.

Born in Savoy of noble parentage, Jacquet, spoiled child of art, enjoyed intimate companionship with singers like Melba, Battistini, Lilli Lehman, Journet, and Victor Maurel. The philanthropist Condé Nast first persuaded Jacquet to teach, and the maestro consented to take on Grace Moore as a pupil. She studied every day including Sundays for two years with Jacquet, and he toured with her on her first concerts. Knowing this, I am always amazed to hear people say that Moore had no technique. Her vocalism she received from Marafiotti, and she learned about musical deportment and interpretation from Jacquet.

Personally I acquired a great deal in the scientific and spiritual approach to singing in Jacquet's studio, where his understanding kindness created a rapport that outshone anything I had ever known. While I am grateful to all who have taught me, I reserve a special place for Maurice Jacquet. More than even the *beauty* of music, he taught me by his own example, *service* to music.

Jacquet's teaching, like all natural things, is simple, but not easy. We complicate everything with our own egos, rendering ourselves incapable of translating natural laws from one sphere to another. In other words, the singer's success depends on how he "plays" with his voice rather than a mechanical process of concentration on exercises.

When he could leave his pupils for a time, Jacquet would tour with me; in the concerts I always persuaded him to play a group of his own compositions, especially the lovely "Les Jardins de Murcie." Jacquet taught me in French, which was an added attraction. He was amused when I told him I had learned it in school. "So many girls study French in school, but they can't speak a sentence," he would retort. "Same with French music; to you it is like a pair of shoes you walk away in."

We are fortunate to have so many great minds from all over the world concentrated here in America. Together with other forces at work, the beautiful American voices, our love of music, abundant opportunities, augur a rich musical future.

The busy month of December took me to Richmond, Virginia, where I sang at the Bankers Association Conference of the Southern States. There would be talks on the American way of handling banking problems, and I was to interpolate several groups of songs as relief from serious matters. As this appearance had to be worked in between others, there was no possibility of delaying to see the interesting historical sites. The early concert was at seven o'clock in the large Masque Theater, and by nine-thirty we were ready to go back to the hotel, pack, and catch the train.

Scarcely in our rooms, we heard the telephone bell ringing wildly; it was the local manager. He knew the dining room was already closed and offered to get us some food at the home of a philanthropic citizen. We could get our train on time, he would see to that. It sounded innocent enough, and we were hungry. Robert Taylor, the bankers' public relations man assigned to us for the evening, joined us; so we felt reasonably safe. The manager's "short distance" kept stretching with each succeeding mile out of town. The golden minutes were running themselves out, yet on and on he drove us on a seventy-five-mile jaunt. Finally we arrived at a castlelike home and were ushered into a living room face to face with an immense pipe organ. The host greeted us warmly with an air of having expected us all the while and quickly introduced his visitor, Charles Courboin, the Belgian organist.

"Will you sing something for us?" beamed our host.

"Oh, I've put the canary to sleep," I said sadly, "but if Mr. Courboin will oblige."

"Indeed, yes," smiled Courboin.

Together we gave Schubert's "Ave Maria" and after the postlude died away, we all sat quietly. Meanwhile, Mr. Manager disappeared; and we became panicky lest we be stranded. Later he reappeared with a highball in hand, but offered us neither food nor drink. As politely as I could, I took leave of my host and stood on the steps, waiting to be driven to the train.

Finally the manager caught on. "Why can't you stay until tomorrow?" he pleaded. "My wife and I will see that you get the morning train." Adamant, I stuck to my guns, and with coattails flying, this hulk of a man raced out of the house, jumped in the car, and began driving us back to Richmond.

At the hotel at last, we picked up our bags and dumped them in the back, while Robert Taylor stood guard against any possible flight of the manager. When we were seated, he went to the desk to check the train.

"You have fifteen minutes you didn't count on. There's a railroad diner," he said, pointing to something that looked like a dive. "I think you can get a sandwich over there. Better do it; there's no diner on the train."

At the exhaustion point, we moved wearily toward the dingy restaurant. Without even looking at the moldy menu, I ordered an egg sandwich and a glass of milk. Robert Taylor stood in the doorway, one eye on us and one on the volatile manager outside. Barely had the sandwich and the milk been placed before us when Robert Taylor pointed his thumb over his shoulder. I grabbed up the sandwich in my paper napkin and ran, leaving Nadea to pay the cashier. Once again we were driving at break-neck speed toward the station. We were going so fast, there wasn't a chance to take even a bite of that sandwich.

In the station finally I thought "Ah, at last!" But just then a Southern banker came up to me. "I beg your pardon, Miss. Permit me to tell you how much I enjoyed your singing." Every step I took the same thing happened. Fortunately, in the darkness, not one of the bankers who stopped me was aware of what was in the precious little white package I was clutching—I was my most cordial. Blessed moment when the train pulled in, and Nadea and I boarded the Pullman.

Robert Taylor hopped on after us for a minute. "You'd make a swell public relations gal; too bad you're a singer." As he hurriedly left, he dropped two cartons of milk on the seat in our drawing room!

After Christmas I sang the first of four concerts in the Wanamaker Grand Court in Philadelphia, when 12,000 people jammed the famous middle aisle and balconies of this truly remarkable store. After concerts that brought me through March, I returned to New York to take part in a special broadcast for Catholic Charities in which Walter Hampden did a dramatic version of the life of Cardinal Hayes, *The Cardinal of Charity*. Then we were off again for a turn at the four-a-day in the Capitol Theater in Washington.

Carter Barron, the motion picture house manager, was not only excited over his scoop but over the fact that immediately after he announced my appearance, his competitor, the Earle, quickly let it be known that Marion Talley would be their attraction. It all could have been coincidence. Nevertheless, it is strange that Talley was under George Engles' management. She had the successful picture *Dark Victory*, but even with a picture Washingtonians hated, *The Lady's From Kentucky* with George Raft, so many people flocked backstage, sending large baskets of flowers and gifts, that a rumor circulated I was born in Washington, D. C.

This was the one time my friend Dr. McNeil could not come to see me. He was very ill so I went to him and when I asked him why he would not go to the hospital, he said with a childlike concern, "I won't be able to light the candles for my wife." Mrs. McNeil, a Catholic, had been dead many years, but every week he faithfully lighted a candle for her at the Blessed Virgin's altar. Touched by the depth of his devotion I said, "Why, Mac, I shall be glad to do it for you. So now it becomes my responsibility." After I left, Dr. Watson Miller wrote me a note of thanks for succeeding where he had failed.

Now I was back in Studio 8H again, standing on the stage where I had sung so often in the past. This time I was surrounded by a symphony orchestra and the Paulist choristers under Father Finn with whom I would sing a Mendelssohn cantata and other hymns.

Archbishop Spellman would officiate and give the papal blessing, and Monsignor Fulton Sheen, a regular speaker on the Catholic Hour since its inception in 1930, would speak again. "Today the Catholic Hour is ten years young. I say 'young,' not old, because age is a climate of the soul, not the measure of years." On the lower stage sat the Papal Marquis, the Knights of Malta and St. Gregory, and far back to the doors the room was crowded with guests.

I sat quietly waiting while the red hand raced around the studio clock, and the director stood watching it, ready to set the broadcast in motion. I was wearing an old-fashioned *bouffant* blue tulle dress with tight bodice, long sleeves, tiered skirt, and a matching veil circled with apple blossoms. After the assembly was seated, Mr. Louis Kenedy, president of the National Council of Catholic Men, presented me with a bouquet of freesia and roses. As I looked around, I suddenly realized I was the only woman among so many men.

At supper afterward in the Rainbow Room high in the lookout of the RCA Building, the Archbishop was singling out one of the Knights of Malta.

"Jessica," His Excellency said, "the little man sitting next to Martin Conboy is a great painter. I remember Müller-Ury from my American college days in Rome. He has painted three popes and was a great favorite of Pius X. You must meet him before you go."

Nadea and Martin Conboy introduced me to the painter as we were leaving. "Tell my sister the Giotto story, Mr. Müller-Ury," she was urging.

"Another time. It's late now, and I rise very early." In the swift, restless, all-seeing glance he gave, I detected his arm in motion, as if he were already painting me.

"May I bring the ladies to your studio?" Mr. Conboy was asking.

"By all means; with pleasure. Next Tuesday afternoon at four?" He was wearing the wide red Maltese band across his chest; it made a rosy reflection in his eyes as he bade us good night.

The following Tuesday, Martin Conboy escorted us to Müller-Ury's studio on West Sixty-seventh Street. The painter received us into the richly appointed, high-ceilinged duplex studio I was later to know so well. On the walls were several copies of paintings by Velásquez: Don Carlos on horseback and the artist painting the infanta. Müller-Ury had copied the pictures in Spain and kept them as technical reference. He had been working all day on a portrait of

Archbishop Spellman that would soon be finished. Later on he did several more.

Now he was showing us portraits of the Havemeyer children, Lord Duveen, Lord Mount Stephens, the elder Morgan, James J. Hill. He had painted everyone of importance in the last thirty-five years, and finally he was showing us what he enjoyed painting for relaxation between portraits. They were pictures of roses of every color and variety—American Beauty, Belle of Portugal, La France, Killarney, Claudius and Boucher-Pierné—arranged in the great porcelains of the Morgan collection later bought and sold by Lord Duveen. We were in another world when he showed us the rose paintings. No one could call them still life—they were portraits of living flowers.

"I went forty times to Amsterdam to study Rembrandt," he told us. "I think I have gone beyond his technique in these canvases."

After that visit I saw the artist a good deal when we were in town. Sometimes he would dine with us and when the urgency of the day's painting was over, he would tell us incredible tales of his fascinating life.

But the Giotto story? The life of the Italian painter had made a profound impression on Müller-Ury when he read it at seventeen. He was very fond of saying, "Giotto said: 'If you wish to paint and you are a genius, then you may marry and partake of life; but if you are merely talented, there will be no time to marry, for you will have to work day and night.'" Müller-Ury believed he was merely talented.

How wonderful to see this renowned artist in the sunset of life preserving all the youthful ardor and devotion to his ideal! To watch him before a canvas, literally playing with the brushes, the years falling from him, to hear him exclaim: "When I paint, I'm the happiest man in the world."

Dan Tuthill kept his word; when I returned at the end of April, there was a radio series ready for me. The furor I had caused by leaving Cities Service, the downright misleading releases of NBC, the intrigue of Sheldon Coons had not been forgotten; in fact, they had gained momentum. Already the newspapers were announcing my return to the air on the Ford Summer Hour series, but when Dan Tuthill gave me the contract to examine, I observed in essence

I would be "auditioning" the first three broadcasts; if they were satisfactory, I would be held over for the twenty-two-week series. This was a blow which dimmed considerably the golden luster of my Star of Stars crown. Besides, *Radio Guide Weekly* published a notice that Vivian della Chiesa was under commitment to stand by in case I "cracked up."

The overwhelming crowds who came to hear me, the excellent notices I had been receiving from music critics over the country, meant absolutely nothing. As a matter of fact, agency men argued that singing so much in large halls had probably wrecked my radio possibilities. There they were acting in reverse, believing prejudice rather than statistics. It was difficult to try to do one's best in the "come on and show us" atmosphere. I knew I was fighting desperately for the life of my career, and even more important for a victory over my slackening personal stamina. After working for years, I was having to make good all over again!

When the first dress rehearsal for the Ford Hour in the rotunda at Dearborn was over, Larry Sizer, then with the N. W. Ayer advertising agency, rushed from the control room onto the stage with "Jessica, you're great! You sound like *two* people." Then coming close so no one else could hear, he whispered, "Confidentially—they led me to believe you had lost your voice!"

Even Herb Rosenthal, who represented the CBS artists except me, was gushy; after the first performance he had nothing but highest praise for my singing. I went on for twenty-two weeks with Leith Stevens, the conductor; James Newell, the California baritone; and Linton Wells, commentator and world traveler.

Twice a week I flew to Detroit for the broadcasts, and with the assignments in between there was never any time to see the unique city Henry Ford had built. Henry and Mrs. Ford attended some of the broadcasts in the rotunda. He seemed pleased when I admired the clean classic lines, the landscaping, and above all the beautiful beacon light on the air field. It was then I noticed his expression change—he looked grave, saddened. I wondered about this, and later Louis Barbiere, one of his secretaries, told me the beacon was a memorial to a flier, and Henry Ford had never gotten over the loss of the young man.

By June the headlines were screaming: First Mass Clash of New

World War—1,000 Dive Bombers Lead Attack on 100-Mile Front—
600,000 Germans in Somme Push—and I was on my way to Toledo
to take part in the high-school students music festival in DeVilbiss
Stadium. With the world moving toward suicide, I was happy to
participate in something constructive. Toledo appreciated my efforts, the 1,100 students who sang with me and the 15,000 people
who turned out to hear us.

Between the Ford Summer Hours in Dearborn, I sang the first
of many concerts in that idyllic music setting, the Potomac Water-
gate, as part of the Sunset Symphonies under Hans Kindler. It was
quickening to sing with this fine orchestra on a barge floating about
a mile from the shore. We faced the Washington Needle and the
Lincoln Memorial; immediately surrounding us and tied to the barge
itself was an informal flotilla of hundreds of boats and canoes, full of
music lovers lolling on pillows and billows. They were decidedly
more comfortable than the audience on shore, sitting on the long, low
stone steps. A goodly portion of the populace of Washington and
vicinity seemed gathered there, for with the 18,000 people assembled, 2,000 were turned away. They waited outside the gate or remained to listen under the Memorial Bridge.

Among many friends was Dr. McNeil who left his sick bed to
come. Since he was the epitome of joy, only a few of us realized how
ill he was. On his white evening jacket he wore all the medals
earned during his forty years in the army. He had not forgotten to
send the lovely orchids I was wearing in my hair. Dr. Watson Miller
of the Veterans Bureau accompanied him.

"You were never better, Jessica, God bless you." Dr. McNeil said
the words with such vital enthusiasm I felt instantly recharged. "And
d'you know something? I've been taking the carrot juice you prescribed and I feel fine."

Dr. Miller smiled, corroborating the story. "He has indeed been
faithful to the regimen."

Now Dr. McNeil was laughing. With his incomparable sense of
humor he said: "We're in the presence of another doctor. Watson,
I want you to salute Dr. Darling Dragonette."

As for me, I fell in love with everyone who came back to see me
—the highest and the lowest brought a sincerity so overwhelming
that I was speechless; it kept me snared, for I wanted to give back

my best in return. In the face of many odds it has been the public
who really keeps my career alive.

Between the flights to Dearborn, I was now sitting to Müller-Ury.
He had decided on a life-size portrait, had chosen the position, the
background, and the gown—an embroidered white organdy with
French blue moiré sash I used for summer concerts. It was a good
deal for both of us to embark on, since we were so busy. Insatiable,
he demanded hours of posing, yet all of them were enjoyable because next to painting, Müller-Ury loved to talk. He worked right
through the summer, and every hour I could spare away from practice and performance, I devoted to him.

Arriving late one Monday evening from a concert in Lancaster,
Pennsylvania, I heard the telephone ringing persistently as I entered
the foyer of my apartment. When I picked up the receiver, the operator said Washington had been ringing all evening, and would I
speak to Dr. Watson Miller?

"Our dear Dr. McNeil died today," he said sadly. "He will be
buried at Arlington on Wednesday. I thought you might like to
know."

A guard of honor of Legionnaires met my plane and escorted me
to the lovely chapel in Arlington where Dr. McNeil, dressed in his
uniform, lay in state between the draped flags. He looked happy
and peaceful. Though he had been inducted into the thirty-third
degree Masons in a private ceremony with General Pershing alone,
and the Masons would have liked to honor their distinguished
brother, they all stepped aside with supreme grace to permit me to
sing Dr. McNeil's favorite hymn, Schubert's "Ave Maria." Then they
wrapped the flag about him and lowered him into his soldier's grave.
Taps sounded through quiet Arlington; as I threw the armful of
flowers I carried over the open earth, the words of Strauss's "Aller-
seelen" sang themselves in my heart:

> Stell' auf den Tisch die duftenden Reseden,
> Die letzten roten Astern trag herbei,
> Und lass uns wieder von der Liebe reden,
> Wie einst im Mai.

CHAPTER 18

"DO YOU HEAR ME, AMERICA?"

Now that an elder-day, gray legendary mist falls over the Forties, we look back in wonder at Broadcasting Day when Norman Corwin and John Latouche lent themselves to the writing of something memorable. We were celebrating the freedom of the air, and a voice from the intricate machine proclaimed:

> I am Radio
> Companion of Sun and Thunder
> Over the American continent . . .
> From the steaming savannahs of the South
> Up to white Alaska
> From the gold-tossing cornfields of the West
> to the incredible Eastern cities
> Do you hear me, America?

John S. Young, personifying the voice, continued:

We are speaking to you from the World's Fair Court of Peace, where famous entertainers and distinguished personages are gathered to celebrate Broadcasting Day, a day set aside jointly by the World's Fair and the Golden Gate Exposition to pay tribute to Freedom of the air—

During the next hour you will hear the voices of scores of your favorite radio artists, voices you have welcomed to your homes time and time again.

You will also hear leaders in many walks of life who will express their opinions freely on the subject of Broadcasting. For this occasion great networks and the independent stations from coast to coast have placed their facilities at the disposal of the Fair, creating a hook-up of over 500 stations, one of the greatest ever formed together.

LISTENERS OF AMERICA, THIS IS RADIO

The familiar voices began to come in from Hollywood, New York, and everywhere—Amos and Andy, Orson Welles, Gertrude Berg, James Melton, Ted Husing, Morton Downey, H. V. Kaltenborn, Major Bowes, Clifton Fadiman, Kate Smith, Walter Van Kirk, Brian

McEntagart, William Green, Quincy Howe, John W. Studebaker, Harvey Gibson, Howard Barlow, Morton Gould, Frank Black, Milton Cross.

And now John Young was announcing: "Jessica Dragonette from the Ford Rotunda in Dearborn." He caught the last part of my "Indian Love Call," an unconscious choice of song, completely appropriate to the occasion. The listeners heard

> Then I will know my dream will come true
> You'll belong to me, I'll belong to you.

We had passed another milestone in the far-flung dream from the long-ago nineteen stations, to this network of 500 stations today, united in a single aim. With a world at war, this broadcast was emanating from the Court of Peace, celebrating a Freedom. "Faith is the substance of things unseen. . . ."

I continued my unbroken cycle of work that summer, but before going to Milwaukee again for "Music under the Stars," I did something I had promised myself for a long time. I had known superficially the score of *Pelléas et Mélisande;* now I would make every measure of the Debussy masterpiece my own. William Tarrasch, another Nazi refugee conductor from the Saxony Opera House, knew the score well and had a reverence for the music; together we accomplished good work in a short time.

As a child in Estelle Liebling's studio, I had confined myself to the scores I would be likely to sing in the future, had I not been sidetracked by radio: *La Bohème, Romeo and Juliet, Rigoletto, Madama Butterfly,* later *Otello* and *Thais,* especially *Thais*—this was one of the scores Jacquet thought I walked away in. However, other teachers preferred to hear me in Italian music. The vowel-laden language is custom-made for the singer, keeping the vocal mechanism unhampered, the singing line flowing, the way clear for a beautiful *emissione*—that wonderful word whose symbol appears over and over again every time we see the crescendo-diminuendo sign in music; the groove into which any language, any singing, fits perfectly.

My friends often ask, "Jessica, where is your fun?"

"Just living is fun for me," I answer, "but having a multitude of interests, and being merely talented, I cannot afford to lend myself to completely hedonistic pursuits." From childhood I have been ac-

customed to the austere timbre of solitude conducive to study and I
have followed a close schedule of practice and performance.

Fighters work out on the road; baseball players have spring training; singers likewise keep fit by adhering to a program of exercise
suited to their particular needs. Beauty, posture, and breathing are
so closely allied that it is difficult to separate them. A proper use of
strong diaphragm muscles in the small of the back is the internal
secret assuring surface suppleness and smooth, graceful carriage. The
hardships of the singer's life could never be endured without this
powerful knowledge. It involves oxidized circulation of the blood
from the crown of the head to the soles of the feet, inducing absence
of physical and mental tensions, making for balance—in other words,
true poise.

Proper breathing tones the body, aerates the senses, and brushes
away the cobwebs of tautness over tired nerves. Before singing my
scales in the morning, I have a breathing bath, and several times
a day I tune up my body, which is my singing instrument. All my
life I have studied breathing, physical grace, and fitness.

I make a game of walking at an appointed time each day, letting
a group of motivating pictures pass clearly through my consciousness, to give a feeling of release from fixed habits. Appropriately I
imagine a dinosaur tail dragging from my spine and my legs trying
to run away from it; this has a tendency to elongate the backbone
and tuck the hips under where they belong. Or I think of wading
in the ocean against a strong current, which imparts a sense of proper
integration of the torso muscles.

The axis of the spine should be long, the head held high, but not
stiff. I imagine the crown of my head reaching up toward a hook
in the sky, Venus perhaps, and I hang, feet scarcely touching the
earth. The fantasy makes for a lighter tread—no sound of heaviness
—and a more graceful carriage, giving a sensation of stretch to the
back of the neck and the lower spine.

To be in athlete-condition to carry on is no mean accomplishment.
For that reason I have enjoyed little social life in general; my career
has been all-consuming.

Interminable dinners are a waste of time for the singer. One eats
too much, subjects oneself to smoke, crowd poisoning, and fatigue.
Naturally, there are exceptions to all rules. Dining out usually gives

the hostess license to call on one to sing. Since I love to please, the most difficult thing in the world for me is to refuse. Yet, I dislike singing in the drawing room except for my closest friends; I prefer to keep my performances for the stage. Nor do I like to practice where I am likely to disturb people—almost never at home but in a studio some distance away—a great disappointment to my family.

Not long ago, the elevator boy in the building where I go to practice, unknown to me, lingered outside the door while I was singing. An hour later when I descended with him, he said completely ignorant of my identity:

"Have you had your audition yet, Miss? You have a fine voice. Keep practicing now, and I'm sure we'll see your name up in lights."

"Thank you, oh, thank you," I answered, blushing. "I'll do all I can."

As I left the building, he smiled after me with the air of an impresario who had made a new discovery, and I smiled back with all the flushed feeling of a high success.

Toward the end of August, the Ford Motor Company asked the whole cast of the Summer Hour, except Linton Wells, their Rouge River Plant reporter, to perform a benefit concert for the Detroit Federation of Musicians celebrating a golden jubilee of music in the city parks. Since the concert was to be held in the music shell on Belle Isle at midweek, I planned to stay over in Dearborn. The summer so far had been unbearably hot, but on the night of the concert, frost drifted down from Canada and settled over the music-haunted island on the Detroit River, hidden from us, but glittering under the cold moon, as it streamed out into the night. Some 40,000 shivering Detroiters gathered and remained enthusiastic to the end.

The performers were clad in flimsy summer costumes that afforded scant protection against the chilling winds. Though I have been accustomed to acting in public like a well-trained race horse, one of those artist creatures who win their blue ribbons for skill, beauty, and deportment in their classes, taking whatever hardships the occasion imposes in showmanship stride, this situation was making a fetish of hardship. When we came offstage between numbers, there was no place to warm up. Huddling about a tree it seemed to us that even the stars in the pale sky were afraid to show their faces, and we remained there shivering until time to go on again.

The audience alone had the secret of mind over matter; they were

loving the music. That was the cue—I might have pneumonia tomorrow, but I couldn't face them wrapped in a cape! James Newill
took matters into his own hands. I was almost thrown off guard during a romantic duet, when I looked up and noticed that under his
evening jacket, he had slipped a cable stitch tennis sweater! Only
in the finale did I throw my red velvet wrap over my frozen shoulders. Oddly enough, I didn't catch pneumonia.

The Summer Hour came to a close toward the end of September,
and less than a month afterward I was embarked on the Saturday
Night Serenade broadcasts. Meanwhile, a number of changes had
taken place. The NBC Artists Bureau was now divorced from radio;
George Engles was out of the picture; Dan Tuthill, who had arranged
this series, was part of the newly formed NCAC Concert Bureau.

On the other hand, I had signed up with Albert Morini. For some
years previously, Mr. Morini had operated in Europe, and each season, on returning to America, he would try to induce me to tour
abroad, starting with a concert at the American Embassy in Paris
when the Duke and Duchess of Windsor were entertained there. In
answer to all his cables I had to tell him my radio obligations made
it impossible for me to leave America.

Driven home by the war, Albert Morini decided to buy out the
old Daniel Mayer Concert Bureau and handle a few American artists along with the remaining European list, among them Tito
Schipa. In talking to Mr. Morini each season—when he was persuading me to go back to Europe with him—I got the impression of
a serious-minded, sensitive, musical man, interested in only the finest
concerts. He did not want to handle his violinist sister, Erica Morini,
because he did not care to trade on family prestige. I thought Mr.
Morini's taste would lead to less strenuous tours. He quickly ran to
type, however, after I was signed with him; in the years under his
management, he booked as high as ten to fifteen times a month between the weekly broadcasts.

Since Saturday Night Serenade had a fairly simple format, requir-
ing minimum rehearsal time, I was free to pursue the busy tours Mr.
Morini mapped out for me. That the broadcast fell on a Saturday
facilitated the concert schedule; I could sing in New York Saturday
night, be off again on Sunday, and return the following Friday. The
latitude such a program afforded me seemed to warrant accepting

a smaller salary than I had ever before received; this fact contradicts the propaganda fed to the public that no sponsor could afford the price I demanded for my services.

The first year I was with Saturday Night Serenade, we did not broadcast over the CBS New York Station, and since New Yorkers could not hear me, they assumed I was not on the air. Nevertheless, we were heard over a large network of stations throughout the rest of the country. My fans thought the venture below the high caliber of my former programs, yet they expressed great pleasure over hearing me sing a few songs a week.

Looking back I am amused at the series of daunting hoops I was put through. The sponsors, Pet Milk for Babies, wanted to be sure I was a character they could send with impunity into every American home. There could be no blots on the escutcheon. They knew I had refused to appear on cigarette ads because I do not smoke. When a beer company approached me with a fine series, they objected on the ground that it would be undignified.

I was continually watched, probed, and investigated. As usual Nadea came in for her share of the brunt; while in reality far more fragile than I, neglecting herself, she hovered over me like a solicitous mother. We were shocked later to learn that Roland Martini, the agency man for Pet Milk, had put a detective on us to ascertain if we were really sisters! The stark truth bewildered him; he didn't know what to make of it. I remember once he said to me: "If you aren't lying, it means you haven't enough intelligence to do so." It was all typical of the narrow circle of radio agency life. Where had they been for the last eleven years?

I found further inducement in Saturday Night Serenade because Gustav Haenschen was the conductor; Emile Coté and his choir, along with William Perry, took part. I remained with the series throughout four and a half years, doing the long concert schedules in between.

Albert Morini went "all out" in the bookings. He would have had me singing every night, had I not complained it was too much with the rugged travel involved. For this he reported me to *Musical America* and *Musical Courier*. Both magazines wrote me scathing letters, asking me how I dared refuse work in a time when most concert artists could not get engagements.

In the face of the Morini concert schedules, accusations were ridiculous. My new season began September 11—eleven days before the Summer Hour closed—and carried on right up to the opening of Saturday Night Serenade. It included hops to Madison, Wisconsin, for a doctors' convention; Port Huron for the initial concert in the Methodist Church Auditorium series; Decatur, Illinois, for the Wesley Brotherhood. Together with the Morini concerts, I sang at air bases and camps opening up everywhere over the country, starting with Westover Field, where they introduced me to my first B-29.

That fall Gayelord Hauser, accustomed to coming to us for Sunday brunch whenever we were in New York, telephoned he would like to bring along a visitor. Nadea and I readily consented and awaited our guests with eagerness. A series of half hourly telephone calls ensued in which Gayelord announced the *status quo.* "Yes, she will come." Then, "No, I don't think she can make it." Again, "She has changed her mind." And finally, "She will come if you can assure her that no one but yourselves alone will be there." It all added up to a kind of frenzied suspense until at last I went to the door myself in answer to the bell.

I found Gayelord standing on the sill alone. Where was his guest? She had evaporated into thin air, playfully hiding. Suddenly, from back of the door leading to my outer hall, she emerged with a laugh that was like a chime of bells. Then in a burst of full glory, with the out-of-nowhereness of her cinema entrances, I saw Greta Garbo, looking exactly as I had known her on the screen; one exception, in life she is far more beautiful.

I shall never know what induced her to come, to shed the shroud of her life's inevitable mystery, to loosen her disinclination to show herself, for however much I had desired it, I had never asked Gayelord to bring her. There she was standing in the center of my doorway, her eyelids hooding her soft blue gaze. In that moment I sensed the actress. At my extended hand she moved toward me, like a swift-footed Diana, and I could see her bright head under the darkness of her large-brimmed hat.

Like children, she and Gayelord fought over his usual place at the table, and she kept asking "Why?" to every question, like a child.

"You serve grapefruit as we do in California," she said with a surprised air. "Where did you learn that?"

"Oh, I've been to California," I bantered. "To Texas, too, where I was offered a grapefruit ranch, if I would accept the strings attached."

This threw her off. She had made up her mind I might be prim and standoffish.

"Oh!" She let fall a gap in the conversation. Then, with an impish pull at Gayelord's pocket handkerchief, she unfolded it and wrapped it around her hair. This set Nadea, naturally inclined that way, off into fantasy. She left the table, came back with armfuls of East Indian tissues—blue, green, purple, white, orange, and old rose—all shot with gold. We draped ourselves like Orientals and proceeded with breakfast.

"I eat only poached eggs," Garbo said timidly. Then whipping out a small package she turned to our maid Adelaide, while she was serving coffee. "I drink only Postum. Here, I brought some."

Adelaide, an indulged member of the family for years, looked scornfully at the proffered box, and to my embarrassment refused it. "Oh, Miss Jess' has Postum, thank you."

This sent us all into gales of laughter, Adelaide into the pantry talking to herself, and Gayelord whispering to Garbo, "Them's African Echoes!" And ever after the name stuck.

Garbo was swift and continually moving; as she sat opposite me at the table, I had ample opportunity to study her finely molded head, her gorgeous eyes, small features, splendid arch of the mouth, the smooth, transparent, grapelike skin. At her strong straight throat she wore a pale peach-colored scarf that cast a pearly patina over her face and eyes. "How can they say she's badly dressed?" I wondered, as I observed her immaculate tailleur of live dark blue; she looked the quintessence of appropriate chic. To the end of this first visit she remained delightfully playful.

"Have you a rubber band?" she asked, in leaving.

"Oh yes," I answered, pulling a handful of red and blue ones from my desk and wondering.

"One will do," she said archly.

"Then do have this red one," I said, stretching it in the buttonhole of her lapel. "I hereby give you the Légion d'Honneur."

This was a signal for her improvising humor again. She came back and jumped up on the bench before the fireplace. "Will you vote for me as President of the United States?" she said. Then patting herself on the chest and flashing her white teeth in a broad smile, "I'm a good man. Besides I'll have to do something important after having been in the films."

She was in a good position for me to see those much maligned feet. They are small, as everything about her appears to be in spite of her height, and she was wearing the softest dark blue leather, low-heeled buckled slippers.

When it was time for them to go, I took a blue hyacinth from a bowl of flowers. "Won't you wear this? It matches your eyes!"

She turned me a cinematic sidelong shoulder in refusal. "I never wear flowers," she smiled, observing that I was carrying the red rose nosegay she and Gayelord had brought me.

This first of many visits happened some months after she had finished *Ninotchka*, but even then I wondered why the films had never used her exquisite playfulness or her fantastic humor. Once at Christmas time, when Gayelord persuaded her to join us at tea in his rooms at the Ritz Towers to meet Harry Ackerman, just when we thought she would never come, she arrived in knickers! As the three of us sat talking, the conversation veered to the swift, progressive strides the Turkish women had made.

"Oh," she said, looking at me painfully as if we were getting in too deep, "shall we have to use the dictionary?"

We could always count on Garbo's being unpredictable. One day when Adelaide was ill and at the last moment could not come to make breakfast, we were frantic. It was Sunday so we could expect no one from employment agencies. We hit upon the brilliant idea of hiring a chef from Longchamps Restaurant. Yes, he would come on the condition we hired him for the whole day. It was an expensive proposition, but we paid the piper rather than disappoint our friends. When the chef arrived, we told him he was only to prepare the food, not serve it; Garbo didn't like to have strangers look at her. He appeared hurt at this and rubbed his hands over his spotless white uniform and rakish high hat as if to say: "But why?"

With a sigh of having completed the impossible, at the first sound of the bell I went to the door. There were Gayelord and Gee Gee.

She dashed in and seemed to sense something strange, or maybe she was just in one of her prankish moods, for without warning she dove into the kitchen frightening the bewildered chef, picked up a silex of coffee and began serving us herself! The chef left shortly afterward with a whole day's pay, and ever since we boast of our forty-dollar breakfast for Garbo!

Another Sunday morning she had already arrived before I had returned from Mass. I was wearing a mink coat; and, as I came into the living room, I walked a little sideways with one shoulder leading in imitation of Garbo entering a scene. Half rising from her chair, she studied me fixedly.

"That's my hat you're wearing. Where did you get that pink felt? And that coat?"

"Why, it was in a window," I said, falling in with her stride and play-acting, "so—I hinted a little."

She put on an understanding expression, posing her head from side to side, and letting out a drawled "O-oo-oh, I see!" Then with a note of conspiracy, "Does he have black eyes?"

"Yes," I answered softly, "and he plays the guitar."

"Well then," she said with subtle emphasis, "it's worth it."

Sometimes, feeling the scenes needed musical accompaniment, I would go to the piano and play.

"Will you sing for me?" She would rush over and say, "Do!"

"I never sing on Sundays."

"Oh, don't say never," she would plead bending over the piano, looking her most persuasive, "Say maybe." Seeing I could not be budged, she began to recite tragically. "Won't you sing for me? I'll have nothing but the burned-out hills when I return to California. Besides, when you write your memoirs, you can tell how you sang for the world-weary."

Nadea and I were knitting wristlets for the British soldiers; beside the dark blue required, we had lively colored yarns in an Indian basket to entice others. Garbo picked up a ball of orange yarn and began knitting furiously at the high point of her elocution.

"No," I cried. "I don't expect to write memoirs; but if I do, I shall say Garbo knitted here."

So it was whenever we came together. Nadea walked with her a great deal and always found her enchantingly playful, intelligent, and skillful in every way. She sent us charming gifts at Christmas and Easter; and, when Nadea was visiting California, Garbo herself drove her to the Farmers Market for luncheon.

One morning at breakfast Garbo asked for a copy of Walt Whitman's *Leaves of Grass* and to our utter surprise began reading one of the obscure poems in her eloquent contralto. Another time, coming to say good-by before leaving for the Coast, she said ruefully, "Now that I'm here, I'm sorry I haven't come more often." A few seconds later, she fell into an amusing imitation of what she heard the night before in *Kiss Me, Kate.* She picked up her skirts and jazzed "True to You in My Fashion."

Everyone who knows Garbo thinks he understands her. I rather think people misunderstand her natural curiosity, her meticulous thoroughness, her suggestibility. From childhood she has been a well-trained actress, and most of her life has been spent before the camera. It is her spontaneous ability to act every scene in life, as well as on the screen, that makes her so fascinating.

Her running away from prying eyes is comprehensible. As we continued to see more and more of her, this aloofness grew less; yet sometimes the habit had its ludicrous aspects. Knowing her to be a sun worshiper like myself, I invited her to sit on our terrace. She accepted readily; but, when she suddenly realized she was sitting on a roof garden, she became aware that people on the terraces two blocks away might see her, and she was terrified. I assured her they were all too busy with their own thoughts to be looking our way. I must have been convincing for later she was so relaxed, she almost went bathing in the fountain pool. Then *I* became worried about what the neighbors might think.

One day, seeing me show some photographs of myself to Gayelord, she exclaimed, "That's cute. Is that me?"

Another day I made her lie on the floor because she was tired. I administered to her, giving her breathing and relaxing exercises, and after a rest she was much better. She looked at me very sweetly. "I shall come from Hollywood for treatments, Dr. Nightingale."

Once, when the maid was running the vacuum cleaner, I answered the telephone but could not hear the name clearly. I kept repeating, "Who is it please?" and the voice kept answering, "Brown, Brown, it's Miss Brown!" Finally, the last exasperated deep-voiced

"Brown" penetrated. It was Garbo incognito as Harriet Brown, telling me she wanted to pay us a call.

One of the tragedies of the time, and something I can never understand is why Hollywood cannot find the right picture for this gifted actress. The Italian fiasco and bad press under Walter Wanger's management was unfair and must have been heartbreaking to the sensitive star. It is not that she is unwilling, for what artist breathes who does not wish to work? She languishes in the best years of her life, away from the realm where she can bring increase to our happiness and enhancement to life.

On my first visit to West Point, starting in a twilight atmosphere where stories frequently end, with endearing sequences already performed, a handsome young officer and I proceeded almost by formula to Flirtation Walk. Flirtation Walk? It sounded like something blinking in neon lights on a theater marquee, like the name of a place written in a flower bed, like a sampler woven in careful cross-stitches, the title of a Hollywood scenario; but I was at the United States Military Academy. I should have heeded the premonition flashed when an officer's precocious daughter shouted after us in a knowing, adolescent voice, "Where're you going? To Flirtation Walk?"

I put my hand over the little book in my coat pocket. After the brilliant showing I had made at tea in Grant Hall, I couldn't follow up with a let-down on this more important mission. There were only brief moments after rehearsal with Captain Resta and the chorus, with whom I had come to sing, to scan *Bugle Notes,* the cadets' bible—but oh! to have a look at it now, to help me on this destination unknown.

I looked up through the silver shutters of the rain at the golden lady tiptoe on the golden ball.

"Do you know her?" questioned my companion.

"Yes, sir," I answered demurely. "They are all fickle but one."

"Well done," he replied, as I stood saluting the statue way above us.

He was totally ignorant of the source of my pat answers. On the parade grounds still, where he dare not offer me his arm, he was very formal as he tried to make conversation.

"The rehearsal went well, and the glee club is looking forward to the concert with you tomorrow afternoon. Colonel Reybold says we will have a full audience from fifty miles around the countryside. We enjoyed the way you danced for us when we weren't quite getting the rhythm of the czardas—and telling us to add that rousing 'Hey' at the end is fun."

"And I'm looking forward to singing with two hundred handsome cadets," I said proudly, "thoroughly happy, too, over the way your conductor, Captain Resta, arranged my songs and *arranged* to have you show me West Point."

It had stopped raining now, though the last vestiges of white snow were still clinging to the sleepy earth. Winter was looking toward April, clasping hands with spring, like children in a game of pulling apart.

"This is Flirtation Walk," Captain Coker said solemnly. Handsomely tall and graceful in his blue-gray uniform, with a smile that lighted his nut-brown eyes, he held the gate open for me to enter. Once inside, he offered me his arm. I instantly obeyed the command and moved toward him. Leading me to a place sheltered by a spreading, overhung rock, he quickly lifted me to the ledge and leaped up beside me. Gently taking my hands in his, he said, "I don't know who taught you, but so far you've been an awfully good pupil. I hope you're aiming at an A plus. I brought you here to tell you a story. Have you ever heard the legend of the rock?"

I confessed I hadn't, but I knew something else was impending! This information has been expurgated from *Bugle Notes*—the secret could only be entrusted from cadet to cadet by word of mouth. Naïve and ignorant as the greenest freshman to the United States Military Academy, I stood listening rapturously to Captain Coker's story. I pursued an ambiguity, maneuvering neither acceptance nor refusal, and kept him guessing.

When I punctuated his sentences with mirthful laughter, he would look at me sternly and say, "My dear, I'm serious."

Then I would answer, according to the book, "Sir, my head being made of African ivory, of hard casement steel—"

This set him laughing, too, but he was not to be put off. "You don't want the rock to fall on our heads, do you, Jessica?"

Seeing no possible escape, I turned my smiling face to him. "Far be it from me," I said, "to break a tradition." . . .

He carried me down the long walk over the snow to the gate, where we turned to each other in a last good-by, to

> A present in whose reign no grief will gnaw
> The heart, and never shall a tender tie
> Be broken.

That evening Nadea and I dined in the Officers Club with the Academy superintendent General Robert E. Eichelberger, Captain Resta, and other staff members. The general told me how sorry he was that he would not be able to attend the concert the next afternoon. Would I not then sit beside him and sing his favorite song? I could not refuse this great soldier and sat crooning in his ear "Carry Me Back to Old Virginny."

All was going according to the impeccable schedule. At the appointed hour, Captain Coker waited outside the officers' dining room to take me to the cadet proms, which the staff did not usually attend. At the morning rehearsal, Colonel Reybold, director of entertainment, had offered also to take Nadea dancing. Later, Captain Resta, knowing nothing of this arrangement, assured him Nadea would remain at the Officers Club after dinner while I went off with Coker. Colonel Reybold, annoyed and puzzled over the on-again, off-again, women-can-never-make-up-their-minds-again, went off to bed. Nadea, meanwhile, impatient to go dancing, inquired about Reybold. Where was he? After a telephone call he rose to the occasion and caught up with us just as Coker and I reached our second prom in the upper class hall. We had a gay whirl, watching the prettiest girls we ever saw, laughing at the way the cadets would gloat over cutting in on Colonel Reybold. Dancing with the dashing colonel in his blue cavalry dress uniform, even to the spurs on his boots, I felt I was living out one of my operetta stories.

After our last waltz, Coker took me aside, ripped three golden buttons from his uniform, slipped them through the cord, and looped them over a page of the dance card he inscribed to me. Colonel Reybold waited impatiently, then led us to the car. The snow was still on the ground and Coker, fearing I might get my feet wet, offered to carry me again.

"It's such a little way," I said, trying to soften my refusal.

His privileges were at an end. Here the rules dictated a quick good night, giving the upper hand to Reybold in revenge for so many cut-ins. "Good night, Coker," he said with finality and hurried me into the car. Through the windshield, I watched the young captain walking swiftly to his quarters in the dark night.

After a stirring of the spirit, the concert went so gloriously that Raymond J. Dulye in the Middletown *Times-Herald* wrote: 5,000 PERSONS ENCHANTED BY MAGNIFICENT ARTISTRY OF JESSICA DRAGONETTE AND WEST POINT BAND.

When the backstage crowd dispersed, Coker came to me. "Wonderful," he said, "you're just wonderful. That's what we all said, to a man." Then taking my hand, "Can't we take a walk before you go to tea? I shan't see you again for a long time. We'll have class week in May. Maybe—"

Colonel Reybold was in the shadows, waiting to take me to the Officers Club; Fred Mitchell was with him, waiting to drive us back to New York City.

"I'll try," I said hopefully to Coker, "and thank you for making a week end at West Point something I'll never forget. Au revoir now."

At the Officers Club there was much *brouhaha* about the concert, the large audience, the spirited singing of the cadet chorus and Captain Resta's music. Later, under cross-examination from one of the colonels, I realized how *au courant* the staff was, despite the apparently unsupervised actions of the cadets.

"Have you enjoyed your visit to West Point, Miss Dragonette?"

"Yes, Colonel, more than I can ever tell you."

"Did you see everything—everything important, I mean?"

"Almost everything, thank you, Colonel."

"Flirtation Walk?"

"Oh, yes."

"With somebody handsome?"

"Very."

"What was his name?"

"Oh, sir! That isn't cricket."

The colonel was having a good time at my expense. "Oh, come now. You can confide in me. I won't tell a soul."

I never saw Coker again. As we left West Point, the presence of

night was beside us; gossamer, star-shining, mysterious, it hung over
the trees and the Hudson, in secret over Indian Rock on Flirtation
Walk, sealing the untarnished moments with its dark, protecting
wings.

Now I was off again into *non sequitur* concert routes that took me
to the deep South: Alabama, Georgia, North Carolina; then west to
Illinois, Indiana, Wisconsin, Pennsylvania, Ohio, Colorado, Utah,
Minnesota, and Michigan. Soon it was Christmas time, when besides
Saturday Night Serenade, I appeared twice on the Musical Ameri-
cana broadcasts with Raymond Paige.

The brutal attack on Pearl Harbor sent us into feverish war prepa-
rations, and I was adding to my itinerary the veteran hospitals and
army camps. Travel was becoming more and more difficult.

After I had sung thirteen of fifteen concerts scheduled for February in Oklahoma, I fell ill. Colonel Lee Gore, army doctor and a
life-time friend, piloted us through the whole trip in the fickle
climate. I learned first hand the truth of Will Rogers' words, "If you
don't like Oklahoma weather, just wait five minutes!"

The natives warned me: "In Oklahoma, dress in a bathing suit
under a fur coat, and be sure you carry an umbrella and galoshes."
They were right. We encountered every kind of climate from steam-
ing heat to icy snows.

My illness derived from fatigue and improper food. I am allergic
to anything fried and suffer from a lack of green vegetables. The
available nourishment left me depleted for the heavy schedule I
was carrying. However, having promised to sing at Will Rogers
Field, I could not bring myself to disappoint the airmen. Although
I was burning with fever, my voice seemed to be affected only in
the lower register below middle G; the high voice was manageable.

I can never forget the voltage of courage received as I passed the
statue of Will Rogers inside the entrance of the air base. Some years
earlier one of my Alaskan fans had sent me a snapshot of him with
Wiley Post when they stopped in Fairbanks on that last fatal flight.

Now I was on the stage talking to a crowd of American airmen.
"Rather than disappoint you," I said, "I've flown in on one wing tonight, so bear with me if my voice is not entirely clear."

The airmen roared with laughter. I went on to tell them that so
far I seemed to be scheduled along the routes of the air bases. They

loved that—and cheered me. I entertained them for a full hour, talking, joking, and singing, asking them to join in.

After I sang my last song, by way of good night I said, "Do you want to know something? This is my birthday; and I can't think of any way I'd rather spend it than being with you."

This brought the house down! Colonel Earl de Ford came upon the stage with his staff, made a little speech of thanks, and pinning the silver command pilot wings on my white gown, he pronounced me first honorary colonel of Will Rogers Field.

As we were leaving, the young captain assigned to me asked me to go dancing at the Sherwin and have a birthday fling. I reluctantly refused, because I had three more concerts and had to conserve waning strength. He was amazed at my conscientiousness.

"Why, you're too good to be true," he said.

"Yes," I answered, with mock seriousness, "too true, dear Captain, to be good."

What a contrast to come from the thunderous tumult of young throated soldiers into the inner sanctum of quietude of a Carmelite monastery! I had promised the Prioress, Mother Teresa of the Child Jesus, I would pay a visit, if ever I was in her vicinity.

I had met her some years before in New York, when from time to time on Sunday afternoons I sang Benediction in the tiny chapel of the little band of discalced Carmelites on Gun Hill Road in the Bronx. These singing moments were greatly appreciated by the Sisters, and afterward they would invite me to talk to them through the iron grille back of which they sat, their faces covered with long black veils. During these visits I learned that Mother Teresa, in her twenty-five years as prioress, had collected money for a new monastery which would soon be built. Plans were hardly announced when she was sent to Oklahoma City to found a new mission. Why Oklahoma? This state was originally converted by the early padres, but lacking churches and missions, many Catholics were lost to the Faith; now they are to be reclaimed by Carmelite prayers. I was talking to Mother Teresa via telephone in her new wooden frame monastery in Oklahoma City. The heavenly quality of her angel voice took my breath away.

"I shall come and sing Benediction this afternoon, Mother."

"That will be a blessing, dear," she answered.

I stopped at the florist to buy some flowers for the altar and when I arrived at the convent, Mother Teresa herself was at the turnstile. "How appropriate, Jessica, to bring red carnations on the feast of the Pentecost. Please put them on the altar yourself."

I arranged the flowers in gold vases on the white altar of the little chapel, unaware that anyone but the Carmelites would attend the Benediction. When I turned to descend the altar steps, I faced a host of people crowded into the small pews, while in front of them knelt the brown-robed, sandaled Carmelite monks and brothers from a neighboring monastery. I had not counted on this, but Mother Teresa had. Between my call to her and my visit, she had telephoned all the friends of the monastery to come to the twilight services.

Dark-eyed Father Vicente Martinez, the Provincial, led the singing monks and brothers in the "Tantum Ergo" after my "O Salutaris." Sometimes I fell silent to listen to the soft curve they gave the Gregorian music. Hearing their voices join with me in the anthems, I was lifted out of myself and forgot I was ill.

After Benediction, Mother Teresa invited Nadea and me to enter the cloister and talk to the community back of the grille. Alone in the bare wooden speakroom, dismantled but for two straight wooden chairs, we stood waiting for Mother Teresa to appear. After a little while we heard the soft rattle of rosaries, and Mother Teresa and her sandaled Sisters filed in, graceful in their beautiful swinging rough serge habits of Carmel brown. We caught our breath seeing the Sisters were all unveiled. What a privilege had been vouchsafed to us!

Mother Teresa, having only recently come to Oklahoma City with two Sisters, now displayed a community of eleven. Three novices, in their white veils, looking like angels of a lower choir, moved toward her in loving veneration. The other Sisters, grouping themselves in twos or threes against the background of the whitewashed walls, became a series of living religious tableaux. While they were abundantly cheerful, their faces revealed their life of deep spirituality and contemplation. They were emulating St. Teresa of Avila, who founded the Convent of Our Lady of Mt. Carmel in the sixteenth century. Accordingly, each Carmel is the sad world's "powerhouse of life" through the dynamism of its perpetual prayers.

Mother Teresa led the conversation in her clear rich soprano. She was vitally interested in every detail of the concerts, the hardship of travel, the Spanish songs I was singing, especially the "Dos Cantares Populares," the words of which go back to Isabella La Catolica in the fifteenth century.

Now the Sisters were saying, "Do not leave us, dear Jessica. Come, join us and sing to our Lord in the chapel."

Nadea, frightened at the efficacy of their powerful prayers, began a violent reaction against the possibility of their "praying-me-in." She began to talk about the rigors of a singer's life, the bare stages, the drafty wings, the rickety stairs in most backstages, the broken keys on the pianos, the dirt picked up on the lovely concert dresses; the convent is peaceful and clean alongside of this other world.

"Isn't Nadea wonderful?" Mother Teresa said. "We love her, too. Yes, dear Nadea, we know—the world is on fire, 'it is in a fever,' as St. Teresa says; that is why we are always praying."

In this rarefied atmosphere where we could scarcely breathe, we realized we were in the presence of ideal souls, "free, perfect, solitary, and pure." These lives, sealed and concealed by the cloister, are liberated in God.

After a three-hour visit, Father Vicente Martinez came to bid us good-by. We found it difficult to leave this heaven on earth, this powerhouse of life. It was letting myself down from the inner planetary spaces, like that night of Arcturus years before. Father Vicente's Valencian eye caught my dilemma. He brought me back to earth quickly. "Be careful," he said. "Mother Teresa's prayers are very powerful."

Three months later, in New York, when I sang at the opening of the new Carmelite monastery on Gun Hill Road, Father Martinez was present; crowds thronged the new chapel and were permitted on that Jubilee Day to see the outer rooms of the cloister. But all thoughts carried me back to the little monastery in Oklahoma City, to the saintly Carmelite whose prayers had made it possible—Mother Teresa of the Child Jesus.

After singing in the beautiful Missouri towns peripheral to the St. Charles River and then in golden Indiana and Illinois, the season was over, and in July I was permitted a few weeks' leave of absence from Saturday Night Serenade. The Earl Zimmermans took us on a western trip, beginning with Colorado; then we went on to Wyoming, where we were the guests of Governor and Mrs. Nels Smith. Wyoming's colorful cowboy governor drove us across the entire state, from fabulous Yellowstone to the Medicine Bow of Owen Wister's *Virginian.* "One is space conscious here—in the middle of the Rockies," I thought, as we drove through hundreds of miles of range country en route to Cody, the home of Buffalo Bill. We stopped in Greybull where we met Arlan Coons, an old newspaperman and delightful radio friend. He pointed out the wonders of the Big Horn Basin, the Bean Festival, the Lilac Town, the extra hour of sunshine that puts more sugar in the beets and brings the highest market prices.

The climax of our trip was my induction as princess into the Crow Indian Tribe at Sheridan. The two-hour ceremony took place at night in the Sheridan Arena. Chief Max Big Man directed the ceremonies and around him stood nine other chiefs; Barney Old Coyote, Bird Well Known, Jack Coversup, Tie-His-Knee, Bird Horse, Good Horse, Deernose, Windfield, and Max Big Man Junior; next, a circle of Indian women in their Crow costumes of antelope skin with the turquoise beaded flower design distinguishing their tribe. Then came dancers and singers, magnificently dressed in feathers, bells, paint, and every imaginable scintillating ornament.

A prayer to the Great Spirit opened the ceremony, followed by the smoking of the peace pipe, then the search for the child to be adopted. Jim Buffalo and Steve Driftwood found me in a hidden place and escorted me to the center of the group while the Indian women formed a wall around me. A turquoise beaded band, decorated with yellow tanager and golden notes, and an eagle feather were placed upon my head. One of the women removed my cloak, and I was revealed in my tribal Indian costume of blue antelope skin. Slim Crane and Joe Not-Afraid led me to the chiefs for approval, and they agreed my name should be Princess Singing Bird after the singing bird of the West. The tom-toms commenced again, and in the protective dances they swore to lay down their lives for the newly adopted, ending with the Blessing of Food dance to the Great Spirit. My aids, Mabel Runs-in-a-Circle and Wild Horse, helped me distribute gifts to my adopted family—bright colored shirts for the chiefs and multicolored handkerchiefs for the women.

Harry Beads led the dance, pointing a wand to the four winds and touching it to Tie-His-Knee's mouth. *"Ho-ko-la,"* he said, a Sioux word meaning, "My friends, let us eat." Only Indian sign language could fittingly express my thanks to Chief Max Big Man for his moving words of welcome into the Crow tribe, so I placed my right hand with fingers down-pointed on my heart, and made a sweeping gesture straight out over an imaginary nose to make the sign which means, "My heart is good." I followed this with another sign, speaking the word *"Ahouahou,"* which means thank you. My beautiful adopted sisters, Myrtle Big Man and her daughter, Phyllis Jefferson, Stella Deernose, and May Old Coyote gathered around me as I sang the "Indian Love Call" and "The Land of the Sky Blue Water" at the close of the ceremony.

In the large square, huge flares lighted up the sapphire night, and I joined in the festival dances with my newly adopted tribe—braves, squaws, and little children.

The high dry air of Colorado and Wyoming greatly benefited my health, and I began the season in fine fettle. However, toward the end of November, one evening after the Saturday Night Serenade broadcast, a sharp pain brought me back from the world of music and held me to reality. When the excruciating suffering continued three days, I became alarmed. Even the doctor, who told me I had appendicitis and must be operated upon at once, did not suspect I was already in an advanced stage of peritonitis, though Dr. Henry T. Chickering found infection in the blood count. In the face of this danger, flaunting a stoical courage, I refused at first to go to the hospital; I did not yet realize how ill I was. Fortunately, I got there just in time. A few more hours would have meant quietus.

"Was it really necessary?" I kept repeating as I lay wrapped in the confusing fog of waning anesthesia. "Was it really necessary, Nadea?" Even in that bewildered postoperative state, while my nurse, Miss Carroll, was wheeling me down the hall, my mind was discharging no scattered, unfettered thoughts, but a load of unified purpose. Was it really necessary to interrupt the continuity of work, the pursuit of perfection?

"Yes, Jessica, it was necessary; be quiet now and rest," Nadea was saying, completely exhausted from the long vigil she had kept with Dr. Martin Pollack outside the operating room.

For ten days I hung between life and death. Faithful Nadea never left my bedside except to answer innumerable calls of solicitous friends and fans everywhere. Arthur McGivney, my counselor, was in constant attendance. John Charles Thomas sent frequent messages from the Coast and the friend he gave me, Dr. Martin Pollack, never missed a day at the hospital. Justice Frank Murphy and Lady Bumgardner, his associate, telegraphed; the newspapers called hourly and issued bulletins—they had my obituary written, ready to print at a moment's notice.

There is nothing like sickness to make one appreciate physicians and nurses; these skillful, kind, hardworking angels of mercy pour out their hidden lives in service.

Dr. Lester Breidenbach, on his daily round of visits, would rally me with, "Do you know your picture was in the paper again today with big headlines?"

"Really, Doctor. Did they say how thirsty I am?"

"Isn't a spoonful of water enough? Well, at least you haven't lost your sense of humor."

At my first removal from the critical list, Rita, my hairdresser of years, insisted upon a minute with me; I cannot recommend her bedside manner. "Too bad," she began, "you didn't die, Miss Dragonette. What a front-page story you would have made: 'YOUNG, BEAUTIFUL, AND FAMOUS'—so romantic. Now you will probably live to be an old lady and spoil everything."

After she left, Rita gave me something to think about as I lay in the bay-windowed hospital room. Her "spoil everything" touched off the stream of concatenated days of my life. If it was time to go, what had I done so far? Time had run out quickly, and only by almost myopic concentration had I been able to accomplish anything. I would like to have given more service to my fellow man, more of my time and singing for charities of various faiths, for children, for the sick and wounded of my country; but there wasn't time. I was consumed now with a desperate desire for another chance. In my supplication, I could feel myself joined by the prayers of millions I had sung to; and I believed I could be spared, just as I believed positive thought helped to heal General Pershing that time I sang in Arizona.

I turned to the lovely bouquets and flower pieces, so many I shared them with the Sisters and other patients in the hospital. One simple bowl of tiny pink roses and daisies I cherished beside me on my night table. Whether by intention or not, I do not know, but beautifully and loosely arranged in the daisies was the sign of the Cross. These flowers, sent by His Excellency, Archbishop Spellman, breathed not only a healing, but they were harbingers of a princely visit a few days later.

When His Excellency arrived, he brought another blessing from His Holiness, Pope Pius XII—a white, yellow, and scarlet ribbony badge from which hung the large gold papal medal.

"This is the *Pro Ecclesia et Pontifice*, Jessica," the Archbishop said quite simply, with a beaming smile.

"But what have I done, Your Excellency?" I said in an awed whisper.

"Just what the medal says, 'Services for Church and Pontiff,'" was the answer he gave with heartening informality.

Trembling at the realization that here was my omen for a second chance, I was too overwhelmed at receiving this great honor to speak. But His Excellency, in warm serenity, raised his episcopal hand in blessing, and the aura of his presence remained long after he was gone. I looked up through the window to see a rift in the winter clouds, and I knew instantly I would be whole again.

CHAPTER 19

SONGS OF THE MACHINE AGE

Now I was sitting up, and young, newly ordained Father Downey, the hospital chaplain, who had shriven and given me Holy Viaticum, came to finish his priestly ministrations. "You have had a narrow escape from death, Jessica. God has spared you to continue your work, but you will have to be careful for a while. I suggest you cancel all contracts for six months."

"Thank you, Father," I said, "you have been kindness itself, but do not ask the impossible. Have I come back from the tomb only to go down into another valley? I shall rest, of course, but the time I have lost must be made up."

Missing only two broadcasts, I was back singing on Saturday Night Serenade fourteen days after my sudden illness, but it was a full year before I recovered robust strength. My colleagues could not believe their eyes; their expression of awed wonderment conveyed the thought they were looking upon a Lazarus coming forth from the grave. That evening I asked Roland Martini if I might sing Schubert's "Ave Maria" as a tributary prayer of thanksgiving for my deliverance from the stormy passage of illness. The audience read my mind, and wrote many letters telling me they had never heard me sing more beautifully.

Though I was regaining strength every minute, I had certain forfeits to pay. Since I insisted on doing the broadcasts, bond concerts, and camp shows, the doctors absolutely forbade me to go abroad for USO. The second day after leaving the hospital, I embarked upon new studies in vocal research which kept me busy for the next three years. It was the thirst for artistic perfection that prompted a consuming desire for further knowledge. Since my life from early childhood had been occupied with professional performance, I had never been able to delve into fundamental studies I deemed necessary to my ambitions. A critical organizing sense of discipline and métier spurred me on like a moral force; I wanted to fit myself to perform supremely in a shifting time. It is up to the artist to be the symbol of permanence in change, of validity amid worthlessness, like the ring of true crystal, an authentic timbre in a hollow-sounding world.

The work with A. E. was a thorough overhauling job; he felt his system would bring out greater loveliness in the quality of my voice. Fired by the service-to-music idea, I followed a tedious course of study in which the mill of the gods ground slowly and exceeding fine. The process was vastly enlightening, but psychologically and physically devastating, for during the process of learning, I was constantly performing.

Though A. E. had much that was interesting to impart, as a teacher he was at the opposite pole to Jacquet. A disappointed man who had suffered a good deal in life, he was dogmatic, erratic, and highly temperamental. He lacked the Frenchman's mellow approach to teaching; there was no contagious enthusiasm that made the pupil absorb naturally and spontaneously, no feeling that sent one out of the studio wanting to conquer the world. To me his influence was dampening and repressive.

While he had in common with all teachers the goal of free emission, his preoccupation was the clear vowel and the spun pianissimo. This ability was the only thing that could keep him on the edge of the piano stool. I found relief from his strait-jacket technique in singing sessions with golden-throated Goëta Lyjünberg, celebrated Wagnerian singer, and later with Maestro Stanislao Mucha.

My convalescence and the increasing difficulty of travel now made the long concert tours impossible. I told Mr. Morini I would be available for only a limited number of engagements. Disregarding the doctor's orders completely, he booked an isolated concert in southern Texas, and when I told him I would not be able to go, he sued me for his commission. Such experiences, common in every singer's life, point out to persons contemplating a professional career the necessity of understanding fundamental commercial practice.

After confining myself to the broadcasts, close-by camps, and absorbing studies, increased strength now permitted more ambitious journeys. Now I was going to Canada. The schedule of publicity events aimed at focusing attention to bond-buying was plentiful and various. On one occasion my colleague was the suave, charmingly casual Walter Pidgeon. That morning we were performing for 11,000 airmen in Manning Depot outside Toronto. Since Shirley Ross from Hollywood and Wittemore and Lowe, a piano team from the U. S. Navy, joined us, our time of performance had to be very carefully allotted. I was asked to sing no more than four songs, but when I finished my last number, the airmen kept insisting on an encore. They were shouting, " 'Danny Boy'—give us 'Danny Boy.' " I looked hopelessly at the stage manager, who seeing it would have been a breach to refuse the clamor, gave me permission to sing.

With a gasp of fright, I turned to Pidgeon, "What shall I do? I know only the Irish lyrics of the Londonderry Air—'Would God I were the tender apple-blossom.' "

Pidgeon was quick to the rescue. *Sotto voce,* he said to me, "Don't worry, Jessica, it's my favorite song. I'll not only accompany you, I'll feed you the words if you stand quite close to the piano."

As the airmen sat back, silently enjoying "Danny Boy," they must have noticed I had shifted my position. I hugged the piano; my ears I cocked to Pidgeon while I poured my heart out in the words he gave me. "Oh, Danny boy, the pipes, the pipes are calling."

As we left Manning Depot, the officer in charge handed me a paper-thin silver compact, ornamented with the blue crest of the Royal Canadian Air Force, *"Per ardua, Ad astra";* as I left Canada, the Canadian Bond Campaign Director gave me another souvenir— a silver dish crested with the ancient Chaucerian seal and the simple words "Jessica Dragonette—Canada thanks you for your generous help."

War activities were taking more and more of my time between broadcasts. I was singing everywhere, at embarkation camps, bond rallies, and hospitals, in each case learning all over again what a morale booster music is. It was not surprising to discover the same wide gamut of musical tastes among servicemen as with the general American public. I sensed, however, a special need of the nostalgic love song, and tried to key my programs to satisfy everybody. In these informal gatherings, sometimes in an improvised center or mess hall, I always asked the servicemen to join in the singing and frequently invited a musical soldier to try a duet with me. This informality lifted us out of ourselves and made them forget for a little while the serious issues in which they were involved.

Continuing my route along the air bases I spent a whole day at Lakehurst, New Jersey, singing a symphony concert in the afternoon and another in the evening with D'Artega. On this occasion, I added never-to-be-forgotten souvenirs—a scarf of used parachute nylon, stamped "U. S. Navy" with my name in golden letters, and the gold Navy wings.

Sometimes, at short notice from the Treasury Department, I would swing across the country between broadcasts to Tucson, Arizona, on a local plane, stopping en route at sixteen airports, to sell war bonds in the few minutes on the ground. In Washington, D. C., with Hans Kindler, the National Symphony Orchestra, and basso Lansing Hatfield, we raised a million dollars in one night. Then, after waiting through indefinite plane connections, I was off again to Arizona, this time to help my brother Frederick, who was bond chairman of Pima County. With a whole show Fred arranged, we sold over eleven million dollars in bonds. From here the Treasury Department sent me over the mountains in a little cratelike four-seat plane to Albuquerque, New Mexico. It was like sitting on a mosquito's back to fly through the awe-inspiring Western mountains at sunset. The population of Albuquerque is eighty-five per cent Mexican, so the $50,000 raised in E bonds was equivalent to the Washington million dollars.

Traveling in wartime continued to be fitful and precarious. I remember it took me a whole day to get to Wilmington, Delaware, to sing at an airbase center, and after the performance, it took the whole night to get back to New York.

The improvised dressing room at the Wilmington center, where I had just a few minutes to dress before going on the stage, I shared with Gypsy Rose Lee and others. Gypsy had arrived the day before and was all ready to go on except for some scarce bobby pins which I gladly contributed. Her delightful sense of humor won me completely. She joked, but objected strenuously to having a man in her dressing room, the captain accompanist, who sat with me in a corner, our backs turned to her while we quietly went over the routine of the music. When I stepped up to the dressing table, she taunted me with tongue in cheek.

"You certainly are the star of this show," she bantered in a deep-toned, husky voice. "I couldn't get a thing I wanted this afternoon. 'No!' the captain kept saying, 'Miss Dragonette would not want the piano there. No, no! It must be exactly here.'"

"Oh, Miss Lee, I'm terribly sorry," I said with concern. "How dreadful! Can I do anything for you now? Please have the stage the way you want it regardless of the piano."

She looked at me with suppressed mischief in her eyes and impishly casting me a knowing glance, she said, "Oh, don't take me seriously, I was just kidding. I know how to get what I want all right."

She was dressed in a skirt and beautiful billowy organdy blouse; her hair in pigtails under a floppy hat—not at all the costume I imagined for her act—but I think this was only how it began!

I left before she performed. The captain raced me out into the snowy night, lest I miss the train—it made no difference if I caught pneumonia after singing; then we sat three hours in the station, waiting for the train. Had I been able to remain, I most certainly would have told Gypsy one of my favorite taxi stories.

The New York taxi drivers are a colorful breed—Broadway bronchos, I call them—for no Western riding I've ever encountered—mountainside tacking, desert canyons, and sagebrush cantering—can equal these wild excursions in the light-dodging, dime-turning, careening cross-town traffic of New York.

Innocently I entered a taxi one day. "Take me to Dean's, please, Fifty-seventh and Fifth Avenue." Then I fell back into my absorbing thoughts.

The loquacious driver awakened me with a hearty laugh. "Yes, ma'am, so you think you're a privileged character because you're wearin' that hat—" (I was wearing the gold fez I'm addicted to, one that Prince Mahmoud gave me)—"Oh, I beg your pardon, I mean fez."

After my errand at Dean's I would speed to my dancing lesson with Josephine and Albert Butler, so besides my music I had *The Thinking Body* by Todd with me—I left them all on the back seat while I dashed into the confectioner's.

"I'll be three minutes," I called over my shoulder.

"That's your story," he rejoined.

When I returned, he said, "You meant what you said, lady; I timed you; you *were just* three minutes—and you're reading *The Thinking Body* by Todd. I wonder what Gypsy Rose Lee would say about that? She's an authoress, y'know."

I pleaded ignorance to Miss Lee's many talents; I just hadn't been around—too busy.

"She puts my mind where I don't like it to go," he said, measuring the effect of his words while he studied me in the driver's mirror.

Hoping to quell his exuberant prattle, I said calmly, "I'm *careful* of what I put in my mind."

At this, he slammed the clutch with a grinding roar. I hung to the strap in desperation, praying I would escape from this madcap unscathed. "Broncho" was too tame for this one!

By now we had arrived at the Butlers' building on Central Park South and I alighted with my music, books, and other impedimenta. As I offered him his fee in a red reptile gloved hand, he let out a war whoop!

"Lady, you're the most mysterious creature who's ever been in my cab. Are you a snake charmer?"

"No," I said, smiling my sweetest and dropping the coins in his palm; with a flourish, I turned and gave him, "A charmer, yes, but *not* a snake charmer!"

After we settled into our wartime stride, as a minuteman of the United States Treasury, I was on call to go anywhere I might be directed. There was that never-to-be-forgotten hasty trip back to Omaha to help sell E bonds. I had to drop my television series for Durez Plastics at Dumont; work collecting money for the United Jewish Appeal campaign; studies with Frances Robinson Duff, the famous dramatic coach whose mother taught Mary Garden. I felt, however, I was doing the most important thing of the moment. All I asked was the assurance of returning to New York immediately after the concert.

I arrived in Omaha the evening before and rehearsed late into the night with an excellent local accompanist. The next day I found myself fatigued to the point of exhaustion. Fearing I might not be able to perform, I began to seek out an osteopathic doctor. In the blind, I called Dr. Delia Lynch who refused to come to the hotel because her office was full of patients. When I explained my mission, she not only came and took care of me, encouraging the circulation, feeding me hard-to-get steak, but she even rode out to her farm and brought back strawberries still hot from the sun. With the help of this incredible woman, I rose "like a young Hercules" to use her own words, and together with the Boys Town Choir we put the E bond drive $700,000 over the top.

Arriving at the airport after the bond concert, with only seventeen minutes to spare, Nadea discovered in checking in, we had no reservations despite the Treasury Department's assurances. Cold, tired, and desperate to return to New York, we had to think quickly. At one o'clock in the morning, Nadea took a chance on telephoning Washington and found Sheldon Turner in the office. "Let me speak to airline reservations," he said. Nadea handed over the telephone.

When the girl came back, she was smiling. "Miss Dragonette, we'll have two places for you on the incoming plane. Sure is quick action, but this is your night for going over the top."

An iridescent glow hangs over middle November, 1944. I addressed the New York Society of Dancing Teachers, at the request of Florence Cowanova, the society's program chairman. Florence knew how much I love the dance, using it always as a form of exercise, an aid to stage deportment, well-being, and rhythmic patterns underlying the singing line. From time to time I had attended the meetings with Florence. There I first introduced myself to Josephine and Albert Butler. The way they held their heads made me think of beings from another planet. I felt they knew something important about posture.

The teachers were interested to learn what the singer had to say about the dance. Later Franklyn Oakley, president of the society, invited me along with Florence and her father to a dinner party at his home. It was entirely unlike me to accept this pleasant diversion to a busy schedule, but an impulse kept urging me on.

The dinner party of eight people were sprightly and pleasantly gay; seated next to my host, I was aware of a tall, handsome cavalier sitting next to Mrs. Oakley. Though there was much general laughter, conversation over the gulf between us was impossible, as we were separated by two guests.

After dinner, while I scanned Mrs. Oakley's *bibelot* collection, Florence came to fetch me. "Nikki Turner has enjoyed meeting you, Jessica, but he has to leave immediately for Ithaca, and he will not go without saying good night to you."

This was quaintly flattering, and unconsciously I moved immediately to bid him good night. He was standing at the door with his coat on and his bowler in his hand.

"I shall be back in two weeks," he said, flashing me a dazzling smile. "I would love to attend your broadcast; will you arrange to have me admitted?"

"Oh, yes," I said perfunctorily, "do come and join us for supper afterward. I'd like you to meet my sister—she's fascinating."

"Thank you very much," he said, "but you won't forget, will you?"

"Of course not," I replied with gusto, observing the way his wavy hair conformed to the high wide forehead, the live dark azure eyes.

He smiled again. "In two weeks then," and he was gone.

Nikki wrote me while he was in Ithaca, saying the afterglow of meeting me had lasted ten days, proving it wasn't a champagne dream. This certainly displayed a sense of humor. The night he came to the broadcast, Gayelord Hauser, Fred Mitchell, and Leonardo were also there. We had supper later and from then on, Nikki seemed bent on crowding out everyone else. While I was greatly attracted to him, I did not take him seriously, thinking he was merely being carried away by a woman of the stage.

It is difficult to ascertain whether a personality in the public eye is loved for herself or as the star. For a long time I could not reconcile marriage with a career. It seemed neither fair to marriage nor to a professional life. The men who fancied themselves in love with me always wanted me to retire. I couldn't expect them to understand that after so much had gone into my music, singing naturally took first place.

I would laugh when Nikki would say in romantic outpourings, "Jessica, I'm going to marry you. Fate has written it in the heavens."

In this sense he was way ahead of me. *"Qui vivra, verra,"* I would say with a shrug of the shoulder à la Madame Brugell.

Sometimes in our hours together when he was in town, between dancing and theater interludes, he would plead, "I know your music has first place; that's as it should be. I would expect to dedicate myself to it, too."

As he came more and more to the broadcasts, the theater audiences in CBS Playhouse No. 2 on West Forty-fifth Street, where we broadcast Saturday Night Serenade, used to watch for him to ascend the stairs and enter the box. Coming backstage, they would say to me, "Who is that young man? He never takes his eyes off you." Or, "We're rooting for that handsome suitor with our fingers crossed. We would really like him to win." I would just smile sweetly and continue full steam ahead with my busy program.

On the Oklahoma trip, while singing in Bartlesville—home of Phillips Petroleum—Mr. and Mrs. Frank Phillips invited me to join them at their fantastic ranch house in the Osage country. As the forty guests sat about the huge open fire after dinner, Mr. Phillips introduced me to jolly Mrs. Perle Mesta, widow of the steel and oil magnate, formerly ambassadress to Luxemburg. She was stunning in a plain black costume, complete with matching tricorn covered with Chantilly lace, which brought out her smiling eyes and her beautiful jewels. When I admired her ensemble, she cooed with pleased expression, "It's Valentina."

Mr. Phillips, bent on impressing his guests with my musical achievements, stood right up and made the most glowing speech of praise; but each time he mentioned my name he stumbled. Politeness dictated a few words of appreciation in return. I thanked him for his hospitality, expressed congratulations for the extraordinary museum housing American art and Indian lore, thanked him for the privilege of tasting "buffalo milk," and finally I said, "But, Mr. Phillips, I do want you to remember my name. Think of it this way and it's very easy. If Mr. Phillips went fishing, would Jessica Drag-a-net?" Everyone laughed, and Mrs. Mesta, leaving immediately for Washington, expressed the hope of seeing me there on my subsequent singing engagements.

She was living now in the old Herbert Hoover house and invited me to an enchantingly gay party she gave for Margaret Truman, after dinner at the Sulgrave Club. It may have been this gala affair that won her the nickname of "Two-Party Perle," because so many celebrities from both sides of the political fence attended. The occasion marked Margaret Truman's social debut and caused a great deal of pro-and-con comment. As co-guest with Margaret was Mrs. Mesta's debutante niece, Betty Tyson. In our group was fabulous Rosa Ponselle, looking like the dark heroine of the dramatic operas associated with her—*La Gioconda* and *Norma*—and her polo-playing husband, Charles Jackson. Since President and Mrs. Truman were not to attend the supper dance, Mrs. Mesta arranged to take a few of us to the White House.

Tea was held in a rich paneled, silver and candlelight-chandeliered room. Mrs. Truman presided in quiet dignity—her simple, friendly manner reminded me of many American mothers I had met, especially the mother of my friend Mildred Palmer Cain, columnist on the Philadelphia *Inquirer*. There was something, too, in her open manner, of Gertrude Stein, the American authoress.

Later, at Mrs. Mesta's party, columnist Mrs. Lyon Boston (Nancy Randolph of the New York *Daily News*) danced almost continuously with Rear-Admiral Giles Stedman and Blevins Davis. Among the two hundred and fifty guests, Margaret Truman was easily the belle of the ball, whirling about with diplomats, senators, servicemen, and Harvard boys; but however many the cut-ins, she would revert to Drew Dudley and Graham Smallwood, who definitely had an edge on the political oldsters. Margaret, not yet graduated from George Washington University, was pretty much a typical attractive American girl, well balanced and fun-loving, though not a social butterfly at heart. She rarely indulged in frivolities, for even then she was planning to study voice, dreaming of a debut at the Met in Verdi's *Rigoletto*.

Among the other debutantes was a girl of such rare dark beauty that seeing her advance toward us, Hal Phyfe, the photographer, with whom I was dancing, caught his breath.

"Don't you remember me, Jessica?" she said. "I met you in Honolulu. I am Commander Heard's daughter."

I thought, "The bud has come to full flower."

The party lasted until the small hours of the morning, and while Nadea and I were having a late breakfast at the Sulgrave Club, I was called to the telephone. New York was trying to reach me. It was Bishop McIntyre of St. Patrick's Cathedral calling. "Miss Dragonette, it would add much to our reception if you would sing next Tuesday evening for our returning Archbishop, now Francis Cardinal Spellman."

It was at the close of a day of ovations for His Eminence, newly come from Rome. His arrival was awaited by many thousands outside the theater at Broadway and Thirty-ninth Street, seeking a glimpse of the prelate who, in the words of Governor Thomas E. Dewey, was being welcomed home as a citizen of New York, of America, and of the world. On the great stage of the Metropolitan Opera House, the eminent churchman was being accorded one of the most enthusiastic receptions in the city's history. Four thousand people from all walks of life, all races and creeds, were represented in the audience that filled every available seat in the opera house; gathered to pay homage to the archdiocese's fourth Prince of the Church, they taxed to capacity the available standing room. From the parishes of the teeming metropolis to the missions in the faraway rural communities of the great See of New York, they came to pay respects to the renowned Cardinal. Seventeen bishops were there headed by the Most Reverend J. Francis A. McIntyre, Vicar General;

Postmaster Robert Hannigan, emissary for President Truman; Governor Dewey, presenting a congratulatory scroll on behalf of the state legislature; Mayor William O'Dwyer, expressing the acclaim of the city; Altman's John S. Burke, chairman of the Cardinal's committee of the laity; and Mrs. James F. McDonnell, pledging devotion of the women of the archdiocese.

The Cardinal stood out as the central figure in this consistory, a hierarchy of church, state, and city. The colorful splendor of red and purple ecclesiastical habiliments mingled with the lay dignitaries' black and white, forming a ranking column that moved to selected places as the full organ rolled out the processional hymn, "Ecce Sacerdos Magnus."

Between the speeches, mine was the golden privilege to give an intonation to this memorable evening, singing solos and in concert with the choristers from St. Patrick's Cathedral, a Schubert Cantata under the direction of my old friend from the wild adventure in Richmond, Charles Courboin. I shall never forget his greeting at rehearsal, "I see you got home all right."

Governor Dewey, in a fine speech that detailed the highlights of the Cardinal's life, emphasizing his American College days in Rome, frequently referred to a word used by an old teacher of His Eminence. The Governor made a refrain of the word "*fantastico*" after recalling each clarion event, culminating in the evening's historical climax. Francis Cardinal Spellman, fingering the pectoral cross, smiled benignly at each reiteration of "*fantastico*," letting flash across his mind a succession of remembrances.

Now His Eminence was rising to speak a gracious "thank you," but before he launched into the pithy subject of rekindling a spiritual flame in a time of almost universal darkness, he paused for a moment, and looking about him he said, "In my wildest flights of imagination I have never pictured myself on the stage of the Metropolitan Opera House. It is indeed '*fantastico*.'"

A few days later, on a letterhead of the Cardinal's residence, I received the following note:

Dear Jessica,

As you know your presence at the Metropolitan Opera House the other evening, together with your beautiful singing, made me and thousands of others very happy. I am sure you know of my gratitude and prayers. With my best wishes and kindest regards, I am,

Very sincerely yours,

F. J. Spellman

Archbishop of New York

Against a backdrop of almost twenty years of national headlines in which radio, industry, and historical progress interplayed, the Cities Service Company, in January, 1946, celebrated its *1001 Nights on the Air*. Still involved with touring, between philanthropies, weekly broadcasts, and concerts I was living through a busy year. No wonder people found it difficult to catch up with me.

One day I was called to the telephone to speak to Lawrence Fitzgerald, former assistant to George Engles in the Artists Bureau. "No one has been able to reach you," he said, introducing himself. "They are interested in having you appear on the Cities Service celebration program. Will you be able to do this?"

"Yes," I answered, "but who is giving me the invitation?"

"We are," he replied, "we who were formerly with NBC. I now book artists for the program, so I hope you don't mind paying me the commission!"

How broadcasting had changed from the days of Merlin Aylesworth! Now there was a wide neutral zone between sponsor and artist, an area, in this case, to which only Larry Fitzgerald had the "password."

After having learned so much the hard way, I still was not alert to the cues. Feeling I was pouring oil on the old troubled waters of NBC, I accepted and readily agreed to the modest terms proposed. From that moment, Mr. Fitzgerald took on a proprietary attitude, posing as my manager.

The title of the celebration, *1001 Nights on the Air,* flattered me. Cities Service had taken it bodily from an article I had written years before. It was appropriate to the cavalcade of music and historical events on this reminiscent program. Ford Bond, announcer, who began his Cities Service engagement the same year I did, was detailing the highlights of the parade of passing years.

The National Broadcasting Company was only three months old when Cities Service, on Friday, February 18, 1927, began the series of broadcasts, which now rank as the oldest sponsored program on the air. The NBC log of that day, for WEAF transmitting studio, states unhappily that it went off the air for three minutes at the start of the program "due to a fuse blowing out."

This was the time of exuberant America, years of booming prosperity, Lindbergh, disarmament conferences, silent man in the White House, sound on the screen, Al Smith and his brown derby, Dempsey versus Tunney and $2,600,000 "gate," the *Graf Zeppelin* crossing the Atlantic, Prohibition, speak-easies, television in the laboratory, and finally market collapse ending an era.

In the years of depression, political upheaval, world economic conference failure, Roosevelt, Gandhi, the death of Edison, Prohibition repealed, doles, and hope around the corner, I emerged on the Cities Service program. Ford Bond was saying it this way: "In January, 1930, Cities Service featured its first soloist Jessica Dragonette. The petite star possessed a beautiful lyric soprano voice, and the hour had hardly been completed before telegrams began pouring in to be followed by thousands of letters."

After my singing "Indian Love Call" at this celebration, Ford Bond made mention of middle January, 1937, when I left the program, and the world began to hear the distant drum of the years of confusion ahead, a setting of the stage for World War II.

Now the program had completely changed from the concert format held to under Rosario Bourdon and Frank Black. As the *Highway of Melody,* under the direction of Paul Lavalle, it featured baritone Leonard Stokes and a choir of singers. Lavalle, an outstanding musician-pupil of Joseph Schillinger, had played in the orchestra under Rosario Bourdon, conspicuously absent that evening, after serving as director for more than ten years.

In the Rainbow Room after the broadcast, a gala crowd of Cities Service people, NBC officials, and newspapermen were foregathered. Ben Gross took Nadea and me aside, leaving Larry Fitzgerald at the table.

"It's all right for Jessica to be in the clouds," Ben Gross was saying, "but no excuse for you, Nadea. Jessica should never be away from this program. Regardless of what anybody has told you, she is here tonight only because every radio editor in the country answered a request sent them by Cities Service and said, on an anniversary program they wanted most to hear Jessica Dragonette."

Nikki Turner, listening in from Buffalo, hearing me sing, with Leonard Stokes, the duet from *Oklahoma!* "People Will Say We're In Love," called me on the telephone to say how much he enjoyed "our song." We had adopted it as our own when the orchestra played it that first night he took me to dinner at Sherry's.

The next day Ben Gross wrote in his column, *Listening In:*

The return of Jessica Dragonette, even for one night, to the program, was a happy event for the oldtime fans—and the new ones, too. . . . As she sang 'Indian Love Song' and joined with the talented Stokes in 'People Will Say We're In Love,' last night, her lyrical voice swept away the cobwebs of time. Those who remembered lived again in the days when Prohibition and not war was the exciting topic of the moment. And, as for the youngsters, they learned just how much they missed by having been born too late!

A few weeks later I asked Roland Martini for a pass to the theater for a special friend from the West Coast. When I mentioned his name, Mr. Martini asked me if he could publicize the fact of this hero being in the theater that evening.

"With pleasure," I said, "if *Life* Magazine has done it, I'm sure you can."

But the incredulous Martini, always the doubting Thomas, thought I was tossing off a rash promise and made alternate provisions in the script. He did not neglect, however, to have a photographer on the spot. When it came time for the theater to be closed before the broadcast, and my guest had not yet arrived, Mr. Martini cast me a deprecating look. I smiled back confidently.

"Don't give up so quickly. Remember he's a Navy man and they always keep their promises."

"*Do* they?"

I knew my guest would not disappoint me because I was a tie in his devotion to his beautiful little sister Anita, who was one of my school friends. She had entertained me on my first trip to California and had gone down to the lighthouse in San Pedro when the keeper, James Edgar Donnelly, insisted on saluting me with three dips of Old Glory as I sailed on the *Lurline* to Honolulu.

I had taken my own precautions by stationing a page to keep a "lookout" at the one unlocked door and permit my guest safe conduct to his seat, no matter what time he arrived. Just as Gus Haenschen stood with poised baton, his eyes on the control room across the stage, ready for the signal to begin, I saw the outline of moving figures in the darkness of the theater. My page was leading a party to the front row. Warren Sweeney, the announcer, made a swift shift of pages at the microphone and Emil Coté shuffled about the music-stand in front of him. Martini looked at me sheepishly through the glare of the control room glass and broke into one of his rare smiles.

"We honor the distinguished guest present in our theater tonight," Warren Sweeney began, "a man who did much to establish morale, give comfort to the men on ships in devastated Pearl Harbor, a Navy chaplain who used a rig as a church for twenty-six years; we salute Captain William A. Maguire with the song he inspired, 'Praise The Lord and Pass The Ammunition.'"

The following week I received the *Radio Guide* trophy as most popular singer on the air.

"This is the eighth time you've received it," Mr. Martini said, as we stood posing for pictures. "Isn't it getting to be a bore?"

"I should say not," I answered with sprightly jauntiness. "The more the merrier—and I love my fans for it."

I had been with Saturday Night Serenade now for four and a half years, and they were getting ready to cut expenses and change their format.

Leaving the program gave me new freedom and wider scope. I could hop-skip-jump in any direction without worrying about being back in New York at the week end for the broadcast. Winging far west beyond the great divide, singing concerts in the Red Rock country of Colorado; in Phoenix, not minding the temperature at 114 degrees; in Canada for concerts and broadcasts; a week in Milwaukee's lake-front Centurama when I had to walk up fifteen flights of stairs because all the fuses in the hotel were blown out; back to Boston for the Christian Doctrine Congress in the packed-to-capacity Boston Garden, where I sat on the stage with the only other woman, ex-Empress Zita of Austria. Back and forth between New York and New England to sing for wool merchants', hotel men's, bankers', doctors' conventions; learning that while they loved all the songs I sang, the immortal "Sweet Sixteen" held first place in their hearts.

Such a schedule was frowned upon by my music advisers. They felt I was spreading myself too thin over a wide surface; I felt I was gaining flexibility in the communicative art for the immediacy of television. Taking part in local events across America whenever the concert schedule permitted, I was in closer personal contact with living audiences who had listened to me on the air. Talking to women I found out how concerned they are with present barbarous world conditions, how determined they are to take their places beside men in the conquest of the universe and building the kind of life we want. They have tossed off the woman's page routine—how-to-look, how-to-eat, how-to-cook, how-to-speak—as a taken-for-granted ritual and are intent on solving the catastrophic debasements that confront us. The world's work, the fight against evil forces, is a never-ending job.

By late October I was booked for a recital in Washington, at the Lisner Auditorium, a splendid music-making hall of Washington University, but off the beaten path and far from the center of the city. I had made every conceivable kind of appearance in the Capital except a recital, so I looked forward with enthusiasm to the opportunity of presenting another artistic facet to Washingtonians. I had selected an unhackneyed program and hoped for the best.

The local committee suggested an ambitious schedule of publicity events to draw a large audience for the coming recital. To every suggestion I was amenable, not realizing what was in store for me; I only asked that all appointments be lined up so I could rest on the day of the concert. Eight assignments, embracing radio and newspaper interviews, photographs, a press party at seven, were arranged. But my plane was grounded and after waiting for weather clearances, I had to abandon the idea of flying. The train didn't arrive in Washington until ten o'clock in the evening. Immediately I was whisked off to dinner with some of the remaining press. Bright and early I was up for fashion pictures in my fairy-tale concert gown of apricot and gold Persian brocade, a fabulous ensemble, including jacket, shoes, gloves, and purse, by the best American designers, Philip Mangone, Mary Liotta, and Palter de Liso; next came a nutri-

tion article for the woman's page, four radio interviews, everything
else I failed to do the previous day.

Things were decidedly rough in the top flight hotel where I was
staying. There was a strike going on, with difficulty in getting food,
compelling me to walk upstairs and to make my own bed. At five
minutes to eight, ready to leave for the concert, I was feeling a bit
shaky after the hectic day, when a newspaper photographer knocked
at the door.

"Miss Dragonette, I'd like to snap your picture making your bed in
that gold creation everybody's talking about. Would you oblige
quickly? There's a murder down the street, and I'm in a hurry!"

The picture, published the next day, reveals the finery and my
pained expression. There were other things to worry about besides
the distance of the auditorium: there was local union trouble between
theater and music hall. For the concert that night, where usually one
stage manager presides, four men sat out the evening backstage.

"Everything happens to me," I thought as we rode out to the auditorium. But once I heard the introduction to Leila's aria from Bizet's
Pearl Fishers, I began to breathe more easily; feeling my voice come
free and clarion clear, I wielded the tonal colors with joy and confidence. As the words flowed, I made a prayer of the Cavatina:

> Comme autrefois dans la nuit sombre
> Caché sous le feuillage épais
> Il veille près de moi dans l'ombre
> Je peux dormir, rêver en pais. . . .

With new-gained courage, I turned a bold Spanish shoulder to the
Joaquin Nin and Turina group, chanting the folk songs in "starkly
realistic fashion" as one critic said, "making bold, almost savage, melodic gestures, while against this strong vocal line Paul Meyer wove
rhapsodic comment and counterpoint at the keyboard." On, on
through the Massenet arias, the Debussy and American songs, and
the encores, then it was time for the rush of backstage congratulations. I could not sleep when I returned to the hotel. The surge of
the day's fantastic events receded from me, but weariness and remorse descended. Perhaps I had not sung the best concert of my
life, as I always wanted each last one to be; passing my hand over
my eyes, I shuddered, "Now, the critics!"

I was awakened by a call from Maryland's Bethesda Naval Hospital, "Won't you come and sing for us? We're so far away we're usually forgotten. Walter Reed gets everything."

I agreed to go, but wondered how I could summon the strength to sing. At breakfast I timidly turned the newspaper to the music page and as I read, I could feel the color come back to my cheeks. Glenn Dillard Gunn's headline was: "MISS DRAGONETTE MARKEDLY SIMILAR TO MARY GARDEN. . . . the resemblance is both physical and spiritual. Miss Dragonette is a Celtic mystic in her art. So was Mary Garden."

New life came galloping back through my veins; Lady Bumgardner and Madeleine Sack were waiting to take us to luncheon. I gathered them up and took them to the Naval Hospital instead, sang in as many wards as I could until train time, which we made by the skin of our teeth—none of us getting anything to eat.

Quite recently Louis Biancolli having requested an interview told me he would have to postpone it because he was closeted with Mary Garden, writing her memoirs. I mentioned Glenn Gunn's analogy to the diva and how the critic hinted that I was, no doubt, aware of the Garden resemblance.

"Do you mind if I show Miss Garden the review?" he asked. "I think she will be interested."

The next time I saw Biancolli, at a Philharmonic concert, surrounded by the singing-student ushers in Carnegie Hall, he said, "Mary Garden told me that anything Glenn Dillard Gunn says is so. 'He really knows better than anyone else. As a young man he was music critic in Chicago during my time; he really knows!'"

Now, reading *Mary Garden's Story* and smiling over what she has to say over critics in general, this is high praise for one critic in particular. Glenn Dillard Gunn's words were dear to me, dearer perhaps, because he was the nearest I ever came to Mary Garden. He knew her in Chicago, but it was from Carl Van Vechten's writings I got a breathing picture of what her living art must have been:

I have watched her many times in the same role . . . and almost as many times I have been blinded by the force of her magnetic, imaginative power, without which no interpreter can hope to become an artist.

And this "highest form of stage art," alas, I have missed.

Some weeks after the Washington concert, in a broadcast ceremony, Station WEAF changed its call letters to WNBC. There was
a line-up of old and new WEAF artists on hand, Jinx Falkenburg,
Tex McCrary, Elaine Malban, Joseph Dunninger, Ben Grauer, Fred
Allen, and others. Governor Dewey spoke a few appropriate words
on this hail-and-farewell occasion, and after a fanfare introduction
by Ben Grauer, I sang a few songs, then retired to the control room
with Governor Dewey and Portland Hoffa to listen to Fred Allen.
Fred twanged an amusingly clever monologue that kept us chuckling every second. When he finished and joined us, Niles Trammel,
president of NBC, scolded him: "Fred, how can you be so wasteful?
This is only a sustaining program. Don't throw away that valuable
material on an unsponsored show!"

Walter Winchell was asking more and more in his column and
broadcasts, "Who is the handsome six-footer bodyguard seen everywhere with Jessica Dragonette? There's romance in the air." Sometimes I wrote Walter denying the rumor and promising to tell him
"when and if it happened."

Nikki was likewise importuning me and found it difficult to reconcile his love at first sight with my lagging heart. His campaign to
win me never flagged; he carried on an ardent, fascinating courtship.
He tried his best to dissolve any hurdles, but I was still vacillating—
and when I finally told Cardinal Spellman I would be married in late
June, His Eminence was skeptical.

"You have already postponed it twice, Jessica. I hope you're really
going to hit home base this time."

On June 28, Nikki and I crowded into the tiny elevator in the
Cardinal's residence, and as we ascended a trembling fright, worse
than any before a broadcast or concert, seized me. Where-to had
I come? Had I made a wise decision entrusting my life to Nikki?
He led me gently to the little chapel on the third floor and as we
entered its jewel-like premises, a peace descended. The blue-green
stained-glass windows sifted the early morning sunlight in a sparkling shower of cellophane streamers over the white satin cushions
on the *prie-dieu* close to the white altar, fragrant with carnations
aurioled by baby breath. The noisy rasp of the city far below us

made no disturbing intrusion on the high sanctuary where we gathered for our nuptials.

Nadea, my matron of honor, wore a lovely pink suit with matching cart-wheel straw and pink lady-slipper orchids; I wore a Paris shantung suit, beige picture straw hat, trimmed with a white silk jersey flowing scarf, and Nikki's exquisite white orchids. Nikki and Count Roger de Palluel, best man, wore dark blue.

Monsignor Kellenberg began vesting the Cardinal for the nuptial Mass. His Eminence reverently kissed each holy vestment, softly intoning the appropriate prayers, as the Monsignor adjusted it. Marking the Ordinary of the Mass in my missal pages—Confiteor, Offertory, Canon—I rejoiced in the lesson conveyed by the ritual that marriage is a sacrament worthy of blessing, praise, and thanksgiving. Robed at length in the white chasuble, His Eminence walked to the foot of the altar. His chanting recalled: "Sing with the spirit, sing also with the understanding." I followed the prayers of the Cardinal Priest and the Priest-Acolyte.

> Blessed are all that fear the Lord, that walk in His Ways
> May the yoke of love and of peace be upon her.
> True and chaste may she wed in Christ.

After the blessing and exchange of rings and the thanksgiving prayers we descended to the dining room, gleaming in white flowers, silver, china, and linen, and at each place a gem-encrusted goblet. Nikki, deeply touched, tried to express his astonished pleasure at the Cardinal's thoughtfulness. His Eminence smiled and quickly came to his rescue. "Why, don't you know, Nick, we've been practicing for weeks?"

At home, Nadea had prepared another wedding feast; kneeling to kiss the episcopal ring, we took leave of our distinguished host. As we opened the grilled iron gate leading to the outer steps of the Cardinal's residence, we faced a barrage of cameras. It had all been so secret—how did the news leak out? I worried about what my newspaper friends—Walter Winchell, Frank Farrell, Antoinette Donnelly, Eddie Mahar—would say. I had promised to tell them when! Between the firing line of flash bulbs, Nikki and I smiling, stood, walked, entered a car; and soon after we drove away, lost again in the East Side traffic.

Nikki's hand on mine, we cut the wedding cake, and as Roger gave a toast, he looked at me and winked. "I was with Igor Cassini last night. I couldn't resist telling him why I had to leave to keep an early morning appointment. I'm afraid, Jessica, I scooped you."

The wedding party saw me off on the plane to California. Nikki would join me in ten days and take me to Santa Barbara for our honeymoon. As I sat alone in the cabin, I opened the little box he had pressed into my hands as we said good-by at La Guardia. I found beautiful solitaire diamond earrings and written on the card,

> Doubt thou the stars are fire,
> Doubt thou the sun doth move,
> Doubt truth to be a liar
> But never doubt I love.

CHAPTER 20

A NEW SONG

As we left the crowded cocktail lounge in the Waldorf's Jade Suite on our way to the ballroom for dinner, William Watts Chaplin, president of the Press Club, our host, gave General Marshall the latest headline: "MOLOTOV OUT AS SOVIET FOREIGN MINISTER; VISHINSKY HIS DEPUTY TAKING OVER POST."

"What do you think of the news hot off the wires, General?" Chaplin asked quietly.

General Marshall's steel blue eyes, no revealing seismograph, looked at Chaplin thoughtfully for a moment; then smilingly he commented: "It's replacing a reckless man with a ruthless man."

As the guests mounted to the dais on the ballroom stage, Chaplin took his place to the left of the evening's guest of honor. Seated along the table were also Warren Austin, our delegate to the United Nations; Lieutenant General Albert C. Wedemeyer, deputy chief of staff; Major General Frederick Osborn, deputy of the U. S. representation of the UN Atomic Energy Commission; Dean Acheson, Secretary of State; Paul Hoffman, administrator of ECA; the Honorable

Wilhelm Munthe de Morgenstierne, ambassador of Norway to the United States; John Foster Dulles, UN adviser; Bernard Baruch; Fritz Kreisler; Elmer Davis; and other recipients of Overseas Press Club awards.

I found my place on the first tier, between Senator Henry Cabot Lodge, Jr. of Massachusetts and New York *Herald Tribune's* prize-winning foreign correspondent, Homer Bigart. After I had finished the "Star-Spangled Banner," Mr. Chaplin thanked me, then turning to the audience with a quizzical smile, he said: "Jessica Dragonette will sing again later in the evening."

There was much activity during the first course at the table directly under the dais where handsome Mrs. Marshall was sitting. I saw her investigating minutely the Crabmeat Louis; then looking up at the General whose eyes were riveted on her, she bobbed her head in three positive jerks. This was a signal, I learned later, that all was well, and no harassing shrimp lurked in the cocktail to plague his allergy.

The speeches were eloquent, serious, and significant. Ambassador de Morgenstierne made the formal announcement that his country that day had taken the first steps toward entrance into the North Atlantic Pact. I thought of de Morgenstierne's speech almost a year later when I sang at a Wings Club Dinner in New York. Then the Honorable Thomas K. Finletter addressed defense ministers, air chiefs of staff, and air attachés of seven of the North Atlantic Pact Nations. Another dream had been realized.

Since the guest of honor at the Overseas Press Club, General Marshall, was retiring as Secretary of State, his successor, Dean Acheson, spoke in genuine sadness and referred to himself as a lieutenant listening for his captain's voice, but hearing only the empty echo of his own coming back to him.

General Marshall's speech was short, keyed to a world careening toward war; he pleaded a universal effort for understanding among the nations. The overseas pressmen, eager to have the reluctant Secretary of State write his memoirs, which he swore he never would, presented him, as an inducement to the task, a gold-plated type-writer. Marshall looked at it admiringly, and we thought for a minute he had been persuaded; then he looked up and countered with, "Gentlemen, I am deeply touched, but I think what I really need is a gold-plated kidney." Everyone laughed, remembering that the General had recently left a kidney in Walter Reed Hospital.

In the quiet intervals, Senator Lodge was a delightful dinner partner, speaking beautiful French and harmonizing *sotto voce* with me some popular French songs. As state dinners have been routine to Senator Lodge, I wondered if he always managed to be so entertaining. At that moment, big Jim Farley stepped up and shook the senator's hand; he bowed to me, adding jovially, "I see you know where to sit, Senator." Nikki, at a table some distance from the dais, seeing us, wondered what in the world was so engrossing.

I had been sworn to secrecy concerning General Marshall's favorite song which I was now about to sing. Though I was happy to have been chosen for this honor, the song seemed unsuitable to his personality and achievements. "What will he think?" I mused. The choice was a touch of genius in this ponderous atmosphere of serious world problems; it proved to me that a statesman is after all human. Standing alone, I spoke a few words before singing. "General Marshall, it is my happy privilege to sing your favorite song tonight. Had the choice been mine, I would now be saluting you with 'My Hero'; but your song adds zest to this festivity. General, as your favorite, 'Buttons and Bows' becomes the theme song of the world."

The two thousand guests roared with laughter, but the General looked frankly puzzled. I sang "Buttons and Bows" with appropriate gestures and had to repeat it while everyone looked to see how the General was taking it. The next day the newspapers said, "Jessica Dragonette by-passed 'Rock of Ages,' the General's real favorite, and sang 'Buttons and Bows' instead." That set me wondering who might have mixed things up.

An opportunity of solving the mystery presented itself some weeks later when I was in Washington for President Truman's birthday party at Anderson House, that distinguished old mansion of the Society of the Cincinnati, where only functions of state are held. Attorney General Tom Clark had planned a surprise party, and after we were all screened by the FBI, we flew to Washington in an army bomber.

Among the sixty guests of Attorney General Tom Clark were some of the statesmen I had already met at the Overseas Press Club. As

I entered the reception hall, General Marshall came forward to greet me.

"You certainly started something. Every place I go, the band plays 'Buttons and Bows.'"

"Well, isn't it your favorite song?" I inquired innocently.

"Not exactly," the General said. "You see my secretary had a good time playing a joke on me. My real favorite is 'Rock of Ages.'"

President Truman was receiving in the patio and I went directly to him with birthday congratulations. "Mr. President, you are looking very well; I am glad to see that grave affairs of state are not wearing you down." Then changing my tone to one of frivolity, I added, "Aren't you afraid to disclose the date of your birthday? We can place you astrologically, Mr. President. You are under the sign of Taurus."

"That's the Bull, isn't it?" he said, straightening his shoulders. "Well, they tell me I can shoot the bull all right."

At dinner I sat with Mrs. Truman, Vice-President Alben W. Barkley, and former Ambassador Joseph Davies. In deference to the President, no doubt, and to José Iturbi, the celebrated Spanish pianist, only a trio of strings and an accordion made dinner music. The musicians strolled around the tables, playing favorite songs. Back of the Veep's chair now, they broke into strains of "Wagon Wheels," and Vice-President Barkley sang in a lusty, sonorous baritone. I applauded until he had to repeat the song.

"You sing so fervently, Mr. Barkley, 'Wagon Wheels' must have some special meaning for you?" I inquired.

"Oh, it's a hymn to me, Miss Jessica," he drawled with true Southern gallantry. "My childhood comes back to me, and I see my father's wagon wheels. We were eight children, and my father worked hard, hauling to and from our farm. On Sundays he placed chairs in the wagon and took Mother and us children twenty miles away to church. I relive my boyhood in Kentucky whenever I sing 'Wagon Wheels.'"

As the President played an unfamiliar Chopin selection, José Iturbi and I sat mystified.

"What is it, José?" I whispered.

"Danged if I know," he shrugged.

Mr. Truman, smiling like the boy who stuck in his thumb and

pulled out a plum, announced, "That's er——er 'Napoleon at Water-loo.'" With infectious humor, the President winked at Iturbi, in a manner of saying: "You don't get my little joke? I mean pianist at Waterloo."

After Robert Merrill, José Iturbi, and I finished performing, Mr. Truman enthusiastically exclaimed to the delighted guests, "That was a fine show, worth ten dollars a head!"

During the dinner plain-clothes men lurked everywhere, even hovering closely about the chief chef in the kitchen. The meal was simple enough to see through, the master cook thought—sliced *filet mignon*, garnished with tomato and cress; asparagus hollandaise; and avocado salad—but one of the FBI men never left his side. Annoyed finally beyond endurance, the chef looked up imploringly as he prepared the strawberry dessert.

"Is there anything wrong, sir? You make me so nervous, I don't know what I'm doing. I don't want to disappoint the guests."

"No," said the stolid FBI man, "there's nothing wrong. I just want to taste one of those big red strawberries flown from Texas for this party. I want to see what's so different about them!"

Under the impression I would be singing early in the evening, I had refrained from partaking of the delicious dinner, but I did not sing until after midnight—and the party was late breaking up. When I got back to the Mayflower Hotel, room service was closed, and the best I could muster, before making a dash for the plane, was some crackers and milk.

Nadea, with her unusual inventive talent, had been working on something that would in time be a boon to feminine beauty, something called the BC, a creation that encourages the principles of good body mechanics. Eager to help her market this extraordinary invention, I decided to call the New York State Chamber of Commerce. Don Mullin, the membership secretary, was kindness itself and suggested I come to see him at 65 Liberty Street. The moment I saw the genius-guided institution, I chided myself for never having taken time out for a visit. It was like the creation of "music in space—frozen music."

After I discussed my mission, Mr. Mullin led me on a tour of the handsome building. As we mounted the steps to the Great Hall, he explained that the Chamber still operates on the English charter established 180 years ago when Cadwallader Colden was acting governor of the colony of New York.

The collection of portraits hanging in the beautifully lighted Great Hall cover the period of its entire history. When I found four portraits by my friend A. Müller-Ury, I began to think that my visit had another purpose besides the "BC."

With a surge of enthusiasm, I said to Mr. Mullin, "I have a portrait of a great American by Müller-Ury that would be at home here. Will you accept it?"

Mr. Mullin, obviously nonplused by my offer, stuttered "You have, but how can that be? Both men were before your time."

I told Mr. Mullin briefly about my friendship with Müller-Ury— he had painted several portraits of me in his last years; how shortly afterward Nadea and I arranged a loan-exhibition of his work for Italian war relief, he fell ill; how Mitchell Samuels, the French gallery's incomparable connoisseur, brought out appropriate treasures to enhance the room where Müller-Ury's portraits of four Popes hung, together with many others including a life-size portrait of Mrs. Theodore Havemeyer that he painted when only nineteen; how I saw him in the hospital lying like a crumpled leaf out of one of his own rose paintings and from then on, how he just faded away; how I could not bear the ruthless disposition of his effects after his death; how his brother came across the ocean to take back to Switzerland certain pictures like the magnificent *Cardinal Mercier*.

Everything else was sold at auction. His books, furniture, pictures, brocades and velvets with which he covered his portraits were carelessly thrown about. Dealers only interested in the handsome frames denuded the pictures. I bought whatever I could in friendship and admiration of the master. Gayelord Hauser, knowing how I revered the artist, later presented several paintings to me. Though I was familiar with most of Müller-Ury's pictures, there were a few unidentified; but I was unwilling to see any of them misplaced or destroyed.

Eager to have them where they would be a lasting memorial, I consulted Hermann Hagedorn, poet and biographer, who identified several. Then I wrote to the respective families giving them first chance to acquire the canvases. In the case of Boyce Thompson, the Newmont Mining Corporation magnate, his daughter showed no interest, and his estate set a modest fee for the privilege of destroying the picture. Outraged at the thought of annihilating Müller-Ury's work, I decided to place the portrait where it would do credit to both men. After Hermann Hagedorn's assertion that it was excellent, I sought out Charles Fanning Ayer, Boyce Thompson's partner for forty years, who pronounced it a living likeness.

That day, in the Chamber, I knew the picture belonged among Americans of distinction, in company with the other Müller-Ury portraits. Now Boyce Thompson hangs close to Alexander Hamilton; and the little gold plaque on the frame, acknowledging the gift, links my name with that of my esteemed friend, Adolpho Felice Müller-Ury.

Finding myself in Boston and its environs again for concerts, I began to think I had reached the saturation point of appearances in New England. Since these were bad pre-concert thoughts, as I drove from Boston to Norwood where I was singing that evening, I shook my head free of them. Looking out the car window at that moment, I noticed the chauffeur was making a detour.

"Anything wrong?" I ejaculated with alarm.

"No, ma'am, but we have to stop, before we go to the hall."

"Stop?" I asked in consternation. "We dare not be late for the concert."

"Well, ma'am, I have instructions to take you to the Sisters' convent first."

"Sisters—" It began to dawn on me that conspiracy was afoot. Trained to be punctilious as to concerts on time, I said, "Who will take the responsibility for beginning late?"

"I will, ma'am," he answered dryly.

Before I could gather my equilibrium, we were in the Sisters' driveway, and soon he was ringing the convent bell. When the door opened, there they were gathered, the whole community of twenty-five Sisters of St. Joseph, waiting and sure I would come to them.

"We wanted a glimpse of you, Jessica," the Superior said, triumphant that her plans had not miscarried, "since we are not allowed to go to hear you."

"Oh! Couldn't we see your gown?" sprightly spoke up one of the Sisters from the back.

"And won't you sing for us before you go?" they all cried.

What else could I do? Throwing off my ermine cape with its face-framing hood, I stood there in the hall among them and sang the "Ave Maria." Then blowing them a kiss, I dashed out into the night and began the concert five minutes late.

The next day I was still reluctant to appear at the Boston Garden for a hospital benefit. Archbishop Cushing's emissary met my scruples with true Bostonian gallantry: "Why, Jessica, we can never have enough of you; Boston without Jessica is like Boston without baked beans."

The sugar coating melted me down, and I agreed to sing at the charity horse show. I had only one gown with me—my concert gown. Packing has long since become a fine art, thanks to the discipline of air travel. The colossal trunks sent ahead with innumerable changes are a thing of the past. I allow myself one gown, wisely selected, that packs well and fits a variety of occasions, with the possibility of emerging from the trunk, fresh and stageable.

On this trip, my singing gown was a pink satin *bouffant* over layers of tulle appliqued with lace flowers, outlined in pearls and brilliants, long and trailing to the floor, with pink satin gloves. I looked like a cherub lifted from a wedding cake into a tanbark ring; and as I walked, with every step I took, I sank into the soft, brown gingerbread turf, my beautiful gown dragging over the horse trails.

While I stood there in the center of the arena, reaching up to pin ribbons on the bridles of winners, the gallant emissary, knight of the evening, received a message. In awed tones he gave it through the microphone to the audience: "Tonight the prize winners will be picked up by television; the equipment is now being installed; this is a historical moment for New England."

A buzzing spread like wildfire in the Garden. People could not believe they were witnessing a show that was being telecast. It added excitement to the zest of competition in the various classes of the horse show. Although the audience thought the telecast was only local, the coaxial cables carried the show to Philadelphia, New York, Cleveland, and Schenectady. Not knowing what I know about TV, it never occurred to anyone that I was anything but thrilled by the occasion, I was thinking I might as well be resigned to making a spectacle of myself in the midst of prize-winning horses, for the gown I was wearing—the pink, shiny confection—was the worst possible choice for TV.

When I arrived home in New York, I had letters of congratulations from the cities of the network, telling me how much they enjoyed the colorful spectacle of the Boston Garden telecast, but most of all, they said, "We loved your gown—perfect for television. You must have spent weeks having it made specially for this occasion."

There is an element of chance in these things, more than right clothes, right make-up, and right lighting, the importance of which cannot be minimized; it is the quality of immediacy, the heart of television. This truism was proven again and again last summer when I made my TV tour appearing on ten different programs in a few short weeks. I found this quality back of the success of Faye Emerson, Ilka Chase, the Fitzgeralds, and above all, Dizzy Dean with whom I appeared at the Stadium after a Yankee-Red Sox ball game. It was strictly an ad-lib show, in which Dizzy Dean commented on the evening's game and asked me simple questions about baseball, in which he expected to find me completely at sea.

"Now, Miss Dragonette, you're a singer and probably don't know a thing about baseball. 'Dyuh ever hear of a screwball?"

"Why, yes—it's just what it says it is, a screw—ball. But I'd rather ask you, Diz, since so many balks were called tonight, the difference between a balk and a walk."

"Say, yuh do know somethin' about th' old diamond, Jessica."

"Yes, I'm fond of saying singing is half a sport and half an art. Only I wish singers had managers like Casey Stengel. Just imagine in the middle of a concert, if a manager could rush out onto the center of the stage and say, 'How do you feel? Tired? Think you can last out this song? Or shall I start warming up someone in the orchestra pit?'"

"And if yuh happen to miss a high note, Jessica?"

"Why he'd come streaking into the arena to register violent complaint that it was strictly a bad pitch from the orchestra!"

"Well, little lady, with your love o' baseball, and my love o' singin', we should get together. How 'bout singin' a duet?"

I had never heard the favorite song of this lovable "natural,"

Dizzy Dean; it had never found its way into my thousand songs repertory, but in an introduction that murdered the king's English, Dizzy announced, "I ain't no Pinza, but Jessica and me'll close the program with a duet—'Wabash Cannonball!'"

As Dizzy jazzed about, I had a hard time keeping up with him, but at least we ended together! The overflowing spontaneity of the colorful sportsman accounted for the excellent telecast of the evening.

What holds for the broadcasting of sight goes for the broadcasting of sound. That quality of immediacy is Mary Margaret McBride's chief charm. Yes, she has other great gifts, but the unfettered flow of sincerity, like a direct current from her heart straight to the heart of the listener, is electric. Her phenomenal memory helps; it enables her to remember many things about her guests. She astonished me recently by telling me what I had said to her in an interview some years earlier:

"I was talking about coffee, Jessica, and you said to me, 'You don't know it, Mary Margaret, but I'm the cream in your coffee.' I was startled at first, but quick as a flash I knew you meant Pet Milk, the program on which you were appearing at that time."

In our self-conscious twentieth century, it is a rare transport to be carried along on the tide of a great multitude gathered for a religious commemoration, and in an age of agnosticism to profess publicly a simple act of faith. All anniversaries, whether romantic, civic, or religious, tie us to our traditional past and pose an ideal for the future. Such moments are pregnant with history, could we but realize them as such in our passage through time.

Late in September of 1947, a request came from His Excellency the Most Reverend John F. O'Hara, C.S.L., distinguished bishop of Buffalo, Military Chancellor of the Armed Forces during the war, former president of Notre Dame University, to sing at the civic reception of the Buffalo Centennial Eucharistic Congress.

I first heard of His Excellency through my friend, John Quincy Adams, a student at the University of Notre Dame during his time. Jack held in highest esteem this scholar whose heart was in his work at the university, yet who accepted in religious obedience the call to the Bishopric of Buffalo.

This centenary year was to be a census in manifestation of faith, a prayerful thanksgiving for all the graces and blessings of the past hundred years. Every seat in the main auditorium of Kleinhans Music Hall was occupied, and the overflow from the more than five-thousand audience was diverted to the Mary Reaton Room where people heard the ceremonies over the public address system. On the brilliantly lighted platform, resplendent in their official garb, were seated six Cardinals from various parts of the world, their Eminences Juan Gualbert Cardinal Guevara of Lima, Peru; Carlos Carmelo Cardinal de Vasconcellos Motta of São Paulo, Brazil; James Cardinal McGuigan of Toronto; Francis Cardinal Spellman of New York; Norman Cardinal Gilroy of Sydney, Australia; Bernard Cardinal Griffin, primate of England; Bishop O'Hara and Mayor Dowd of Buffalo. This was the first time in American history that six Cardinals sat together. It was moving to look out over the crowded hall where one could almost touch the taut silence of concentration, the earnest reaching out to God. "Lord, to whom shall we go," their presence said, "against the evil injustice and oppression everywhere?"

Bishop O'Hara, in his welcoming speech, stressed the need of prayer "in this hour of the world's desperation" and called attention to the central theme of the Congress, a profession of faith in the Holy Eucharist—"my delight is to be with the children of men." Through faith, His Excellency continued, "the purposes of God shall be carried out in the hearts and deeds of men." Then, he quoted from President Truman's words in a letter to Pope Pius XII:

I believe that the greatest need of the world today, fundamental to all else, is a renewal of faith—I seek to encourage renewed faith in the dignity and worth of the human person in all lands, to the end that the individuals' sacred rights, inherent to his relationship to God and his fellowmen, will be respected in every land.

In the spirit of the President's words, Bishop O'Hara continued: "From every part of our hemisphere and from lands across the sea, prelates and princes of the Church kneel with farmers, factory workers, carpenters, grain shovelers, businessmen, lawyers, doctors, fathers, mothers, and children of the diocese of Buffalo in a humble petition that 'peace on earth to men of good will may reign.'"

Between the addresses of welcome, the Buffalo Philharmonic Orchestra, directed by Frederick A. Ressel, accompanied me in Verdi's "Ave Maria," Bach's "Prière," and Franck's "Panis Angelicus."

I was deeply touched a few days later by a letter from Bishop O'Hara:

Words fail me when I try to express my gratitude for your inspiring contribution to our Eucharistic Congress. The offering of your beautiful voice to God's service thrilled a vast multitude, and assured a deep reverence for the events of the Congress. . . .

This was the realization of my great hope in going to Buffalo—humbly to serve in song.

Spain, long-distance friend of my soul, whose music has ever been an angelus bell stirring my heart to prayer, was to honor me for promoting Spanish music on the air and in my concerts throughout the country. Father Vicente Martinez, the Carmelite Provincial from Valencia, Spain, whom I had met during the Oklahoma concert tour, recommended me for this distinction.

When I opened the announcement from Señor German Baraibar, chargé d'affaires, telling me that in the name of the Spanish government, he would confer upon me its highest civilian honor, the ribbon of the Order of Isabella the Catholic, my mind moved like a swift planchette over the many Spanish souvenirs of my life—my childhood when I was first fascinated by the thought of Columbus in the Genoa background of my mother; the expressiveness of the Iberian idiom; my Spanish school friends; my introduction of Spanish music to the air; the excitement that spreads through my concert audiences over the programed Spanish music.

Though I have never set foot in Spain, I have traveled there in imagination, moving easily from century to century and place to place. Andalusia, Valencia, Madrid live in me through their dances and folk songs, lighting the map of Spain like a thousand stars of blinding fire in which I have seen the elegance and rich qualities of the native Spanish heart and mind. The flower of this abundance I have come to recognize in Isabella, Columbus, Ponce de León, St. Teresa of Avila, and Velàsquez.

Traveling over our southwest country, I have traced the wide periphery wherein the early padres labored, as the names of some of our American states and cities bear witness: California, Colorado, Florida, Los Angeles, San Francisco, Saint Augustine, Sacramento, Santa Barbara, Santa Clara. Memories of Isabella came to me when visiting the San Xavier mission in Tucson, Arizona, where I pondered on the crouching lions in the altar rail, remembering our very continent was discovered by Spain. This lightning current, igniting the fuel of my imagination, found expression in the Spanish acceptance speech I delivered at the embassy.

Father Vicente, proud beyond words of my work in Spanish music and of the honor bestowed, had offered to supervise my talk; he rehearsed me until no shadow of flaw remained, and I worked hard to shine brilliantly among his distinguished countrymen.

The exquisite embassy was a little Spain with its Moresque fountains and flowers, its beautifully appointed reception rooms where the gay Spanish paintings on the walls came alive and seemed to mingle with the colorful gathering of three hundred guests. Francis Cardinal Spellman was a magnetic center who drew about him Ambassador José Felipe Lequerica, Doctor Joseph F. Thorning wearing the rosette of the Grand Cross of the Order of Isabella La Catolica, and delegates from the diplomatic corps—Honduran Ambassador and Señora Caceres, Dominican Ambassador and Señora de Thomen, Ecuadorean Ambassador and Señora Dillon, Colombian Ambassador and Señora Restrepo-Jaramillo. Captain Frank Farrell, dashing in his uniform and decorations, was soon engaged with Señoritas Anita and Teresa Baraibar, daughters of the host and hostess, true Spanish popular beauties, newly arrived from their homeland. Their blossoming younger sister Alicia eagerly presented me with a large bouquet of fragrant crimson carnations tied in the gold and red embassy colors.

Later, in the pale green ballroom, I sang a group of Spanish folk songs—malagueñas, jotas, granadinas, sietas. Immediately afterward, Ambassador Lequerica pinned the beautiful decoration on my white satin princess gown.

His Eminence rose and, as he looked at it beside the papal medal I was wearing, he said, "Congratulations, Jessica, they go very well together."

At the buffet reception we mingled with other prominent guests: Lady Bumgardner who brought regrets from Justice Frank Murphy

77

who was ill; Colonel and Mrs. Wendell Johnson, Colonel and Mrs. Consuelo A. Sloane from our embassy in Spain; and the Polish artist Jan Boleslaw Czedekowski, widely known for his portraits of the late General George S. Patton, Jr.

Almost tearful with joy, I sat apart from the others filling out the official questionnaires. Father Vicente was prodding me. "Go on, Jessica, put down Army and Navy wings."

Hesitatingly I wrote, while a young diplomat, only recently from Spain, peering over my shoulder, full of exuberant gusto, whispered, "What—not the Marines? By the way, I expected to enjoy your singing, but when you said you would speak, I thought 'Uh-uh, that's something else again!'" Then, giving me the glad eye, "But I take it back—it was swell!"

Nikki, tall and striking in full dress, was host to friends from New York who accompanied me, Frank Riesenberger, Augustus Bundy, Arthur McGivney, Madeleine Sack, Josephine Anderson of Milwaukee, Nadea, and Vera Edmondson, a devoted air friend from San Francisco. Señor Baraibar disappeared for a moment and came back with something reserved only for special occasions.

"A parting *adios*," he announced gaily, "for that plane ride back to New York; a bottle of *Viejissimo*, an old brandy distilled from Jerez." Frank Riesenberger, by far the most knowing connoisseur among us, pronounced it the rarest palate delight he had ever experienced. Titian-haired, blue-eyed Señora Baraiba, full of charm to the last, stood at the embassy door, waving *"Hasta la vista"* as we drove away from this magic visit to a castle in Spain.

An early call to army and air force recruiting summoned me to the Wing Ding in Boston. After flying in Esso's private world-worthy plane—its exterior painted with flags of the one hundred nations visited on its around the globe good-will-trade-tour, we attended several AFA social reunions, where we met General Carl A. Spaatz, first chief of staff, USAF, Lieutenant General Nathan F. Twining, deputy chief of staff, Personnel USAF, Major General Laurence S. Kuter, commander of the Military Air Transport Service, and many other air force officers and heroes. Then we rehearsed for a midnight performance at one of the Boston theaters.

The mammoth stage show, attended by airmen and their families, was in reality a recruiting broadcast. Tex McCrary, a devoted member of AFA, and his wife, vivacious Jinx Falkenburg, piloted the program, emceeing the stars of the show; among them: funny-man Sid Caesar, comedienne Denise Darcel, Edward Arnold, John Conte, and Marlo Stevens. Stripper Ann Corio took off nothing but her wrap, saying, "You know how it is in Boston, boys!" Together with my songs, as an honorary Air Force colonel, I was given the privilege of introducing and saluting with "A Wonderful Guy" the Congressional Medal of Honor men whom the audience wildly cheered.

Early the next morning we enplaned for New York, and when I arrived home, there was notice of a registered letter waiting for me. The letter explained that by singing for the Wing Ding, I had violated the American Guild of Variety Artists' rules, forbidding members to perform at benefits without permission, and summoning me to appear at a hearing.

In a few weeks, I found myself with other offenders before the association board of four men and my old friend, Gypsy Rose Lee. I tried to give her a smile of greeting, as I sat down at the table, but she was coldly circumspect, looking neither right nor left; very soon, with a serious incisiveness that bowled me over, she began expounding the necessity of hewing to the line.

"You've got to look below the surface in these things," she said, like a stern Portia. "I know two actors who were taken in by a group working for the Purple Heart. The gate was $40,000, and the Purple Heart got $1,000!"

Under the cross-examination that lasted for two hours, each arbiter piled up evidence against the offending performers. Then we were given an opportunity of defending ourselves. Colonel Louis Duval, the recruiting officer, spoke in our behalf, restating that by performing at the Wing Ding, we had answered a patriotic call to appear on a recruiting broadcast in Boston.

"What have you to say for yourself, Miss Dragonette?" asked Joe Laurie, Jr., one of the judges.

"I'm sorry if unwittingly I broke the rules. But as an honorary colonel in the air force, I felt I was acting in the line of duty."

The board smiled at this. "Shall we have to salute you, Colonel?" asked another judge.

This was comforting after Gypsy's cold shoulder. "That would be in order, gentlemen," I answered courageously.

Presently the board went out of the room and left us sitting there while they deliberated our fate. Nervously awaiting their return, sick with apprehension at the thought of the impending heavy fine, fearful lest justice miscarry, I sat there silently praying.

Suddenly the door opened, and a spokesman for the board announced, "We all feel you have acted in a patriotic way, with no intention to violate the rules; but in the future, when in doubt, call AGVA."

I could not forget the brave fighting men I had met in camps, bases, hospitals over the country; the imprint of their youth, thwarted hopes and dreams, their untimely deaths on the field of battle would not be shaken from my mind, and I lost no opportunity to salute them whenever possible. So it happened that some weeks after the Boston Wing Ding I seriously considered an invitation from General Tuckerman to speak at the reunion dinner of the First Cavalry Division; yet I did not see how I could fit this into my busy schedule.

"I am leaving early Sunday morning for a three-day engagement in Syracuse," I told General Tuckerman when he called me late Friday evening. He did not let go easily. "We have a great organization, Miss Dragonette, our history goes back to General Robert E. Lee and General Custer; we were first in Japan and Korea. We're not asking you to sing, you know, we're asking you to speak."

"To speak," I said, raising my voice at the strange thought. "Very well, General, if you think I can be of service, I will be there."

I kept wondering about this odd request. It was late and very difficult to find any bureau open at that hour that could give me historical data on the First Cavalry Division of the United States. In desperation I called the New York *World-Telegram,* and a highly accommodating night telephone operator managed to get all the information I required.

"Who are the Congressional Medal of Honor men of World War II, Miss Brown?" I said as she was giving me First Cavalry Division data. She read off the list, and when she came to Sgt. Troy A. McGill, I gasped.

"Are you there, Miss Dragonette?" came her anxious voice. "What's wrong?"

I had apparently communicated my amazement to the operator. I couldn't believe my ears as she went on reading—Ada, Oklahoma, Congressional Medal of Honor posthumously received, March 4, 1944. Here was my tie-in with the First Cavalry Division. Trembling with emotion when the operator finished giving me the details I needed, I found it difficult to thank her for her extraordinary help. . . .

In a resplendent ballroom of the Hotel Biltmore, at the gay dinner dance reunion, I was in the company of General Hillary L. Wyman, chief of staff, First Army, Major General Verne D. Mudge, Major General Innis P. Swift, and next to me sat chairman Colonel W. J. Bradley.

Just before I spoke Colonel Bradley questioned me: "Miss Dragonette, it's awfully good of you to do this for us, but I wonder why you do? I am sure if I were you I wouldn't take the time out."

Just then General Tuckerman was approaching to lead me to the platform, and as I left I said, "Colonel, I'll be speaking in a few minutes and then I think you'll understand."

While the brilliant audience stood, I recalled to them the curious fate that brought us together. "When I was selling bonds in Tulsa, Oklahoma, during the war, a quiet mannered sergeant drove me in a jeep through the streets. I was photographed with him as well as other servicemen, and managed to keep the pictures. Some years later the sergeant's mother wrote me, inquiring if by any chance I still had the picture taken with her son, as there was none other in existence. Since he had been killed in the war, and the Oklahoma State Capitol wanted his photograph for their Hall of Fame, she was writing me as a last resort. I was happy to be able to supply the picture.

"That quiet mannered sergeant had lost his life in heroic action on Momote Airstrip—Los Negros Island. Early in the morning the Japs attacked, and all the night men with one exception were killed or wounded. Sergeant McGill fired his weapon until it ceased to function and with complete disregard of his own safety, knowing he faced certain death, he left his foxhole and using his rifle as club engaged in hand to hand combat until he was killed by the enemy. For this heroic action he received the Congressional Medal of Honor.

"To Sergeant Troy McGill and all the brave fighting men of the

First Cavalry Division who fell in battle I would like to dedicate the 'Star-Spangled Banner.'"

As I resumed my place beside Colonel Bradley, a gentleman sitting close by came toward me. It was Brigadier General Hugh F. T. Hoffman. "I was McGill's commanding officer; I had to take a lot of young men out to get killed."

The horror of the General's sad words was softened at that moment by a young captain who asked eagerly, "Did you really know him, Miss Dragonette? Or was it just a page out of General Tuckerman's journal? I loved the way you told the story; you see, McGill was my buddy."

Late in 1949, Austin Wilder, no longer with Columbia Concerts, but now on his own, having so successfully managed the Maggie Teyte tours in America, came to see me one day.

"I can do the same thing for you, Jessica," he urged. "Besides the concerts I have a plan to dovetail other engagements, booking through Music Corporation of America. They control most of the entertainment field, and I would be there to see you were not lost in the shuffle of a large organization." Mr. Wilder proceeded to arrange an appointment with Charles Miller, one of the Big Three of MCA.

"Austin Wilder tells me you have a ready-made audience in every state in the Union," he in turn greeted me. "I would like to sign you up exclusively." Caught up in Mr. Miller's enthusiasm, I thought favorably of the proposed contract beginning in the concert division, while the radio and television departments worked for me. "Paul Gregory is the head of concerts," he continued. "He's a good man, and I'd like you to have a talk with him at once."

Gregory was personable, high pressured and very interested. Nevertheless, I could see after a short time he was only feeling his way in this new field MCA was trying to develop.

Anxious to co-operate with him, I began giving him workable suggestions—most important among them a project which has since been taken up by every recording company and singers in all categories: twelve months before the Holy Year of 1950, I encouraged him to record a volume of religious songs. Not only was it timely, I told him, but such a volume would be welcomed by thousands of people. With the impending Holy Year, this would institute a trend toward religious music, conducive to peace of mind.

Paul Gregory was like a happy boy, reporting his accomplishment with Columbia: "I have succeeded in selling the idea to Goddard Liebersen, director of the Masterworks Division. You should feel proud. Out of the fifteen I presented to him, you are the only artist he signed. Liebersen wondered, though, what had become of you. He put it down to bad management. I must see what I can do to remedy that."

We had taken only the first step when suddenly that maddening process of change peculiar to large organizations occurred. No sooner had the contract with Columbia been signed when a shift in the company policy took recordings out of Gregory's department, and that was the end of his interest in the records. I could expect no help from Austin Wilder. Unfortunately, an eye operation forced him to retire completely from business.

It was quite understandable Gregory would not want to work for a cause that did not redound to his benefit; few men are willing to cast bread upon the waters. Nevertheless, it was disappointing to my dearest hopes to be trapped in the delaying snares of red tape and to be forced to decode his equivocal words.

More and more I began to realize I was only marking time at MCA and could do much better on my own, so I asked Charles Miller to release me from my contract. However, since Paul Gregory was the spearhead of the records, I continued to call him to ascertain a definite recording date. Again and again he put me off, evasive and unconcerned. Finally, exasperated by such callousness, I called Columbia's Director of the Masterworks Division, Richard Gilbert.

"Have you spoken with Mr. Gregory?" were his first words to me. "I thought he had arranged the whole thing."

"Mr. Gilbert, let's not go back and forth," I pleaded. "We've wasted enough time already. *When* do we record?"

The next day Mr. Gilbert set the recording time: "We have only three available dates left. If you want to make the records, they will have to be made then."

"Very well, I shall be there," I answered, realizing full well that the hours fell immediately upon my return from a strenuous two weeks' singing in Montreal.

On my way to the first recording session I was so discouraged I had to spur myself on. After expending all my energy pushing the records, I found myself disheartened by this wall of indifference. "Salute the arriving moment with your eyes," I kept saying, holding my head erect and looking forward to each second of singing.

A ray of hope arrived in the person of Tyler Turner of the Masterworks Division of Columbia. He put me at ease immediately; with his able assistance, we finished the eight selections in two sessions, Avenir de Monfred accompanying me on the Hammond organ.

Mr. Turner suggested calling the album "Ave Maria," since that lovely tribute of many hearts in many lands was the first selection. This was a great lift to my waning spirits. I took heart and for the first time I really believed the records would be released. The other songs included the oft-repeated, simple devotional hymns sung by congregations everywhere: "Panis Lingua" of Thomas Aquinas sung to Gregorian chant, mode 3; "Panis Angelicus" of César Franck; and among the others the English version of the "Te Deum" ("Holy God, We Praise Thy Name").

"Would you mind repeating the 'Holy God,' Miss Dragonette?" said taut-strung, ascetic looking Tyler Turner. "That take sounds too torchy!"

I was amused, remembering how often I had been accused of a too pure style in singing. Was Mr. Turner teasing me? Anyway we did another "take."

A good six months of Holy Year were over before the records were released. Tyler Turner mounted a master copy for Cardinal Spellman, soon to leave on a Roman pilgrimage, and His Eminence invited Goddard Liebersen to luncheon for the presentation.

As we sat at table, Liebersen, making an opening wedge in the conversation, announced, "Artists are such good businessmen."

At this I laughed. "Are you really serious, Mr. Liebersen? I can't imagine your lovely wife Zorina a 'good businessman.' Perhaps you mean *some* artists."

"Well, take Kostelanetz, for example," he went on, "he knows all the good eating places in town. Artists most always have to take a hand in their own affairs."

I let fall a pause in the conversation. I was thinking of the artist as a one-man concern in conflict with the multiple-staffed business organization. As we sat for a while in the pleasant drawing room, after leaving the table, Mr. Liebersen's mood changed to brooding.

"I received a letter today calling me a Catholic-lover. Apparently someone had read in the paper I would be lunching with Your Eminence. Such prejudice goes against the grain," his eyes smoldered. "One actually feels physical about it."

The Cardinal's expression became one of compassion, and he gave Mr. Liebersen a healing glance. "I'll let you read a few of my letters some time," he let fall gently.

While we stood grouped for a photograph in a presentation scene of the master copy "Ave Maria" record, the Cardinal examined the aluminum disk buried in lucite set off in a red velvet shadow box.

"Lovely," said the Cardinal, "I would like to hear it"; then regretfully he added, "oh, I see I can't play it."

Thwarted to the last, I tried once more, and just as the ocean liner for Rome was about to leave the pier in New York, I managed, with Tyler Turner's help, to rush a playable record to the departing Cardinal for His Holiness, Pius XII.

The threaded shuttle weaving in and out of the multipatterned tapestry of life was now forming the dark, ominous shape of continued conflict in Korea. Would a third world war be inevitable? These were sad thoughts at Christmas while I was on my way to appear at the Olympia Theatre in Miami, Florida, and later in Nassau, Bahamas, during December, 1950, and January, 1951. I arrived in Florida a day ahead of schedule to make transcriptions for the Army and Air Force Christmas recruiting broadcasts.

Captain William F. Jordan, the commanding officer, and Modeste Alloo, Miami Symphony conductor, under whom I had formerly appeared in concerts, met me at the airport during a pouring rain, and we went immediately to the studios to record. The incongruity struck me with full force—how to reconcile Christmas with recruiting—but since we could not avoid what we most dreaded—war—we were here to give all we had for our country's ideals, to stem off the forces of destruction.

I chose the simplest songs for the transcriptions, songs that raised no barrier between hearts, songs that would unite us at home with those far away, in a bond of love that would outlast the prevailing

tragedy: "Ave Maria" was my prayer; "White Christmas," my wish
that our boys might soon return; and "Holy Night," my hope for
peace.

When I was finished, Captain Jordan came to me. "You are very
kind to give us so much time," he said with a winning smile, "to
do this tedious job."

Studying the young soldier on leave from Korea, I wondered if
what he had lived through had mellowed his sensitivity and awareness. "What I have done, Captain, seems so little in comparison with
your job," I answered.

"Will you wear this recruiting brassard?" he inquired, offering me
the rich blue and white arm band. "It is worn only by those members
of the Army and Air Force who are considered outstanding. These
men are the showcase of our services, and we hereby appoint you
an honorary recruiter."

The Florida weather during our stay in Miami was fitful, windy,
and cold, with the exception of Christmas Day which dawned sunny
and warm. I was winding up my engagement at the four-a-day Olympia Theatre; soon Nikki would come from New York to join me and
together we would go to the Bahamas for vacation as well as singing.

"This is the first mild day we've had. I'd like to take a dip in the
pool," said Nadea, bubbling with pent-up anticipation.

"Take advantage of it by all means," I encouraged her. "You'll be
leaving here in two days for icy New York."

When she came back later to the theater, where I lived daily from
eleven-thirty in the morning until midnight, she told me how happy
she was with her first swim in months. At that moment, the call-bell
rang, and, dressed in my red tulle gown, I descended the steps and
stood at attention in the wings for my entrance in the Yuletide pro-
logue. Nadea would follow shortly to listen while I was on stage. In
the blackout on the closing line, "Sleep in heavenly peace," I
walked offstage.

Two dancers quickly surrounded me and in horrified tones announced, "Your sister has fallen down the stairs—she's—"

I didn't wait until they had finished; in a daze I ran up the steps
to the landing where she was sitting. "Nadea, dear Nadea, are you
terribly hurt? Tell me if you can move your feet."

She could only murmur softly, "I cannot move."

I could see, from the green shadows under her eyes, she had had a terrible shock. When the doctor came, we had to take her to the only hospital that had an X-ray room open. It was then we learned she had not only fractured a vertebra, but several others were also compressed. In trying to save herself on the slippery steps and reaching out to grab the distant balustrade, she threw herself back against the jagged concrete. This meant she would have to stay in the hospital, lying on her back for eight weeks. I hung upon Dr. Edwin Preston's words, but it was several days before he could tell me what I was waiting to hear.

"We are certain now," he said, solemnly, "she will not be paralyzed, but it will take a long time to heal."

I was forlorn about leaving her in the Florida hospital while I went off singing in Nassau, but Nadea was a good soldier about it. Professional people understand the laws of the theater. Now she is at home, all this time slowly mending, and though I have sorely missed her constant help in many affairs, my whole concern has been her complete recovery.

Listening to the radio and viewing TV today, many recapitulations come to mind. The period is a quite different one looking back to November, 1926, and to the silver anniversary of network broadcasting, November, 1951. The cavalcade of events recorded by radio in the intervening years is a vivid story of our cataclysmic age.

Studying the radio period-piece of 1951, I have the same dream as long ago—"something of its own"—companies of excellent artists, working in sustained effort for the best entertainment in the greatest medium ever conceived. It is not the easy road of depending on actors borrowed from other fields for a day, to lend the advertisement of their names; not the constant interruption of good programs arrested in their flight to the best by arbitrary radio polls.

The "Mister and Missus" program currently in fashion is good in the sense that woman more and more takes her place side by side with man in the world's work. However, in the glib, patly casual argot, the irreducible formula of who married whom, who didn't, who dunit, who's lullabying, who's seen in the soft lights of El Morocco, the Stork Club, and Lindy's, a false urbanity harnesses the vitality of a universal medium to the narrow strip of Broadway.

Looking back, I bless my parents for a goodly heritage, for bending the twig, and the devoted nuns for nurturing the flower of my
faith, giving me a discipline, a way of life without which I would
never be able to weather the storms. Looking forward there are again
three beautiful, talented sisters, as when this story began—Carmé,
Leila, and Jessica, daughters of my late brother Nicholas.

Were I prone to pessimism, reflecting on my shining effort to develop "something of its own" for radio and seeing its partial cul-
mination today in the fascinating commercials, I might consider my
time wasted. And yet—rather do I see in this accomplishment, the
beginnings of the folk songs of industry, as distinct a part of the
American substratum as the Negro spiritual was in its time.

> All the dirt, all the grit,
> Sweeper gets it every bit
> For it beats, as it sweeps, as it cleans—

we used to sing on the Hoover Sentinels. Cranes, dynamos, cement
mixers, bread factories, vacuum cleaners have an airy and romantic
existence. Now every machine has commenced to sing!

Industry tends toward the development of a new music. A crack
train of the West goes crashing out "on the air" in a composition
which gives all the giant breathing and huff-puff of the limited starting and flying smoke trails across the continent. A great rush of oil
out of a geyser becomes the musical trademark of a petroleum
company. (Remember, it was something like this that I suggested to
Cities Service long ago.) Music is no less music because it is mercantile—no less important because it is not profound. Music is a divine
food, nourishing life at every turn.

Looking back, the task involved in giving the public good entertainment and the industrialist advertising at the same time has taken
much skill and imagination. The commercial ballad, sung at the beginning and end of a radio hour, has acquired status and personality. We broadcasters have been privileged to tap a new vein of inspiration in an age teeming with new material, strange sounds of new
objects: the whirring of motors in airplanes, the rhythms of huge,
purposeful turbines like fiery planets on their pathways. The counterpoint of intricate machines has attuned our ears to a new sensitivity.

This awareness might have been long delayed, had it not been for the twentieth-century *deus ex machina*—RADIO.

In all this joy of achievement there is a regret that the dramatic trend now reaching its peak has almost succeeded in crowding out music; in radio's future this will be remedied, for what can match the healing alchemy of music, that poetry of the air; and what language is so many-tongued? Let us hope our electronics will lead us to supersonic music "molten as notes that rose in Palestrina's soul"; permitting us, at last, to hear the surpassing beauty of the music of the spheres "that move," as Milton says, "in melodious time," and "make up full consort to the angelic symphony."

Perfect communication—the dream of the ages—has been fulfilled. Yet a drift of pinions, could we but hear them, beat at our frustration-shuttered globe; they are the restive wings of the Angel of Peace, bearing the olive branch, eager to sound a trumpet call of triumph, to proclaim a message for which the ear of the microphone was created, to which I dedicate myself anew, the song of peace and love to our waiting world.